Appleseeds and Beer Cans
Man and Nature in Literature

Appleseeds and Beer Cans
Man and Nature in Literature

C. Michael Wells
Alan R. Velie, University of Oklahoma
Donita Williams Walker, University of Oklahoma

Goodyear Publishing Company, Inc.
Pacific Palisades, California

Library of Congress Cataloging in Publication Data

Wells, C   Michael, comp.
    Apple seeds and beer cans.

    1.   Human ecology—Literary collections.   I.   Velie,
Alan R., 1937–   joint comp.   II.   Walker, Donita
Williams, 1944–   joint comp.   III.   Title.
PN6071.H78W4   808.8'03   73–85499
ISBN 0–87260–076–5

Copyright © 1974 by
Goodyear Publishing Company, Inc.
Pacific Palisades, California

Current printing (last digit):
10 9 8 7 6 5 4 3 2 1

ISBN: 0–87620–076–5
Y 0765–1

Library of Congress Catalog Card Number: 73–85499

To Mike, who taught us the ecological attitude

Contents

Chapter Four
Man and Nature—The Common Bond 71

Part Two
Failures 121

Chapter Five
The Vanishing Wilderness 124

Chapter Six
Our Synthetic Environment   152

Chapter Seven
Man and Beast   158

Chapter Eight
The Perils of Pollution   177

Chapter Nine
Urban Blight   196

Part Three
Where Did We Go Wrong? 213

Chapter Ten
People Are No Damn Good 218

Chapter Eleven
Virtue is the Root of All Evil 244

Chapter Twelve
The Promethean Bind 251

Part Four
Solutions: Variations on a Theme of the Simple Life 271

Preface

*While England endeavors to cure the
potato-rot, will not any endeavor to
cure the brain-rot, which prevails
so much more widely and fatally?*
                              Henry David Thoreau

Much has been written about ecology lately, particularly about environmental crises. Most of it has dealt with ecology from a scientific point of view, stressing facts and figures about oil spills and air pollution. Carefully marshalled statistics show us precisely how bad things have become. The appeal, although often a highly emotional one, is basically to our reason: if we are to save our environment and ourselves, we must use our heads. Furthermore, ecological writing is usually man-oriented. The "quality of life" generally refers to human life.

This anthology takes a different approach. The selections are not tightly reasoned scientific articles; most are works of art: poems, essays, short stories, selections from novels. Their appeal is not primarily to the reason, but to the imagination and the feelings. Hopefully, the appeal to man's deepest feelings can work a fundamental change in his attitude toward the world he lives in—not merely a facile decision to change his detergent or to use unleaded gasoline.

A few of the pieces are openly didactic, but most are simply infused with the spirit of ecology. What is that spirit? Basically it is the sense of the interrelationship of man and his environment—the idea that man is meant to fit into a greater scheme of things, and that his life is richest when he exists harmoniously with the world around him.

As our approach is chiefly through works of art, the selections are often impressionistic, even surrealistic accounts of ecological disasters rather than factual reports. For example, Laurence Lieberman's "Orange County Plague" gives a vivid and gripping picture of logging as murder:

Mid-day. A mammoth Redwood creeps on wheels. Four lanes of autos,
Reluctant, bestow reverence; the giant's funeral
Hearse shambles. The corpse, exposed,
Has not begun to smell.
Tree-flesh, unembalmed, won't rust
Or rot. Tree bodies outlast tree souls.

It should not be surprising that men of letters are interested in ecological problems. Traditionally they have loved nature, and have often served as the conscience of the race. Although poems or novels may seem a futile way of attacking a problem as serious as the current ecological crisis, they can be very effective. Poets, said Shelley, are the "unacknowledged legislators of the world." Dickens did more to reform the abuses of Victorian England than any contemporary politician. In our country, Harriet Beecher Stowe's *Uncle Tom's Cabin* contributed greatly to the destruction of slavery. Today, poets like Gary Snyder and novelists like Richard Brautigan, with their unique way of seeing things and their powerful way of dramatizing what they see, exert considerable influence on public opinion, and so play an important role in the fight to preserve the environment.

Finally, scientific articles, however powerful, are usually soon forgotten. Works of art are more likely to survive. As Henry Austin Dobson wrote:

All passes. Art alone
Enduring stays to us.

The pieces we include here will live long after us, continuing the fight for a better world.

Part
One

The
Ecological
Attitude

In the scenery of Spring nothing is better, nothing worse;
The flowering branches are some long, some short.

Anonymous[1]

The ecological attitude is a frame of mind, a way of thinking, of seeing things, and perhaps most of all, a way of feeling. In this chapter, pieces from a diversity of nations, periods, and cultures stress the idea that life is sacred, all things are interrelated, and nothing is ugly or inconsequential.

The chapter begins with a selection from the Bhagavad-Gita, the gospel of Hinduism. OM, the word that is God, reveals that "part of myself is the God within every creature." The idea, common also to Buddhism, that God lives within all creatures and things, is deeply ingrained in the Eastern mind, and reflected in much Oriental literature. For instance, Hung Tzu-ch'iang, a sixteenth-century Chinese poet, writes:

> Sitting by a teapoy in a room bathed with pure breezes and moonbeams, one can read the mind of Heaven in every thing.[2]

Expressions of the immanence of God occur in Western literature as well. In Gerard Manley Hopkins' "God's Grandeur," OM becomes the Holy Ghost, who "over the bent/World broods with warm breast and ah! bright wings."

Even in the pieces that are not religious in the orthodox sense—that is, those which do not refer to a deity—there is a sense of the sacredness of life. In "The Flame of Life," W. H. Hudson speaks of

> . . . the wonderfulness and eternal mystery of life itself; this formative, informing energy—this flame that burns in and

---

[1] Quoted by R. H. Blyth in *Zen in English Literature and Oriental Classics* 1942, The Hokuseido Press, Tokyo, p. 33.

[2] Hung Tzu-ch'iang, from Chao-tze-chiang, *A Chinese Garden of Serenity*, p. 18 © 1959 by Peter Pauper Press. Reprinted by permission.

shines through the case, the habit, which in lighting another dies, and albeit dying yet endures forever . . .[3]

The idea that life, all life, is sacred leads to the idea of interrelatedness of things. In the scheme of the whole, all parts fit and function together harmoniously. In seeing a part, one can understand the whole. William Blake's "Auguries of Innocence" is a classic expression of this:

To see a World in a Grain of Sand
And a Heaven in a Wild Flower,
Hold Infinity in the palm of your hand
And Eternity in an hour.

The Chinese poet Hakurakuten expresses the same theme:

One speck of dust contains the whole earth; when one flower opens, the whole world comes into being.

Perhaps Emerson puts it most forcefully and concisely:

Nothing is fair or good alone.

Emerson's point, of course, is that an object or creature is useful or beautiful only if it functions as part of the entire natural order, which Emerson referred to as the Unity, a phrase often used by Oriental thinkers as well.

The theme of the relationship of seemingly diverse objects is common in Japanese poetry. For example, this anonymous poem:

The cicada sings
In the rotten willow.
Antares, the fire star,
Rolls in the west. [4]

[3] W. H. Hudson, "The Flame of Life" in *The Book of a Naturalist.*

[4] Anonymous Japanese poem from *The Four Seasons,* Basho et al. Peter Pauper Press. © 1958.

The cicada and the star are juxtaposed without explicit connection, but the implication is clear: the minute and tremendous, the near and far, are integrally related. So delicate yet strong is this bond between all things in creation that, as Francis Thompson says:

> . . . thou canst not stir a flower
> Without troubling of a star

A concomitant of these attitudes is the idea that nothing is ugly or inconsequential. Illustrative of this is Rikeiho's story of the man who grieved at the death of a dog but thought nothing of the death of lice. His religious instructor told him:

> Now you go home and quietly meditate on this, and when you see that the horns of a snail are the same as those of a bull, the wren of equal value with the mighty Rukh, then come, and we'll talk of religion again.[5]

The temporal aspect of the ecological attitude is that the sequence of events is an ever-repeating cycle. The system is closed and, like a circle, perfect. In *House Made of Dawn*, Scott Momaday tells how the Indians of the American Southwest lived their lives in accordance with this cycle. In "The Return of the Rivers," Richard Brautigan describes the cyclical relationship of rivers and oceans. The poem begins with a passage from Ecclesiastes and ends with a modern, surrealistic image:

> All the rivers run into the sea.
> yet the sea is not full;
> unto the place from whence the rivers come,
> thither they return again . . .

> A slow rain sizzles
> on the river
> like a pan
> full of frying flowers,

[5]Riheiko, from R. H. Blyth, in *Zen in English Literature and Oriental Classics,* 1942. The Hokuseido Press, Tokyo.

and with each drop
of rain
the ocean
begins again.[6]

This then is the ecological attitude: the idea that life is sacred, that all things are interrelated, that nothing is ugly or inconsequential, and that the processes of life are part of an ever-repeating cycle. But its most powerful and concise statement is not a list of the main points; it is a poem like "The Spider," written by Sugawara no Michizane in the late ninth century:

There is craft in this smallest insect,
With strands of web spinning out his thoughts;
In his tiny body finding rest,

And with the wind lightly turning.
Before the eaves he stakes out his broad earth;
For a moment on the fence top lives through his life.
When you know that all beings are even thus,
You will know what creation is made of.[7]

[6]From *The Pill Versus the Springhill Mine Disaster* by Richard Brautigan. A Seymour Lawrence Book/Delacorte Press. Reprinted by permission of the publisher.

[7]From *The Anthology of Japanese Literature,* edited by Donald Keene. Copyright © 1955 by Grove Press. Reprinted by permission of Grove Press.

CHAPTER ONE
Spiritual Foundations of the Ecological Attitude

Part of myself is the God within every creature.

Bhagavad-Gita

All things by immortal power,
Near or far,
Hiddenly
To each other linked are,
That thou canst not stir a flower
Without troubling of a star.

Francis Thompson
"The Mistress of Vision"

BHAGAVAD-GITA[1]
Anonymous

The Bhagavad-Gita (The Song of God) is as central to Hinduism as the Sermon on the Mount is to Christianity. Originally it was a section of the Hindu epic the *Mahabharata*. It is written in the form of a conversation between the warrior Arjuna and his charioteer, Krishna, the "Blessed Lord" of the Hindus.

O Arjuna, I am the divine seed of all lives. In this world, nothing animate or inanimate exists without me.

The light that lives in the sun,
Lighting all the world,
The light of the moon,
The light that is in fire:
Know that light to be mine.

My energy enters the earth,
Sustaining all that lives:
I become the moon,
Giver of water and sap,
To feed the plants and the trees.

I am the essence of the waters,
The shining of the sun and the moon:
OM in all the Vedas,
The word that is God.
It is I who resound in the ether
And am potent in man.
I am the sacred smell of the earth,
The light of the fire,
Life of all lives,
Austerity of ascetics.

[1] From *Bhagavad-Gita*, Swami Prabhavananda and Christopher Isherwood translators, Vedanta Press, 1944, 1951. Reprinted by permission of Vedanta Society of Southern California.

Know me, eternal seed
Of everything that grows:
The intelligence of those who understand,
The vigour of the active.
In the strong, I am strength
Unhindered by lust
And the objects of craving:
I am all that a man may desire
Without transgressing
The law of his nature.

GOD'S GRANDEUR
Gerard Manley Hopkins

Gerard Manley Hopkins (1844–1888) was a Victorian poet noteworthy for the power of his religious feelings and his stylistic audacity. Hopkins became a Jesuit in 1868, and his poetry from that time on reflects his spiritual joys and struggles.

The world is charged with the grandeur of God.
*   It will flame out, like shining from shook foil;*
*   It gathers to a greatness, like the ooze of oil*
Crushed. Why do men then now not reck his rod?
Generations have trod, have trod, have trod;
*   And all is seared with trade; bleared, smeared with toil;*
*   And wears man's smudge and shares man's smell: the soil*
Is bare now, nor can foot feel, being shod.

And for all this, nature is never spent;
*   There lives the dearest freshness deep down things;*
And though the last lights off the black West went
*   Oh, morning, at the brown brink eastward, springs—*
Because the Holy Ghost over the bent
*   World broods with warm breast and with ah! bright wings.*

AN ESSAY ON MAN from Book I
Alexander Pope

Alexander Pope (1688–1744) was the greatest English poet of the Augustan period. His best-known works include *An Essay on Criticism, The Rape of the Lock, The Dunciad,* and *An Essay on Man.* Pope's poetry exhibits the neoclassical tendency toward didacticism, satire, and rational argument.

> *See, thro' this air, this ocean, and this earth,*
> *All matter quick, and bursting into birth.*
> *Above, how high progressive life may go!*
> *Around, how wide! how deep extend below!*
> *Vast chain of being! which from God began,*
> *Natures ethereal, human, angel, man,*
> *Beast, bird, fish, insect, what no eye can see,*
> *No glass can reach; from Infinite to thee,*
> *From thee to nothing.—On superior powers*
> *Were we to press, inferior might on ours:*
> *Or in the full creation leave a void,*
> *Where one step broken, the great scale's destroyed:*
> *From Nature's chain whatever link you strike,*
> *Tenth or ten thousandth, breaks the chain alike.*
>   *And, if each system in gradation roll*
> *Alike essential to th' amazing whole,*
> *The least confusion but in one, not all*
> *That system only, but the whole must fall.*
> *Let earth unbalanced from her orbit fly,*
> *Planets and suns run lawless thro' the sky;*
> *Let ruling angels from their spheres be hurled,*
> *Being on being wrecked, and world on world;*
> *Heaven's whole foundations to their center nod,*
> *And Nature tremble to the throne of God.*
> *All this dread order break—from whom? for thee?*
> *Vile worm!—Oh madness! pride! impiety!*
>   *What if the foot, ordained the dust to tread,*
> *Or hand, to toil, aspired to be the head?*

What if the head, the eye, or ear repined
To serve more engines to the ruling mind?
Just as absurd for any part to claim
To be another, in this general frame:
Just as absurd, to mourn the tasks or pains,
The great directing Mind of All ordains.
    All are but parts of one stupendous whole,
Whose body Nature is, and God the soul;
That, changed thro' all, and yet in all the same;
Great in the earth, as in th' ethereal frame;
Warms in the sun, refreshes in the breeze,
Glows in the stars, and blossoms in the trees,
Lives thro' all life, extends thro' all extent,
Spreads undivided, operates unspent;
Breathes in our soul, informs our mortal part,
As full, as perfect, in a hair as heart,
As full, as perfect, in vile man that mourns,
As the rapt seraph that that adores and burns:
To him no high, no low, no great, no small;
He fills, he bounds, connects, and equals all.

Lines from TINTERN ABBEY
William Wordsworth

    William Wordsworth (1770–1850) was an English Romantic poet. The Romantics in general, and Wordsworth in particular, had an aversion to urbanized civilization, and a deep love and reverence for nature. Wordsworth's best-known works are *The Prelude*, a long autobiographical poem, "Tintern Abbey," printed below, and "Ode on Intimations of Immortality" which, like "Tintern Abbey," treats man's ability to achieve communion with nature.

Five years have past; five summers, with the length
Of five long winters! and again I hear
These waters, rolling from their mountain-springs
With a soft inland murmur.—Once again

Do I behold these steep and lofty cliffs,
That on a wild secluded scene impress
Thoughts of more deep seclusion; and connect
The landscape with the quiet of the sky.
The day is come when I again repose
Here, under this dark sycamore, and view
These plots of cottage-ground, these orchard-tufts,
Which at this season, with their unripe fruits,
Are clad in one green hue, and lose themselves
'Mid groves and copses. Once again I see
These hedge-rows, hardly hedge-rows, little lines
Of sportive wood run wild: these pastoral farms,
Green to the very door; and wreaths of smoke
Sent up, in silence, from among the trees!
With some uncertain notice, as might seem
Of vagrant dwellers in the houseless woods,
Or of some Hermit's cave, where by his fire
The Hermit sits alone.

                              These beauteous forms,
Through a long absence, have not been to me
As is a landscape to a blind man's eye:
But oft, in lonely rooms, and 'mid the din
Of towns and cities, I have owed to them,
In hours of weariness, sensations sweet,
Felt in the blood, and felt along the heart;
And passing even into my purer mind,
With tranquil restoration:—feelings too
Of unremembered pleasure: such, perhaps,
As have no slight or trivial influence
On that best portion of a good man's life,
His little, nameless, unremembered, acts
Of kindness and of love. Nor less, I trust,
To them I may have owed another gift,
Of aspect more sublime; that blessed mood,
In which the burthen of the mystery,
In which the heavy and the weary weight
Of all this unintelligible world,
Is lightened:—that serene and blessed mood,
In which the affections gently lead us on,—

Until, the breath of this corporeal frame
And even the motion of our human blood
Almost suspended, we are laid asleep
In body, and become a living soul:
While with an eye made quiet by the power
Of harmony, and the deep power of joy,
We see into the life of things.

                          If this
Be but a vain belief, yet, oh! how oft—
In darkness and amid the many shapes
Of joyless daylight; when the fretful stir
Unprofitable, and the fever of the world,
Have hung upon the beatings of my heart—
How oft, in spirit, have I turned to thee,
O sylvan Wye! thou wanderer thro' the woods,
How often has my spirit turned to thee!

          And now, with gleams of half-extinguished thought
With many recognitions dim and faint,
And somewhat of a sad perplexity,
The picture of the mind revives again:
While here I stand, not only with the sense
Of present pleasure, but with pleasing thoughts
That in this moment there is life and food
For future years. And so I dare to hope,
Though changed, no doubt, from what I was when first
I came among these hills; when like a roe
I bounded o'er the mountains, by the sides
Of the deep rivers, and the lonely streams,
Wherever nature led: more like a man
Flying from something that he dreads than one
Who sought the thing he loved. For nature then
(The coarser pleasures of my boyish days,
And their glad animal movements all gone by)
To me was all in all.—I cannot paint
What then I was. The sounding cataract
Haunted me like a passion: the tall rock,

The mountain, and the deep and gloomy wood,
Their colours and their forms, were then to me
An appetite; a feeling and a love,
That had no need for a remoter charm,
By thought supplied, nor any interest
Unborrowed from the eye.—That time is past,
And all its aching joys are now no more,
And all its dizzy raptures. Not for this
Faint I, nor mourn nor murmur; other gifts
Have followed; for such loss, I would believe,
Abundant recompense. For I have learned
To look on nature, not as in the hour
Of thoughtless youth; but hearing oftentimes
The still, sad music of humanity,
Nor harsh nor grating, though of ample power
To chasten and subdue. And I have felt
A presence that disturbs me with the joy
Of elevated thoughts; a sense sublime
Of something far more deeply interfused,
Whose dwelling is the light of setting suns,
And the round ocean and the living air,
And the blue sky, and in the mind of man:
A motion and a spirit, that impels
All thinking things, all objects of all thought,
And rolls through all things. Therefore am I still
A lover of the meadows and the woods,
And mountains; and of all that we behold
From this green earth; of all the mighty world
Of eye, and ear,—both what they half create,
And what perceive; well pleased to recognise
In nature and the language of the sense
The anchor of my purest thoughts, the nurse,
The guide, the guardian of my heart, and soul
Of all my moral being.

                    Nor perchance,
If I were not thus taught, should I the more
Suffer my genial spirits to decay:
For thou art with me here upon the banks
Of this fair river; thou my dearest Friend,

My dear, dear Friend; and in thy voice I catch
The language of my former heart, and read
My former pleasures in the shooting lights
Of thy wild eyes. Oh! yet a little while
May I behold in thee what I was once,
My dear, dear Sister! and this prayer I make,
Knowing that Nature never did betray
The heart that loved her; 'tis her privilege,
Through all the years of this our life, to lead
From joy to joy: for she can so inform
The mind that is within us, so impress
With quietness and beauty, and so feed

With lofty thoughts, that neither evil tongues,
Rash judgments, nor the sneers of selfish men,
Nor greetings where no kindness is, nor all
The dreary intercourse of daily life,
Shall e'er prevail against us, or disturb
Our cheerful faith, that all which we behold
Is full of blessings. Therefore let the moon
Shine on thee in thy solitary walk;
And let the misty mountain-winds be free
To blow against thee: and, in after years,
When these wild ecstasies shall be matured
Into a sober pleasure; when thy mind
Shall be a mansion for all lovely forms,
Thy memory be as a dwelling-place
For all sweet sounds and harmonies; oh! then,
If solitude, or fear, or pain, or grief
Should be thy portion, with what healing thoughts
Of tender joy wilt thou remember me,
And these my exhortations! Nor, perchance—
If I should be where I no more can hear
Thy voice, nor catch from thy wild eyes these gleams
Of past existence—wilt thou then forget
That on the banks of this delightful stream
We stood together; and that I, so long

A worshipper of Nature, hither came
Unwearied in that service: rather say
With warmer love—oh! with far deeper zeal
Of holier love. Nor wilt thou then forget
That after many wanderings, many years
Of absence, these steep woods and lofty cliffs,
And this green pastoral landscape, were to me
More dear, both for themselves and for thy sake!

NATURE
Ralph Waldo Emerson

Ralph Waldo Emerson (1803–1882) was an essayist, philosopher, and poet of the New England Transcendentalists, a group inspired by the Romantic movement in Europe, and especially by the philosophy of Kant. Like the Romantics, the Transcendentalists had a deep reverence for nature.

I. Nature

To go into solitude, a man needs to retire as much from his chamber as from society. I am not solitary whilst I read and write, though nobody is with me. But if a man would be alone, let him look at the stars. The rays that come from those heavenly worlds will separate between him and what he touches. One might think the atmosphere was made transparent with this design, to give man, in the heavenly bodies, the perpetual presence of the sublime. Seen in the streets of cities, how great they are! If the stars should appear one night in a thousand years, how would men believe and adore; and preserve for many generations the remembrance of the city of God which had been shown! But every night come out these envoys of beauty, and light the universe with their admonishing smile.

The stars awaken a certain reverence, because though always present, they are inaccessible; but all natural objects make a kindred impression, when the mind is open to their influence. Nature never wears a mean appearance. Neither does the wisest man extort her secret, and lose his curiosity by finding out all her perfection. Nature never became a toy to a wise spirit. The flowers, the animals, the mountains, reflected the wisdom of his best hour, as much as they had delighted the simplicity of his childhood.

When we speak of nature in this manner, we have a distinct but most poetical sense in the mind. We mean the integrity of impression made by manifold natural objects. It is this which distinguishes the stick of timber of the wood-cutter from the tree of the poet. The charming landscape which I saw this morning is indubitably made up of some twenty or thirty farms. Miller owns this field, Locke that, and Manning the woodland beyond. But none of them owns the landscape. There is a property in the horizon which no man has but he whose eye can integrate all the parts, that is, the poet. This is the best part of these men's farms, yet to this their warranty-deeds give no title.

To speak truly, few adult persons can see nature. Most persons do not see the sun. At least they have a very superficial seeing. The sun illuminates only the eye of the man, but shines into the eye and the heart of the child. The lover of nature is he whose inward and outward senses are still truly adjusted to each other, who has retained the spirit of infancy even into the era of manhood. His intercourse with heaven and earth becomes part of his daily food. In the presence of nature a wild delight runs through the man, in spite of real sorrows. Nature says,—he is my creature, and maugre all his impertinent griefs, he shall be glad with me. Not the sun or the summer alone, but every hour and season yields its tribute of delight; for every hour and change corresponds to and authorizes a different state of the mind, from breathless noon to grimmest midnight. Nature is a setting that fits equally well a comic or a mourning piece. In good health, the air is a cordial of incredible virtue. Crossing a bare common, in snow puddles, at twilight, under a clouded sky, without having in my thoughts any occurrence of special good fortune, I have enjoyed a perfect exhilaration. I am glad to the brink of fear. In the woods, too, a man casts off his years, as the snake his slough, and at what period soever of life, is always a child. In the woods is perpetual youth. Within these plantations of God, a decorum and sanctity reign, a perennial festival is dressed, and the guest sees not how he should tire of them in a thousand years. In the woods, we return to reason and faith. There I feel that nothing can befall me in life,—no disgrace, no calamity (leaving me my eyes), which nature cannot repair. Standing on the bare ground,—my head bathed by the blithe air, and uplifted into infinite space,—all mean egotism vanishes. I become a transparent eyeball; I am nothing; I see all; the currents of the Universal Being circulate through me; I am part or parcel of God. The name of the nearest friend sounds then foreign and accidental: to be brothers, to be acquaintances,—master or servant, is then a trifle and a disturbance. I am the lover of uncontained and immortal beauty. In the wilderness, I find something more dear and connate than in streets or villages. In the tranquil landscape, and especially in the distant line of the horizon, man beholds somewhat as beautiful as his own nature.

The greatest delight which the fields and woods minister is the suggestion of an occult relation between man and the vegetable. I am not alone and unacknowledged. They nod to me, and I to them. The waving of the boughs in the storm is new to me and old. It takes me by surprise, and yet is not unknown. Its effect is like that of a higher thought or a better emotion coming over me, when I deemed I was thinking justly or doing right.

Yet it is certain that the power to produce this delight does not reside in nature, but in man, or in a harmony of both. It is necessary to use these pleasures with great temperance. For nature is not always tricked in holiday attire, but the same scene which yesterday breathed perfume and glittered as for the frolic of the nymphs, is overspread with melancholy to-day. Nature always wears the colors of the spirit. To a man laboring under calamity, the heat of his own fire hath sadness in it. Then there is a kind of contempt of the landscape felt by him who has just lost by death a dear friend. The sky is less grand as it shuts down over less worth in the population.

V. Discipline　　＊　＊　＊

Sensible objects conform to the premonitions of Reason and reflect the conscience. All things are moral; and in their boundless changes have an unceasing reference to spiritual nature. Therefore is nature glorious with form, color, and motion; that every globe in the remotest heaven, every chemical change from the rudest crystal up to the laws of life, every change of vegetation from the first principle of growth in the eye of a leaf, to the tropical forest and antediluvian coal-mine, every animal function from the sponge up to Hercules, shall hint or thunder to man the laws of right and wrong, and echo the Ten Commandments. Therefore is Nature ever the ally of Religion: lends all her pomp and riches to the religious sentiment. Prophet and priest, David, Isaiah, Jesus, have drawn deeply from this source. This ethical character so penetrates the bone and marrow of nature, as to seem the end for which it was made. Whatever private purpose is answered by any member or part, this is its public and universal function, and is never omitted. Nothing in nature is exhausted in its first use. When a thing has served an end to the uttermost, it is wholly new for an ulterior service. In God, every end is converted into a new means. Thus the use of commodity, regarded by itself, is mean and squalid. But it is to the mind an education in the doctrine of Use, namely, that a thing is good only so far as it serves; that a conspiring of parts and efforts to the production of an end is essential to any being. The first and gross manifestation of this truth is our inevitable and hated training in values and wants, in corn and meat.

It has already been illustrated, that every natural process is a version of a moral sentence. The moral law lies at the centre of nature and radiates to the circumference. It is the pith and marrow of every substance, every relation, and every process. All things with which we deal, preach to us. What is a farm but a mute gospel? The chaff and the wheat, weeds and plants, blight, rain, insects, sun,—it is a sacred emblem from the first furrow of spring to the last stack which the snow of winter overtakes in the fields. But the sailor, the shepherd, the miner, the merchant, in their several resorts, have each an experience precisely parallel, and leading to the same conclusion: because all organizations are radically alike. Nor can it be doubted that this moral sentiment which thus scents the air, grows in the grain, and impregnates the waters of the world, is caught by man and sinks into his soul. The moral influence of nature upon every individual is that amount of truth which it illustrates to him. Who can estimate this? Who can guess how much firmness the sea-beaten rock has taught the fisherman? how much tranquillity has been reflected to man from the azure sky, over whose unspotted deeps the winds forevermore drive flocks of stormy clouds, and leave no wrinkle or stain? how much industry and providence and affection we have caught from the pantomime of brutes? What a searching preacher of self-command is the varying phenomenon of Health!

Herein is especially apprehended the unity of Nature,—the unity in variety,—which meets us everywhere. All the endless variety of things make an identical impression. Xenophanes complained in his old age, that, look where he would, all things hastened back to Unity. He was weary of seeing the same entity in the tedious variety of forms. The fable of Proteus has a cordial truth. A leaf, a drop, a crystal, a moment of time, is related to the whole, and partakes of the perfection of the whole. Each particle is a microcosm, and faithfully renders the likeness of the world.

Not only resemblances exist in things whose analogy is obvious, as when we detect the type of the human hand in the flipper of the fossil saurus, but also in objects wherein there is great superficial unlikeness. Thus, architecture is called "frozen music" by De Staël and Goethe. Vitruvius thought an architect should be a musician. "A Gothic church," said Coleridge, "is a petrified religion." Michelangelo maintained, that, to an architect, a knowledge of anatomy is essential. In Haydn's oratorios, the notes present to the imagination not only motions, as of the snake, the stag, and the elephant, but colors also; as the green grass. The law of harmonic sound reappears in the harmonic colors. The granite is differenced in its laws only by the more or less of heat from the river that wears it away. The river, as it flows, resembles the air that flows over it; the air resembles the light which traverses it with more subtile currents; the light resembles the heat which rides with it through Space. Each creature is only a modification of the other; the likeness in them is more than the difference, and their radical law is one and the same. A rule of one art, or a law of one organization, holds true throughout nature. So intimate is this Unity, that, it is easily seen, it lies under the undermost garment of Nature, and betrays its source in Universal Spirit. For it pervades Thought also. Every universal truth which we express in words, implies or supposes every other truth. *Omne verum vero consonat.* It is like a great circle on a sphere, comprising all possible circles; which, however, may be drawn and comprise it in like manner. Every such truth is the absolute Ens seen from one side. But it has innumerable sides.

The central Unity is still more conspicuous in actions. Words are finite organs of the infinite mind. They cannot cover the dimensions of what is in truth. They break, chop, and impoverish it. An action is the perfection and publication of thought. A right action seems to fill the eye, and to be related to all nature. "The wise man, in doing one thing, does all; or, in the one thing he does rightly, he sees the likeness of all which is done rightly."

EACH AND ALL
Ralph Waldo Emerson

Little thinks, in the field, yon red-cloaked clown[2]
Of thee from the hilltop looking down;
The heifer that lows in the upland farm,
Far-heard, lows not thine ear to charm;
The sexton, tolling his bell at noon,
Deems not that great Napoleon
Stops his horse, and lists with delight,
Whilst his files sweep round yon Alpine height;
Nor knowest thou what argument
Thy life to thy neighbor's creed has lent.
All are needed by each one;
Nothing is fair or good alone.
I thought the sparrow's note from heaven,
Singing at dawn on the alder bough;
I brought him home, in his nest, at even;
He sings the song, but it cheers not now,
For I did not bring home the river and sky;—
He sang to my ear,—they sang to my eye.
The delicate shells lay on the shore;
The bubbles of the latest wave
Fresh pearls to their enamel gave,
And the bellowing of the savage sea
Greeted their safe escape to me.
I wiped away the weeds and foam,
I fetched my sea-born treasures home;
But the poor, unsightly, noisome things
Had left their beauty on the shore

[2]Rustic, man from the country, not a buffoon in whiteface.

With the sun and the sand and the wild uproar.
The lover watched his graceful maid,
As 'mid the virgin train she strayed,
Nor knew her beauty's best attire
Was woven still by the snow-white choir.
At last she came to his hermitage,
Like the bird from the woodlands to the cage;—
The gay enchantment was undone,
A gentle wife, but fairy none.
Then I said, "I covet truth;
Beauty is unripe childhood's cheat;
I leave it behind with the games of youth."—
As I spoke, beneath my feet
The ground pine curled its pretty wreath,
Running over the club moss burs;
I inhaled the violet's breath;
Around me stood the oaks and firs;
Pine cones and acorns lay on the ground;
Over me soared the eternal sky,
Full of light and of deity;
Again I say, again I heard,
The rolling river, the morning bird;—
Beauty through my senses stole;
I yielded myself to the perfect whole.

TO A WATERFOWL
William Cullen Bryant

William Cullen Bryant (1794–1878) was the leading American poet in the early years of the nineteenth century. "To a Waterfowl," often considered Bryant's masterpiece, stresses the bond between God and nature. God is the protecting power that guides the waterfowl—and man as well. Other poems on the relationship of man and nature include "Inscription for the Entrance to a Wood," "I Cannot Forget with What Fervid Devotion," "Green River," and "A Forest Hymn."

Whither, 'midst falling dew,
While glow the heavens with the last steps of day,
Far, through their rosy depths, dost thou pursue
　　　Thy solitary way?

Vainly the fowler's eye
Might mark thy distant flight, to do thee wrong,
As, darkly seen against the crimson sky,
　　　Thy figure floats along.

Seek'st thou the plashy brink
Of weedy lake, or marge of river wide,
Or where the rocking billows rise and sink
　　　On the chafed ocean side?

There is a Power, whose care
Teaches thy way along that pathless coast,—
The desert and illimitable air,
　　　Lone wandering, but not lost.

All day thy wings have fann'd,
At that far height, the cold thin atmosphere;
Yet stoop not, weary, to the welcome land,
　　　Though the dark night is near.

And soon that toil shall end,
Soon shalt thou find a summer home, and rest,
And scream among thy fellows; reeds shall bend,
　　　Soon, o'er thy sheltered nest.

Thou'rt gone, the abyss of heaven
Hath swallowed up thy form, yet, on my heart
Deeply hath sunk the lesson thou hast given,
　　　And shall not soon depart.

He, who, from zone to zone,
Guides through the boundless sky thy certain flight,
In the long way that I must trace alone,
　　　Will lead my steps aright.

SMOKEY THE BEAR SUTRA
Gary Snyder

Gary Snyder (1930–) is a San Francisco–born poet whose love of life and the earth is an inspiration to the ecology movement. His best-known works are *Earth House Hold* (the title plays on the root meaning of ecology), a collection of Snyder's travel journals, written in prose and verse, and *The Back Country,* a volume of poems which reflect such diverse experiences as logging in the northwest and studying Zen in a Japanese monastery. "As a poet," Snyder has said, "I hold the most archaic values on earth. They go back to the late Paleolithic; the fertility of the soil, the magic of animals, the power-vision in solitude, the terrifying initiation and rebirth; the love and ecstasy of the dance, the common work of the tribe."

Once in the Jurassic, about 150 million years ago,
the Great Sun Buddha in this corner of the Infinite
Void gave a great Discourse to all the assembled elements
and energies: to the standing beings, the walking beings,
the flying beings, and the sitting beings—even grasses,
to the number of thirteen billion, each one born from a
seed, were assembled there: a Discourse concerning
Enlightenment on the planet Earth.

"In some future time, there will be a continent called
America. It will have great centers of power called
such as Pyramid Lake, Walden Pond, Mt. Rainier, Big Sur,
Everglades, and so forth; and powerful nerves and channels
such as Columbia River, Mississippi River, and Grand Canyon.
The human race in that era will get into troubles all over
its head, and practically wreck everything in spite of
its own strong intelligent Buddha-nature."

"The twisting strata of the great mountains and the pulsings
of great volcanoes are my love burning deep in the earth.
My obstinate compassion is schist and basalt and
granite, to be mountains, to bring down the rain. In that

future American Era I shall enter a new form: to cure
the world of loveless knowledge that seeks with blind hunger;
and mindless rage eating food that will not fill it."

And he showed himself in his true form of

SMOKEY THE BEAR.

A handsome smokey-colored brown bear standing on his
hind legs, showing that he is aroused and watchful.

Bearing in his right paw the Shovel that digs to the
truth beneath appearances; cuts the roots of useless attach-
ments, and flings damp sand on the fires of greed and war;

His left paw in the Mudra of Comradely Display—indicating
that all creatures have the full right to live to their limits
and that deer, rabbits, chipmunks, snakes, dandelions,
and lizards all grow in the realm of the Dharma;

Wearing the blue work overalls symbolic of slaves and
laborers, the countless men oppressed by a civilization
that claims to save but only destroys;

Wearing the broad-brimmed hat of the West, symbolic of
the forces that guard the Wilderness, which is the Natural
State of the Dharma and the True Path of man on earth:
all true paths lead through mountains

With a halo of smoke and flame behind, the forest fires
of the kali yuga, fires caused by the stupidity of those
who think things can be gained and lost whereas in truth all
is contained vast and free in the Blue Sky and Green Earth
of One Mind;

Round bellied to show his kind nature and that the great
earth has food enough for everyone who loves her and trusts
her;

Trampling underfoot wasteful freeways and needless
suburbs; smashing the worms of capitalism and totalitarianism;

Indicating the Task: his followers, becoming free of cars,
houses, canned food, universities, and shoes, master the
Three Mysteries of their own Body, Speech, and Mind: and
fearlessly chop down the rotten trees and prune out the
sick limbs of this country America and then burn the leftover
trash.

Wrathful but Calm, Austere but Comic, Smokey the Bear will
Illuminate those who would help him; but for those who would
hinder or slander him,

HE WILL PUT THEM OUT.

Thus his great Mantra:

Namah samanta vajranam chanda maharoshana
Sphataya hum traka ham mam

"I DEDICATE MYSELF TO THE UNIVERSAL DIAMOND
BE THIS RAGING FURY DESTROYED"

And he will protect those who love woods and rivers,
Gods and animals, hobos and madmen, prisoners and sick
people, musicians, playful women, and hopeful children;

And if anyone is threatened by advertising, air pollution,
or the police, they should chant SMOKEY THE BEAR'S
WAR SPELL:

DROWN THEIR BUTTS
CRUSH THEIR BUTTS
DROWN THEIR BUTTS
CRUSH THEIR BUTTS

And SMOKEY THE BEAR will surely appear to put the enemy out
with his vajra-shovel.

Now those who recite this Sutra and then try to put it in
        practice will accumulate merit as countless as the sands
        of Arizona and Nevada,
Will help save the planet Earth from total oil slick,
Will enter the age of harmony of man and nature,
Will win the tender love and caresses of men, women, and
        beasts,
Will always have ripe blackberries to eat and a sunny spot
        under a pine tree to sit at,

AND IN THE END WILL WIN
HIGHEST PERFECT ENLIGHTENMENT.

            thus have we heard.

                        (may be reproduced free forever)

CHAPTER TWO
Large and Small: Whatever Lives Is Holy

'Tis Nature's law
That none, the meanest of created things,
Of forms created the most vile and brute,
The dullest or more noxious, should exist
Divorced from good—a spirit and pulse of good,
A life and soul, to every mode of being
Inseparably linked.

William Wordsworth
"The Old Cumberland Beggar"

I believe a leaf of grass is no less than the journey-work of the stars,
And the pismire is equally perfect, and a grain of sand, and the egg of
the wren,
And the tree-toad is a chef-d'oeuvre for the highest,
And the running blackberry would adorn the parlors of heaven,
And the narrowest hinge in my hand puts to scorn all machinery,
And the cow crunching with depress'd head surpasses any statue,
And a mouse is miracle enough to stagger sextillions of infidels.

Walt Whitman
"Song of Myself"

AUGURIES OF INNOCENCE
William Blake

William Blake (1757–1827) was one of the earliest of the English Romantic poets. His best-known works include "Songs of Innocence" and "Songs of Experience," collections of lyric poems, and the highly mystical prose poem, "The Marriage of Heaven and Hell."

Although generally optimistic and deeply religious, Blake's most powerful verse is the product of his indignation at human callousness and cruelty. His later work, strongly influenced by Swedish religious philosopher Emanuel Swedenborg, is marked by an intensely visionary mysticism. Although chiefly known today for his poetry, Blake was also one of England's great painters.

To see a World in a Grain of Sand
And a Heaven in a Wild Flower,
Hold Infinity in the palm of your hand
And Eternity in an hour.

A Robin Red breast in a Cage
Puts all Heaven in a Rage.
A dove house fill'd with doves & Pigeons
Shudders Hell thro' all its regions.
A dog starv'd at his Master's Gate
Predicts the ruin of the State.
A Horse misus'd upon the Road
Calls to Heaven for Human blood.

Each outcry of the hunted Hare
A fibre from the Brain does tear.
A Skylark wounded in the wing,
A Cherubim does cease to sing.
The Game Cock clip'd & arm'd for fight
Does the Rising Sun affright.
Every Wolf's & Lion's howl
Raises from Hell a Human Soul.
The wild deer, wand'ring here & there,
Keeps the Human Soul from Care.
The Lamb misus'd breeds Public strife
And yet forgives the Butcher's Knife.
The Bat that flits at close of Eve
Has left the Brain that won't Believe.
The Owl that calls upon the Night
Speaks the Unbeliever's fright.
He who shall hurt the little Wren
Shall never be belov'd by Men.
He who the Ox to wrath has mov'd
Shall never be by Woman lov'd.
The wanton Boy that kills the Fly
Shall feel the Spider's enmity.
He who torments the Chafer's sprite
Weaves a Bower in endless Night.
The Caterpiller on the Leaf
Repeats to thee thy Mother's grief.
Kill not the Moth nor Butterfly,
For the Last Judgment draweth nigh.

THE FLAME OF LIFE[1]
W. H. Hudson

William Henry Hudson (1841–1922) was born in Argentina of
American parents. He grew up in South America, then emigrated
to England, where he became a naturalized citizen in 1900. He is

[1] W. H. Hudson, "The Flame of Life" in *The Book of a Naturalist*.

remembered for *Green Mansions,* a romantic novel set in the South American jungle. His best works, however, were nonfiction—autobiographical and nature writing, which include *Far Away and Long Ago, A Traveller in Little Things,* and *The Book of a Naturalist.*

Adders were common at a place where I was staying at a farm in the New Forest, but I had never seen one near the house until one sultry afternoon in July, when coming into a path which led from the farm-yard into and through a hazel copse, I came upon one lying in the middle of the path. It was a large adder, so sluggish that it made no attempt to escape, but turned and struck at me when I approached it. I thought of the little children, for this was the very spot where they came to play and hunt for fowls' eggs every afternoon; the adder, if left there, might be a danger to them; it was necessary either to kill or remove it. Then it occurred to me that to remove it would be useless, since if the creature's place was there, it would infallibly return to it from any distance. The homing instinct is strong in the adder and in most serpents. And so to end the matter I killed and buried it, and went on my way. My way was through the copse and over a fence and ditch on the other side, and I was no sooner over the ditch than I beheld a second adder, bigger than the last and just as sluggish. It was, however, not strange, as in July the female adder is often like that, especially in sultry thunderous weather. I teased it to make it move away, then picked it up to examine it, after which I released it and watched it gliding slowly away into the shadow of the bushes. And, watching it, I became conscious of a change in my mental attitude towards the living things that were so much to me, my chief happiness having always been in observing their ways. The curiosity was not diminished, but the feeling that had gone with it for a very long time past was changed from what it had been when I was sportsman and collector, always killing things. The serpent gliding away before me was nothing but a worm with poison fangs in its head and a dangerous habit of striking at unwary legs—a creature to be crushed with the heel and no more thought about. I had lost something precious, not, I should say, in any ethical sense, seeing that we are in a world where we must kill to live, but valuable in my special case, to me as a field-naturalist. Abstention from killing had made me a better observer and a happier being, on account of the new or different feeling towards animal life which it had engendered. And what was this new feeling

—wherein did it differ from the old of my shooting and collecting days, seeing that since childhood I had always had the same intense interest in all wild life? The power, beauty, and grace of the wild creature, its perfect harmony in nature, the exquisite correspondence between organism, form, and faculties, and the environment, with the plasticity and intelligence for the readjustment of the vital machinery, daily, hourly, momentarily, to meet all changes in the conditions, all contingencies; and thus, amidst perpetual mutations and conflict with hostile and destructive forces, to perpetuate a form, a type, a species for thousands and millions of years!—all this was always present to my mind; yet even so it was but a lesser element in the complete feeling. The main thing was the wonderfulness and eternal mystery of life itself; this formative, informing energy—this flame that burns in and shines through the case, the habit, which in lighting another dies, and albeit dying yet endures for ever; and the sense, too, that this flame of life was one, and of my kinship with it in all its appearances, in all organic shapes, however different from the human. Nay, the very fact that the forms were unhuman but served to heighten the interest;—the roe-deer, the leopard and wild horse, the swallow cleaving the air, the butterfly toying with a flower, and the dragon-fly dreaming on the river; the monster whale, the silver flying-fish, and the nautilus with rose- and purple-tinted sails spread to the wind.

STILL[2]
A. R. Ammons

A. R. Ammons (1926–) was born in North Carolina and presently teaches at Cornell. His best-known collections of verse are *Expressions of Sea Level* and *Corson's Inlet*. American landscape in its many forms is a major concern of Ammons's poetry.

I said I will find what is lowly
and put the roots of my identity
down there:

[2]Reprinted from *Expressions of Sea Level* by A. R. Ammons (Columbus: Ohio State University Press, 1963). The poem "Still" by A. R. Ammons, was first published in 1963 in the *Emerson Review*. It subsequently appeared in *Expressions of Sea Level*, by A. R. Ammons, published by the Ohio State University Press. Copyright © 1963 by the Ohio State University Press.

each day I'll wake up
and find the lowly nearby,
        and handy focus and reminder,
a ready measure of my significance,
the voice by which I would be heard,
the wills, the kinds of selfishness
        I could
freely adopt as my own:

but though I have looked everywhere,
        I can find nothing
        to give myself to:
        everything is

magnificent with existence, is in
surfeit of glory:
nothing is diminished,
nothing has been diminished for me:

I said what is more lowly than the grass:
        ah, underneath,
        a ground-crust of dry-burnt moss:
        I looked at it closely
and said this can be my habitat: but
nestling in I
found
        below the brown exterior
        green mechanisms beyond intellect
awaiting resurrection in rain: so I got up

and ran saying there is nothing lowly in the universe:
I found a beggar:
he had stumps for legs: nobody was paying
him any attention: everybody went on by:
        I nestled in and found his life:
there, love shook his body like a devastation:

I said

> *though I have looked everywhere*
> *I can find nothing lowly*
> *in the universe:*

I whirled through transfigurations up and down,
transfigurations of size and shape and place:
> *at one sudden point came still,*
> *stood in wonder:*
moss, beggar, weed, tick, pine, self, magnificent
> *with being!*

WORLD[3]
A. R. Ammons

Breakers at high tide shoot
spray over the jetty boulders
that collects in shallow chips, depressions,

evening the surface to run-off level:
of these possible worlds of held water,
most can't outlast the interim tideless

drought, so are clear, sterile, encased with
salt: one in particular, though, a hole,
providing depth with little surface,

keeps water through the hottest day:
a slime of green algae extends into that
tiny sea, and animals tiny enough to be in a

world there breed and dart and breathe and
die: so we are here in this plant-created oxygen,
drinking this sweet rain, consuming this green.

[3] Reprinted from A. R. Ammons: *Corson's Inlet.* Copyright © 1965 by Cornell University. Used by permission of Cornell University Press.

OF LICE AND MEN[4]
Yikyubo,
translated by R. H. Blyth

Yikyubo (1168–1241) was a Korean poet, musician, and prime minister.

A friend of mine came and said, "Yesterday evening I saw some rascal beat to death a dog which was wandering about there. It was such a pitiful sight, and I was so upset by it, I resolved never to touch dog's flesh again." I said to him, "Last night I saw a man sitting by the fire cracking lice and burning them. I was so upset I made up my mind never to kill another louse." My friend said indignantly, "A louse is a very small thing; what I saw was a big animal done to death and because I felt so grieved, I told you about it. Why do you answer me so facetiously?" I replied, "All things with life and breath, from common men to oxen, horses, pigs, sheep, down to insects, mole-crickets and ants,—all, without exception, love life and hate death. Do you imagine for a moment that big animals only dislike to die and the little ones don't mind it? Thus the death of a louse is no different from that of a dog. This is quite clear; why should you suppose I was talking flippantly? Bite your own ten fingers and see. The thumb hurts; but how about the rest of the fingers? In one body there is no distinction between large and small members. All that has blood and flesh feels the same pain. So it is with all things that have received life and breath: how can you think that one hates death and another finds it pleasant? Now you go home and quietly meditate on this, and when you see that the horns of a snail are the same as those of a bull, the wren of equal value with the mighty Rukh, then come, and we'll talk of religion again."

[4]Yikyubo, from R. H. Blyth, in *Zen in English Literature and Oriental Classics,* 1942. The Hokusiedo Press, Tokyo. The title is the author's; the selection was originally untitled.

HYLA BROOK[5]
Robert Frost

Robert Frost (1875–1963) wrote most of his poetry about his native New England farm country. His work is characterized by a keen insight into the people and the land. Frost demanded that his verse be simple and honest, and he achieved this effect by a skillful use of simple diction and colloquial speech rhythms.

By June our brook's run out of song and speed.
Sought for much after that, it will be found
Either to have gone groping underground
(And taken with it all the Hyla breed
That shouted in the mist a month ago,
Like ghost of sleigh bells in a ghost of snow)—
Or flourished and come up in jewelweed,
Weak foliage that is blown upon and bent,
Even against the way its waters went.
Its bed is left a faded paper sheet
Of dead leaves stuck together by the heat—
A brook to none but who remember long.
This as it will be seen is other far
Than with brooks taken otherwhere in song.
We love the things we love for what they are.

BIRDS OF SORROW [Utō][6]
Seami Motokiyo
translated by Meredith Weatherby and Bruce Rogers

Birds of Sorrow is a Nō play. Nō is a nonrealistic form of drama in which the actors wear stylized costumes, dialog is mainly chanted to the accompaniment of drums and flute, and dancing plays

[5]From *The Poetry of Robert Frost* edited by Edward Connery Lathem. Copyright 1916, 1923, © 1969 by Holt, Rinehart and Winston, Inc. Copyright 1942, 1944, 1951 by Robert Frost. Copyright © 1970 by Lesley Frost Ballentine. Reprinted by permission of Holt, Rinehart and Winston, Inc.

[6]Reprinted by permission of Meredith Weatherby and Bruce Rogers, translators.

an important part. Seami Motokiyo (1363–1443) was the principal figure in the development of Nō drama and the author of most of the Nō plays which are still performed.

The original title of the play, "Utō," is usually written in Japanese with three ideographs which may be loosely translated as "virtue-knowing bird." The utō or utōyasukata of early legends is a species of sea bird found in northern Japan and widely hunted for the delectability of its flesh. According to tradition, the parent bird of the species hides its young so well in the sand that even it cannot find them and, when bringing them food, calls them with the cry "Utō," to which they reply with the cry "Yasukata." Hunters catch both parent birds and the young by imitating these cries. It is also said that the parent birds weep tears of blood upon seeing their young taken, and that hunters must wear large hats and raincloaks to protect themselves from the falling tears, the touch of which causes sickness and death. Because of its traits the bird becomes an apt symbol for the Buddhist tenet that the taking of life in any form whatsoever is a sin.

Persons
A Buddhist Monk
The Ghost of a Dead Hunter
The Hunter's Wife
The Hunter's Child
A Villager
Chorus

PART I

Place: Tateyamā, a high mountain in Central Honshū, near the Sea of Japan. Time: The month of April.

(The stage is completely bare. Two drummers and a flute player come through the curtain and, passing down the Bridge, take their usual seats at the rear of the stage. They are followed in silence by the Wife and Child. The Wife wears the mask and wig of a middle-aged woman; her inner kimono is the color of dried autumn leaves, over which is a kimono with a small pattern and a long

outer kimono in somber colors which trails behind her on the floor. The Child, apparently six or eight years of age, wears a hakama and a brightly embroidered outer kimono over a scarlet inner kimono. They seat themselves near the Waki's Pillar. The Monk enters, accompanied by the introductory flute music. He is wearing a dark kimono and a peaked cowl of brocade which flows down over his shoulders, and carries a rosary. He passes down the Bridge onto the stage, where he stops at the Name-Saying Seat and, facing the audience, introduces himself.)

Monk: I am a wandering monk, making a pilgrimage throughout the provinces. I have never yet visited the village of Soto no Hama in Michinoku. Thinking on this, I was recently minded to go to Soto no Hama. And as the occasion is indeed favorable, I am planning to stop in passing and practice religious austerities upon Tateyama.

(Takes two steps forward, indicating he has arrived at the foot of the mountain.)

Coming swiftly along the road, already I have arrived here at Tateyama. With serene and reverent heart I now shall visit the mountain.

(Goes to center of stage, indicating he has climbed to the summit.)

But lo! upon arriving here on Tateyama, my eyes do indeed behold a living Hell. And the heart of even the boldest man must quail before this fell sight, more frightful even than demons and fiends. Here the countless mountain trails, grim and precipitous, split asunder as if to lead down into the Realm of Ravenous Ghosts, and down into the Realm of Bestiality.

(Describing his actions.) So saying, he is overcome with the memory of his past sins and for a time is unable to restrain the starting tears. Then, penitent, he descends to the foot of the mountain . . . to the foot of the mountain, penitent. . . .

(The Monk goes toward the Chorus, indicating he has returned to the foot of the mountain. He turns and faces the Bridge. The curtain is swept back and a voice is heard from the blackness of the Mirror Room beyond the curtain. It is the Ghost of the Dead Hunter who speaks, calling out as though he has been running after the Monk.)

Hunter: Hallo-o! Hallo-o! Wait, O worthy monk, for I must speak with you.
Monk: What is it you want with me?

(The Hunter enters. He is seen now in his mortal form, wearing the mask of a pleasant old man and a white wig. He wears a plain, tea-colored outer kimono of rough weave over garments of solid brown and light green. He moves slowly down the Bridge as he speaks.)

Hunter: If you are going down to Michinoku, pray take a message there. I am one who was a hunter of Soto no Hama and who died in the past year's autumn. I beseech you to visit the home of my wife and child and to tell them to offer up for me the cloak of straw and the sedge-hat which are there.
Monk: This is a strange request that I hear. To carry the message is a simple thing, but if I address her thus without any proof, like the falling of sudden rain from an empty sky, is it likely that she will believe?
Hunter: Indeed, you are right. Without some certain sign or token, it would surely be of no avail.

(The Hunter has been advancing along the Bridge; he pauses now at the First Pine and bows his head dejectedly. Then an idea comes to him and he raises his head.)

Ah! Now I remember—this was the kimono which I was wearing at the very hour of death.
(Describing his actions.) And thereupon he tears a sleeve from the kimono which he is wearing, a kimono made of hemp like that of Kiso long ago, and worn in the days of his life.

(The Hunter removes the left sleeve of his kimono, touches it to his forehead, and then holds it out in both hands toward the Monk.)

Chorus: He says, "This give as a token." And so saying, gives it with tears to the wandering monk . . . with tears, to the wandering monk. . . .

(The Monk goes to the Hunter at the First Pine and takes the sleeve, then turns and comes onto the stage, while the Hunter starts along the Bridge toward the curtain.)

They bid farewell. The footsteps of the monk lead away toward Michinoku, down through the flaming, budding trees of spring, far and far away, amid the rising smoke and clouds of Tateyama, until his figure too becomes like a wisp of cloud.

(The Monk continues toward the front of the stage. The Hunter brings his hand to his forehead in a gesture of weeping. Then he turns around on the Bridge and looks long toward the stage, shading his eyes with his hand.)

The dead one weeps and weeps, watching the monk depart, and then vanishes, no one knows where . . . no one knows where. . . .

(The Hunter has turned and continued along the Bridge. Now the curtain is swept back and he moves into the blackness beyond the curtain.)

INTERLUDE

Place: Soto no Hama, a fishing village on the northernmost coast of Honshū) several hundred miles from Tateyama.

(There has been a slight pause on the stage, during which time the Monk is understood to be traveling to Michinoku. Now he goes to the Name-Saying Seat, where he turns and addresses the actor who has been sitting motionless at the Kyōgen's Seat during Part I.)

Monk: Are you a native of Soto no Hama?

(The Villager rises and stands on the Bridge near the First Pine. He is wearing a simple plaid kimono and a kamishimo of brocade.)

Villager: Yes, I am. May I help you?

Monk: Please show me the house here of the hunter who died last autumn.

Villager: Why, of course. The dead hunter's house is that one you see there inside that high stockade made of crisscrossed bamboo. You can reach it in a moment if you please.

Monk: I understand. Thank you for your kindness. I shall go there at once and pay a visit.

Villager: If there is anything else I can do for you, please say so.

Monk: Thank you very much.

Villager: You are very welcome.

(The Villager resumes his seat. Later he makes an unobtrusive exit.)

PART II

Place: The home of the dead Hunter, both the interior and exterior being understood to be visible.

(The Monk has moved to the Stage Attendant's Pillar, where he pauses. The Wife speaks, as if to herself, from her seat at the Waki's Pillar.)

Wife: Truly, long have I known this world to be a fleeting thing, becoming dreamlike even as it passes. But now more than ever before.

To what avail was my troth plighted? Now death has cut the ties which bound me to my husband. And this beloved child, left behind him like a footstep at the parting, only makes my grief more endless. . . . Oh, how can a mother's heart endure such sorrow?

(The Wife makes a gesture of weeping. The Monk has put the sleeve which he held into the breastfold of his kimono and has been advancing slowly toward the stage. Reaching the Shite's Pillar, he stops and turns toward the Wife, indicating he has reached the house.)

    Monk: Pray let me in.

    Wife: Who is there?

    Monk: I am a wandering monk, making a pilgrimage throughout the provinces. While I was practicing religious austerities upon Tateyama there came a weird old man and said, "If you are going down to Michinoku, please take a message. I am one who was a hunter of Soto no Hama and who died in the past year's autumn. Visit the home of my wife and child and tell them to offer up for me the cloak of straw and sedge-hat which are there." I replied, "If I address her thus without any proof, out of a clear sky, she surely will not believe." Thereupon he loosened and gave to me a sleeve of the hempen kimono he wore. I have journeyed and carried it with me until now. Perchance it is a token which will call memories to your heart.

    Wife: Surely this is a dream. Or else a piteous thing. Like unto the song of the cuckoo, heard at early morning, bringing back from Hell a last message from the dead, so now with these tidings that I hear from my departed one. And even as I listen, the tears are springing in my eyes.

(Making gesture of weeping.)

Nevertheless, it is too strange a thing, passing all belief. And therefore, crude though it be and lowly as cloth woven of wistaria bark, I will bring out his kimono. . . .

(A stage attendant comes to the Wife where she sits and gives her the folded kimono without a sleeve which the Hunter was wearing in Part I. She holds it up on her outstretched arms toward the Monk.)

    Monk: That kimono long treasured as a memory of him . . . this sleeve long carried. . . .

(The Monk takes out the sleeve and holds it out toward the Wife.)

      Wife: Upon taking them out. . . .
      Monk: . . . and comparing them well. . . .

(The Monk looks fixedly at the kimono which the Wife is holding.)

      Chorus: . . . there can be no doubt left.

(The Monk comes to the Wife and lays the sleeve in her arms upon the kimono. She bends her head over the articles, examining them closely, while the Chorus speaks for her.)

The cloth is the same—thin, crude stuff, for summer's wearing . . . thin, crude stuff for summer's wearing. And see! a sleeve is gone—this sleeve exactly fits. . . . It comes from him! O so dearly longed for. . . .

(The Wife bows low over the garments in a gesture of weeping. The Chorus now explains the actions of the Monk as he takes a large, black-lacquered hat from a stage attendant at the Flute Pillar, brings it to the very front of the stage and, placing it on the floor, kneels before it facing the audience.)

And forthwith does the Monk chant countless prayers of requiem. And especially, even as the dead one had entreated, does he offer up that very cloak of straw, offer up that very hat of sedge.

(The Monk rubs his rosary between his palms over the hat and intones a Buddhist Sutra.)

      Monk: "Hail, O Spirit. May you be delivered from the endless round of incarnations. May you attain the instantaneous enlightenment of Buddhahood."

(Rising, the Monk goes and takes a seat near the Flute Pillar. There is an interval of music accompanied by cries of the drummers. The curtain is swept back and the Hunter appears, now in supernatural form. He wears a tragic mask of a gaunt old man, just human enough in appearance to be unearthly, and an unkempt black wig which flares wildly down over his shoulders. Over his outer kimono, dappled with white and gray, he wears a short apron made of white and brown feathers. He carries a long stick and a fan. He comes slowly down the Bridge, as though summoned by the Monk's prayers. Reaching the Shite's Pillar, he stops and chants an old poem.)

Hunter: "At Soto no Hama of Michinoku there is the sound of birds, tenderly calling, tenderly cherishing—'*Utō*,' sing the parents in the sky, '*Yasukata*,' the young answer from the beaches."

(The Hunter makes a gesture indicating he is drawing near the house.)

Even as the Holy Sutra says, "Behold but once the *sotoba*, and be delivered for all time from the Three Evil Paths, beset by beasts and demons and hungry ghosts." Truly then a *sotoba* is a blessed thing, a memorial tablet carved fivefold, the five elements of the Buddha Body, the mere sight of which can save. But how much more if it be a *sotoba* raised expressly for my own sake, if a requiem be said in my own name.

For even in the icy Hell of the Scarlet Lotus the Fire of Holy Wisdom is not extinguished. For even in the Hell of Raging Fire the Waters of Dharma still quench.

And, nevertheless, still the burden of sin heaps high upon this flesh. . . . When may this soul find peace? . . . When can the birds find their stolen young? . . . O the killing!

(The Hunter turns and holds out his arms beseechingly toward the Monk.)

Chorus: In the sunlight of Buddha, the All Compassionate, the sins of man become like dew upon the grass: make the blessing-bestowing Sun to shine on me, O monk.

(The Hunter drops his arms and turns back toward the audience. The Chorus now describes the locale, while the Hunter makes a slow tour round the stage, revisiting the scenes of his earthly life.)

The place is Michinoku. The place is Michinoku. And here, in a lonely fishing village, upon an inlet of the sea, fenced round as though on the Isle of Hedges—now by the interlacing lower branches of the pine trees which follow along the strand, now by the salt reeds which grow drooping and matted in the ebb and flow of the tide—here at Soto no Hama stands the rush-mat hut. A humble dwelling, its roof so sparsely thatched. But now when the moon shines through the thatch into the room—a home for one's heart. Oh! truly a home for one's heart.

(The Hunter returns now to the Name-Saying Seat, where he leans motionless on his stick, looking toward the Wife and Child, indicating he has reached the house. The Wife and Child raise their heads and look toward the Hunter.)

Wife: Softly! the shape will vanish if you but say a single word.

(They rise and the Wife leads the Child a few steps toward the Hunter, describing her actions.)

The mother and child clasp hands . . . and there is nought but weeping.

(Leaving the Child standing, the Wife returns to her original position, kneels and weeps.)

Hunter: Alas! in other days this was the wife of my bed, the child of my heart. But now we are estranged forever—like the parent bird I cry *"Uto"* and, waiting with beating heart, never hear the answering *"Yasukata."* Why? oh, why did I kill them? For even as my child is beloved, just so must the birds and beasts yearn for their young. And now when I long to stroke the hair of my son Chiyodo and say, "Oh, how I have missed thee!" . . .

(The Hunter extends his arms and suddenly rushes toward the Child. But at each step of the Hunter, the Child falls back a step, as though some unseen object were keeping a fixed distance between them. It is the legendary cloud-barrier of earthly lusts which obscures the Sun of Buddha and prevents sinful spirits from visiting the earth. The Child takes a seat beside the Wife, and the Hunter returns to the center of the stage and stands with his back to the Wife and Child, indicating he has been unable to enter the house and can no longer see inside.)

Chorus: . . . the shadows of my earthly lusts do rush before my eyes—a cloud of grief now rolls between us, a grievous cloud now hangs about.

(The Hunter makes a gesture of weeping.)

I cannot see him! Just now he was standing there, my child, sturdy and strong as a young pine. . . .
Fugitive and fleeting . . . whither? . . . where? . . . I cannot find the hat—lost in the forests of the country of Tsu, in the shade of the spreading pine of Wada. I cannot reach the cloak—the flood tears, falling, drench my sleeves as might the spray from the waterfall at Minō. I cannot see the blessed *sotoba*,

(The Hunter makes slow circles round the stage, indicating his efforts to see through the cloud, and then stamps his foot in frustration.)

Who is this that stands outside, unable to enter his own home, barred from his wife and child, from cloak and hat, yes even from the *sotoba*? . . . "Having returned to Matsushima, to Ojima, I do not see the rush-mat huts on the islands—the villages are desolate, by the waves laid waste." . . . The song is old, but now it is I, I who cannot find, cannot enter the rush-mat hut. . . .
The bird of Soto no Hama, unable to find its nest . . . raising its voice in grief . . . nought but weeping. . . .

(The Hunter circles slowly to the Shite's Pillar, where he kneels and makes a gesture of weeping.)

The vague and boundless past, dreamlike. . . . It was from the ruin of these past pleasures, from these evil days, that I descended to the Yellow Springs, to the bitter waters of Hell. . . .

(Still kneeling, the Hunter raises his head.)

> **Hunter:** My path of life led from birth far out beyond the four estates of man—I was neither scholar, farmer, artisan, nor merchant.
> **Chorus:** Nor did I delight in life's four pleasures—music nor chess, books nor paintings.
> **Hunter:** There was only the coming of day, the coming of night—and the killing!
> **Chorus:** Thoughtless, wasting the slow spring days in hunting—days meant for the leisurely enjoyment of living. But still the lust for killing was unappeased. And so when the nights of autumn became long and long, I kept them alight, sleepless, with my fishing flares.
> **Hunter:** Unheedful of the ninety days of summer's heat. . . .
> **Chorus:** . . . of the cold of winter's mornings. . . .

(The Chorus now begins a description of the Hunter's past life. The Hunter, still kneeling, gradually begins to look from side to side, slowly, as though seeing the scenes being described.)

"The hunter pursues the deer and does not see the mountains," says the proverb. And truly so it was with me—thinking only of bait and snares, I was like one drugged by the day lily, oblivious to every pain of the body, to every sorrow of the heart. Lashed by wind and wave, even as is the great sand dune of Sue-no-Matsuyama . . . my garments wet and dripping as are the rocks which stand offshore, forever in the ebbing and flowing of the tide . . . coursing the beaches, crossing the

sea even to the shores of the farther islands . . . my flesh burnt as
though I had approached too near the salt-kilns of Chika. . . .
Still and always I pursued my evil ways, forgetful of the days of
retribution, heedless of all regret.

*(The Hunter touches his hands together in the conventional gesture which
introduces a principal dance, bows his head and rises, grasping his stick. He
begins gradually to keep rhythm with the music, but without yet moving from
place.)*

Now the ways of murdering birds are many, but this scheme by which
these pitiful ones are taken. . . .
    Hunter: . . . can there be one more heartless than this?

*(The Hunter now begins moving slowly about the stage, searching, keeping
time with the music.)*

    Chorus: You stupid, foolish bird! If only you had built your
nest with feathers, high in the treetops of the forests, forests dense as
that which lies about the Peak of Tsukuba . . . if only you had woven
floating cradles upon the waves. . . . But no! here upon the beaches, as
broad and sandy as those upon which wild geese settle for a moment's
rest in their northward flight, you raise your young. And here, O bird
of sorrow, you think to hide them. But then I, calling *"Utō,"* come . . .
they answer *"Yasukata"* . . . and the nestlings are taken. It is as simple
as this!

*(Still searching, the Hunter has started toward the Bridge, but when the
Chorus gives the cry of "Utō" he pauses at the Name-Saying Seat and listens.
And at the cry "Yasukata" he whirls back toward the stage, as though hearing
the birds in the nest. He stamps his foot once and in the midst of a profound
silence gives the bird call.)*

    Hunter: *Utō!*

*(The Hunter strikes the stage with his stick and begins a pantomime of the hunt
which preceded his death. The dance begins slowly with the discovery and*

pursuit of the birds and gradually mounts in ferocity to their capture and killing. At first the Hunter raises his stick in the direction of the Waki's Pillar, as though the imaginary birds are concealed in that vicinity, and brings it down to frighten them from the nest. The young birds are then understood to run toward the Bridge. He follows and, stopping near the Bridge, turns his body in an arc as though searching the horizon. Finally discovering the birds near the First Pine, he again flushes them with a wave of his stick. They run toward the front of the stage, with the Hunter in pursuit, wildly brandishing his stick. He catches up with them near the hat, which is still at the front of the stage, and brings his stick down with two sharp blows upon the stage, indicating the killing of the birds. Then he closes the movement with two stamps of the feet.)

Chorus: From the sky the parent bird is weeping tears of blood.

(The emotion of the dance now suddenly changes. The Hunter falls back a few steps and looks up fearfully. Then, hurling away his stick, he runs and snatches up the hat.)

From the sky fall tears of blood. And I, covering myself with the sedge-hat, with the cloak of straw, try to escape the falling tears, dodging now this way, now that.

(Holding the hat in both hands above his head and moving it rapidly from side to side. Then sinking for a moment to his knees.)

But alas! these are not the enchanted cloak and hat which make invisible their wearer.

(Rising and moving toward the Waki's Pillar.)

Faster and faster fall the tears of blood, until my body cannot shape their mortal touch, until the world turns crimson before my eyes—crimson as the fabled Bridge of Maple Leaves, formed of magpie wings across the sky and at the dawn stained red by the tears of two parting lover-stars.

(Throws the hat violently aside and takes out fan. The Chorus now turns from a description of past events to a recital of the tortures which the Hunter is undergoing in Hell. The dance becomes quieter now, the Hunter using the fan to indicate the actions described. The fan is a large white one on which is painted a bird in flight.)

In the earthly world I thought it only an easy prey, this bird, only an easy prey. But now here in Hell it has become a gruesome phantom-bird, pursuing the sinner, honking from its beak of iron, beating its mighty wings, sharpening its claws of copper. It tears at my eyeballs, it rends my flesh. I would cry out, but choking amid the shrieking flames and smoke, can make no sound.

(The Hunter runs wildly about the stage, in agony.)

Is it not for the sin of killing the voiceless birds that I myself now have no voice? Is it not for slaughtering the moulting, earth-bound birds that I cannot now flee?

(The Hunter has started moving rapidly toward the Facing Pillar when suddenly he seems unable to move and sinks to his knees, cowering in the center of the stage.)

Hunter: The gentle bird has become a falcon, a hawk!
Chorus: And I!—I have become a pheasant, vainly seeking shelter, as though in a snowstorm on the hunting fields of Gatano, fleeing in vain over the earth, fearing also the sky, harassed by falcons above and tormented by dogs below.

(The Hunter rises and, looking up toward the sky and down to the earth, moves slowly, defeatedly, toward the Shite's Pillar.)

Ah! the killing of those birds! this heavy heart which never knows a moment's peace! this body endlessly in pain!

(The Hunter stops at the Shite's Pillar and, turning, points a finger at the Monk.)

Please help me, O worthy monk. Please help me. . . .

(The Hunter drops his arms, and the Chorus chants the conventional ending of a Nō play.)

And thereupon the spirit fades and is gone. . . .

(The Hunter stamps his feet, indicating he has disappeared, that the play is done. He walks slowly down the Bridge and through the curtain, followed in turn by the other actors and the musicians. The Chorus exits by the Hurry Door, and again the stage is left bare.)

A WHITE HERON
Sarah Orne Jewett

Sarah Orne Jewett (1849–1909) was an American novelist, short story writer, and poet associated with the local-color school.

I

The woods were already filled with shadows one June evening, just before eight o'clock, though a bright sunset still glimmered faintly among the trunks of the trees. A little girl was driving home her cow, a plodding, dilatory, provoking creature in her behavior, but a valued companion for all that. They were going away from whatever light there was, and striking deep into the woods, but their feet were familiar with the path, and it was no matter whether their eyes could see it or not.

There was hardly a night the summer through when the old cow could be found waiting at the pasture bars; on the contrary, it was her greatest pleasure to hide herself away among the huckleberry bushes, and though she wore a loud bell she had made the discovery that if one stood perfectly still it would not ring. So Sylvia had to hunt for her until she found her, and call Co'! Co'! with never an answering Moo, until her childish patience was quite spent. If the creature had not given good milk and plenty of it, the case would have seemed very different to her owners. Besides, Sylvia had all the time there was, and very little use to make of it. Sometimes in pleasant weather it was a consolation to look upon the cow's pranks as an intelligent attempt to play hide and seek, and as the child had no playmates she lent herself to this amusement with a good deal of zeal. Though this chase had been so long that the weary animal herself had given an unusual signal of her whereabouts, Sylvia had only laughed when she came upon Mistress Moolly at the swampside, and urged her affectionately homeward with a twig of birch leaves. The old cow was not inclined to wander farther, she even turned in the right direction for once as they left the pasture, and stepped along the road at a good pace. She was quite ready to be milked now, and seldom stopped to browse. Sylvia wondered what her grandmother would say because they were so late. It was a great while since she had left home at half-past five o'clock, but everybody knew the difficulty of making this errand a short one. Mrs. Tilley had chased the hornéd torment too many summer evenings herself to blame any one else for lingering, and was only thankful as she waited that she had Sylvia, nowadays, to give such valuable assistance. The good woman suspected that Sylvia loitered occasionally on her own account; there never was such a child for straying about out-of-doors since the world was made! Everybody said that it was a good change for a little maid who had tried to grow for eight years in a crowded manufacturing town, but as for Sylvia herself, it seemed as if she never had been alive at all before she came to live at the farm. She thought often with wistful compassion of a wretched geranium that belonged to a town neighbor.

"'Afraid of folks,'" old Mrs. Tilley said to herself, with a smile, after she had made the unlikely choice of Sylvia from her daughter's houseful of children, and was returning to the farm. "'Afraid of folks,' they said! I guess she won't be troubled no great with 'em up to the old place!" When they reached the door of the lonely house and stopped to unlock it, and the cat came to purr loudly, and rub against them, a deserted pussy, indeed, but fat with young robins, Sylvia whispered that this was a beautiful place to live in, and she never should wish to go home.

The companions followed the shady woodroad, the cow taking slow steps and the child very fast ones. The cow stopped long at the brook to drink, as if the pasture were not half a swamp, and Sylvia stood still and waited, letting her bare feet cool themselves in the shoal water, while the great twilight moths struck softly against her. She waded on through the brook as the cow moved away, and listened to the thrushes with a heart that beat fast with pleasure. There was a stirring in the great boughs overhead. They were full of little birds and beasts that seemed to be wide awake, and going about their world, or else saying good-night to each other in sleepy twitters. Sylvia herself felt sleepy as she walked along. However, it was not much farther to the house, and the air was soft and sweet. She was not often in the woods so late as this, and it made her feel as if she were a part of the gray shadows and the moving leaves. She was just thinking how long it seemed since she first came to the farm a year ago, and wondering if everything went on in the noisy town just the same as when she was there; the thought of the great red-faced boy who used to chase and frighten her made her hurry along the path to escape from the shadow of the trees.

Suddenly this little woods-girl is horror-stricken to hear a clear whistle not very far away. Not a bird's-whistle, which would have a sort of friendliness, but a boy's whistle, determined, and somewhat aggressive. Sylvia left the cow to whatever sad fate might await her, and stepped discreetly aside into the bushes, but she was just too late. The enemy had discovered her, and called out in a very cheerful and persuasive tone, "Halloa, little girl, how far is it to the road?" and trembling Sylvia answered almost inaudibly, "A good ways."

She did not dare to look boldly at the tall young man, who carried a gun over his shoulder, but she came out of her bush and again followed the cow, while he walked alongside.

"I have been hunting for some birds," the stranger said kindly, "and I have lost my way, and need a friend very much. Don't be afraid," he added gallantly. "Speak up and tell me what your name is, and whether you think I can spend the night at your house, and go out gunning early in the morning."

Sylvia was more alarmed than before. Would not her grandmother consider her much to blame? But who could have foreseen such an accident as this? It did not seem to be her fault, and she hung her head as if the stem of it were broken, but managed to answer "Sylvy," with much effort when her companion again asked her name.

Mrs. Tilley was standing in the doorway when the trio came into view. The cow gave a loud moo by way of explanation.

"Yes, you'd better speak up for yourself, you old trial! Where'd she tucked herself away this time, Sylvy?" But Sylvia kept an awed silence; she knew by instinct that her grandmother did not comprehend the gravity of the situation. She must be mistaking the stranger for one of the farmer-lads of the region.

The young man stood his gun beside the door, and dropped a lumpy game-bag beside it; then he bade Mrs. Tilley good-evening, and repeated his wayfarer's story, and asked if he could have a night's lodging.

"Put me anywhere you like," he said. "I must be off early in the morning, before day; but I am very hungry, indeed. You can give me some milk at any rate, that's plain."

"Dear sakes, yes," responded the hostess, whose long slumbering hospitality seemed to be easily awakened. "You might fare better if you went out to the main road a mile or so, but you're welcome to what we've got. I'll milk right off, and you make yourself at home. You can sleep on husks or feathers," she proffered graciously. "I raised them all myself. There's good pasturing for geese just below here towards the ma'sh. Now step round and set a plate for the gentleman, Sylvy!" And Sylvia promptly stepped. She was glad to have something to do, and she was hungry herself.

It was a surprise to find so clean and comfortable a little dwelling in this New England wilderness. The young man had known the horrors of its most primitive housekeeping, and the dreary squalor of that level of society which does not rebel at the companionship of hens. This was the best thrift of an old-fashioned farmstead, though on such a small scale that it seemed like a hermitage. He listened eagerly to the old woman's quaint talk, he watched Sylvia's pale face and shining gray eyes with ever growing enthusiasm, and insisted that this was the best supper he had eaten for a month, and afterward the new-made friends sat down in the door-way together while the moon came up.

Soon it would be berry-time, and Sylvia was a great help at picking. The cow was a good milker, though a plaguy thing to keep track of, the hostess gossiped frankly, adding presently that she had buried four children, so Sylvia's mother, and a son (who might be dead) in California were all the children she had left. "Dan, my boy, was a great hand to go gunning," she explained sadly. "I never wanted for pa'tridges or gray squer'ls while he was to home. He's been a great wand'rer, I expect, and he's no hand to write letters. There, I don't blame him, I'd ha' seen the world myself if it had been so I could."

"Sylvy takes after him," the grandmother continued affectionately, after a minute's pause. "There ain't a foot o' ground she don't know her way over, and the wild creaturs counts her one o' themselves. Squer'ls she'll tame to come an' feed right out o' her hands, and all sorts o' birds. Last winter she got the jaybirds to bangeing here, and I believe she'd 'a' scanted herself of her own meals to have plenty to throw out amongst 'em, if I hadn't kep' watch. Anything but crows, I tell her, I'm willin' to help support—though Dan he had a tamed one o' them that did seem to have reason same as folks. It was round here a good spell after he went away. Dan an' his father they didn't hitch,—but he never held up his head ag'in after Dan had dared him an' gone off."

The guest did not notice this hint of family sorrows in his eager interest in something else.

"So Sylvy knows all about birds, does she?" he exclaimed, as he looked round at the little girl who sat, very demure but increasingly sleepy, in the moonlight. "I am making a collection of birds myself. I have been at it every since I was a boy." (Mrs. Tilley smiled.) "There are two or three very rare ones I have been hunting for these five years. I mean to get them on my own ground if they can be found."

"Do you cage 'em up?" asked Mrs. Tilley doubtfully, in response to this enthusiastic announcement.

"Oh no, they're stuffed and preserved, dozens and dozens of them," said the ornithologist, "and I have shot or snared every one myself. I caught a glimpse of a white heron a few miles from here on

Saturday, and I have followed it in this direction. They have never been found in this district at all. The little white heron, it is," and he turned again to look at Sylvia with the hope of discovering that the rare bird was one of her acquaintances.

But Sylvia was watching a hop-toad in the narrow footpath.

"You would know the heron if you saw it," the stranger continued eagerly. "A queer tall white bird with soft feathers and long thin legs. And it would have a nest perhaps in the top of a high tree, made of sticks, something like a hawk's nest."

Sylvia's heart gave a wild beat; she knew that strange white bird, and had once stolen softly near where it stood in some bright green swamp grass, away over at the other side of the woods. There was an open place where the sunshine always seemed strangely yellow and hot, where tall, nodding rushes grew, and her grandmother had warned her that she might sink in the soft black mud underneath and never be heard of more. Not far beyond were the salt marshes just this side the sea itself, which Sylvia wondered and dreamed much about, but never had seen, whose great voice could sometimes be heard above the noise of the woods on stormy nights.

"I can't think of anything I should like so much as to find that heron's nest," the handsome stranger was saying. "I would give ten dollars to anybody who could show it to me," he added desperately, "and I mean to spend my whole vacation hunting for it if need be. Perhaps it was only migrating, or had been chased out of its own region by some bird of prey."

Mrs. Tilley gave amazed attention to all this, but Sylvia still watched the toad, not divining, as she might have done at some calmer time, that the creature wished to get to its hole under the door-step, and was much hindered by the unusual spectators at that hour of the evening. No amount of thought, that night, could decide how many wished-for treasures the ten dollars, so lightly spoken of, would buy.

The next day the young sportsman hovered about the woods, and Sylvia kept him company, having lost her first fear of the friendly lad, who proved to be most kind and sympathetic. He told her many things about the birds and what they knew and where they lived and what they did with themselves. And he gave her a jack-knife, which she thought as great a treasure as if she were a desert-islander. All day long he did not once make her troubled or afraid except when he brought down some unsuspecting singing creature from its bough. Sylvia would have liked him vastly better without his gun; she could not understand why he killed the very birds he seemed to like so much. But as the day waned, Sylvia still watched the young man with loving admiration. She had never seen anybody so charming and delightful; the woman's heart, asleep in the child, was vaguely thrilled by a dream of love. Some premonition of that great power stirred and swayed these young creatures who traversed the solemn woodlands with soft-footed silent care. They stopped to listen to a bird's song; they pressed forward again eagerly, parting the branches—speaking to each other rarely and in whispers; the young man going first and Sylvia following, fascinated, a few steps behind, with her gray eyes dark with excitement.

She grieved because the longed-for white heron was elusive, but she did not lead the guest, she only followed, and there was no such thing as speaking first. The sound of her own unquestioned voice would have terrified her—it was hard enough to answer yes or no when there was need of that. At last evening began to fall, and they drove the cow home together, and Sylvia smiled with pleasure when they came to the place where she heard the whistle and was afraid only the night before.

II

Half a mile from home, at the farther edge of the woods, where the land was highest, a great pine-tree stood, the last of its generation. Whether it was left for a boundary mark, or for what reason, no one could say; the woodchoppers who had felled its mates were dead and gone long ago, and a whole forest of sturdy trees, pines and oaks and maples, had grown again. But the stately head of this old pine towered above them all and made a landmark for sea and shore miles and miles away. Sylvia knew it well. She had always believed that whoever climbed to the top of it could see the ocean; and the little girl had often laid her hand on the great rough trunk and looked up wistfully at those dark boughs that the wind always stirred, no matter how hot and still the air might be below. Now she thought of the tree with a new excitement, for why, if one climbed it at break of day could not one see all the world, and easily discover from whence the white heron flew, and mark the place, and find the hidden nest?

What a spirit of adventure, what wild ambition! What fancied triumph and delight and glory for the later morning when she could make known the secret! It was almost too real and too great for the childish heart to bear.

All night the door of the little house stood open and the whippoorwills came and sang upon the very step. The young sportsman and his old hostess were sound asleep, but Sylvia's great design kept her broad awake and watching. She forgot to think of sleep. The short summer night seemed as long as the winter darkness, and at last when the whippoorwills ceased, and she was afraid the morning would after all come too soon, she stole out of the house and followed the pasture path through the woods, hastening toward the open ground beyond, listening with a sense of comfort and companionship to the drowsy twitter of a half-awakened bird, whose perch she had jarred in passing. Alas, if the great wave of human interest which flooded for the first time this dull little life should sweep away the satisfactions of an existence heart to heart with nature and the dumb life of the forest!

There was the huge tree asleep yet in the paling moonlight, and small and silly Sylvia began with utmost bravery to mount to the top of it, with tingling, eager blood coursing the channels of her whole frame, with her bare feet and fingers, that pinched and held like bird's claws to the monstrous ladder reaching up, up, almost to the sky itself. First she must mount the white oak tree that grew alongside, where she was almost lost among the dark branches and the green leaves heavy and wet with dew; a bird fluttered off its nest, and a red squirrel ran to and fro and scolded pettishly at the harmless housebreaker. Sylvia felt her way easily. She had often climbed there, and knew that higher still one of the oak's upper branches chafed against the pine trunk, just where its lower boughs were set close together. There, when she made the dangerous pass from one tree to the other, the great enterprise would really begin.

She crept out along the swaying oak limb at last, and took the daring step across into the old pine-tree. The way was harder than she thought; she must reach far and hold fast, the sharp dry twigs caught and held her and scratched her like angry talons, the pitch made her thin little fingers clumsy and stiff as she went round and round the tree's great stem, higher and higher upward. The sparrows and robins in the woods below were beginning to wake and twitter to the dawn, yet it seemed much lighter there aloft in the pine-tree, and the child knew she must hurry if her project were to be of any use.

The tree seemed to lengthen itself out as she went up, and to reach farther and farther upward. It was like a great main-mast to the voyaging earth; it must truly have been amazed that morning through all its ponderous frame as it felt this determined spark of human spirit wending its way from higher branch to branch. Who knows how steadily the least twigs held themselves to advantage this light, weak creature on her way! The old pine must have loved his new dependent. More than all the hawks, and bats, and moths, and even the sweet voiced thrushes, was the brave, beating heart of the solitary gray-eyed child. And the tree stood still and frowned away the winds that June morning while the dawn grew bright in the east.

Sylvia's face was like a pale star, if one had seen it from the ground, when the last thorny bough was past, and she stood trembling and tired but wholly triumphant, high in the treetop. Yes, there was the sea with the dawning sun making a golden dazzle over it, and toward that glorious east flew two hawks with slow-moving pinions. How low they looked in the air from that height when one had only seen them before far up, and dark against the blue sky. Their gray feathers were as soft as moths; they seemed only a little way from the tree, and Sylvia felt as if she too could go flying away among the clouds. Westward, the woodlands and farms reached miles and miles into the distance; here and there were church steeples, and white villages, truly it was a vast and awesome world!

The birds sang louder and louder. At last the sun came up bewilderingly bright. Sylvia could see the white sails of ships out at sea, and the clouds that were purple and rose-colored and yellow at first began to fade away. Where was the white heron's nest in the sea of green branches, and was this wonderful sight and pageant of the world the only reward for having climbed to such a giddy height? Now look down again, Sylvia, where the green marsh is set among the shining birches and dark hemlocks; there where you saw the white heron once you will see him again; look, look! a white spot of him like a single floating feather comes up from the dead hemlock and grows larger, and rises, and comes close at last, and goes by the landmark pine with steady sweep of wing and outstretched slender neck and crested head. And wait! wait! do not move a foot or a finger, little girl, do not send an arrow of light and consciousness from your two eager eyes, for the heron has perched on a pine bough not far beyond yours, and cries back to his mate on the nest and plumes his feathers for the new day!

The child gives a long sigh a minute later when a company of shouting cat-birds comes also to the tree, and vexed by their fluttering and lawlessness the solemn heron goes away. She knows his secret now, the wild, light, slender bird that floats and wavers, and goes back like an arrow presently to his home in the green world beneath. Then Sylvia, well satisfied, makes her perilous way down again, not daring to look far below the branch she stands on, ready to cry sometimes because her fingers ache and her lamed feet slip. Wondering over and over again what the stranger would say to her, and what he would think when she told him how to find his way straight to the heron's nest.

"Sylvy, Sylvy!" called the busy old grandmother again and again, but nobody answered, and the small husk bed was empty and Sylvia had disappeared.

The guest waked from a dream, and remembering his day's pleasure hurried to dress himself that might it sooner begin. He was sure from the way the shy little girl looked once or twice yesterday that she had at least seen the white heron, and now she must really be made to tell. Here she comes now, paler than ever, and her worn old frock is torn and tattered, and smeared with pine pitch. The grandmother and the sportsman stand in the door together and question her, and the splendid moment has come to speak of the dead hemlock-tree by the green marsh.

But Sylvia does not speak after all, though the old grandmother fretfully rebukes her, and the young man's kind, appealing eyes are looking straight in her own. He can make them rich with money; he has promised it, and they are poor now. He is so well worth making happy, and he waits to hear the story she can tell.

No, she must keep silence! What is it that suddenly forbids her and makes her dumb? Has she been nine years growing and now, when the great world for the first time puts out a hand to her, must she thrust it aside for a bird's sake? The murmur of the pine's green branches is in her ears, she remembers how the white heron came flying through the golden air and how they watched the sea and the morning together, and Sylvia cannot speak; she cannot tell the heron's secret and give its life away.

Dear loyalty, that suffered a sharp pang as the guest went away disappointed later in the day, that could have served and followed him and loved him as a dog loves! Many a night Sylvia heard the echo of his whistle haunting the pasture path as she came home with the loitering cow. She forgot even her sorrow at the sharp report of his gun and the sight of thrushes and sparrows dropping silent to the ground, their songs hushed and their pretty feathers stained and wet with blood. Were the birds better friends than their hunter might have been,—who can tell? Whatever treasures were lost to her, woodlands and summer-time, remember! Bring your gifts and graces and tell your secrets to this lonely country child!

THE GUEST[7]
Bert Almon

Bert Almon was born in east Texas in 1943. He received a doctorate in English from the University of New Mexico, writing a thesis on Gary Snyder. His first book of poems, published in 1968, is entitled *The Return*.

two eyes in the dark
past the edge of firelight
in the dim circle of warmth

I see eyes, don't know them
coming close to the inner circle
let me put another log on

for yellow eyes in the dark

[7]"The Guest" is reprinted by permission of Bert Almon. Copyright ©1970 by the author.

CHAPTER THREE
The Eternal Rhythm

One generation passeth away, and another generation cometh:
but the earth abideth forever.
The sun also riseth, and the sun goeth down, and hasteth to his
place where he arose.
The wind goeth toward the south, and turneth about unto the
north; it whirleth about continually, and the wind returneth
again according to his circuits.
All the rivers run into the sea; yet the sea is not full; unto the
place from whence the rivers come, thither they return again.

Ecclesiastes 1:4–7

THE RETURN OF THE RIVERS[1]
Richard Brautigan

Richard Brautigan (1935–), San Francisco poet and novelist, catapulted into fame with his novel/travel memoir *Trout Fishing in America*, a series of semiconnected, semicoherent surrealistic sketches of life in western America. Brautigan's sketches and poems reveal, beneath their fantasy, a love of nature and concern for its preservation.

All the rivers run into the sea;
yet the sea is not full;
unto the place from whence the rivers come,
thither they return again.

It is raining today
in the mountains.

It is a warm green rain
with love
in its pockets
for spring is here,
and does not dream
of death.

Birds happen music
like clocks ticking heavens
in a land
where children love spiders,
and let them sleep
in their hair.

A slow rain sizzles
on the river
like a pan
full of frying flowers,
and with each drop
of rain
the ocean
begins again.

[1]From *The Pill Versus the Springhill Mine Disaster* by Richard Brautigan. Copyright © 1968 by Richard Brautigan. A Seymour Lawrence Book/Delacorte Press. Reprinted by permission of the publisher.

EXPRESSIONS OF SEA LEVEL[2]
A. R. Ammons

Peripherally the ocean
marks itself
        against the gauging land
it erodes and
builds:

it is hard to name
the changeless:
speech without words,
        silence renders it:
and mid-ocean,

sky sealed unbroken to sea,
        there is no way to know
the ocean's speech,
intervolved and markless,
breaking against

        no boulder-held fingerland:
broken, surf things are expressions:
the sea speaks far from its core,
far from its center relinquishes the
long-held roar:

of any mid-sea
speech, the yielding resistances
of wind and water, spray,
swells, whitecaps, moans,
        it is a dream the sea makes,

[2]Reprinted from *Expressions of Sea Level*, by A. R. Ammons (Columbus: Ohio State University Press, 1963). The poem "Expressions of Sea Level," by A. R. Ammons, was first published in *Poetry* in 1963. It subsequently appeared in *Expressions of Sea Level* by A. R. Ammons, published by the Ohio State University Press. Copyright © 1963 by A. R. Ammons.

an inner problem, a self-deep
dark and private anguish
            revealed in small,
by hints, to
keen watchers on the shore:

only with the staid land
is the level conversation really held:
only in the meeting of rock and
            sea is
hard relevance shattered into light:

upbeach the clam shell
            holds smooth dry sand,
remembrance of tide:
water can go at
least that high: in

            the night, if you stay
to watch, or
if you come tomorrow at the right time,
you can see the shell caught
again in wash, the
sand turbulence changed,
new sand left smooth: if
the shell washes loose,
flops over,
            buries its rim in flux,

it will not be silence for
a shell that spoke: the
            half-buried back will
tell how the ocean dreamed
breakers against the land:

into the salt marshes the water comes fast with rising tide:
an inch of rise spreads by yards
        through tidal creeks, round fingerways of land:
the marsh grasses stem-logged
combine wind and water motions,
        slow from dry trembling
to heavier motions of wind translated through
cushioned stems; tide-held slant of grasses
        bent into the wind:

        is there a point of rest where
        the tide turns: is there one
        infinitely tiny higher touch
on the legs of egrets, the
skin of back, bay-eddy reeds:

        is there an instant when fullness is,
        without loss, complete: is there a
        statement perfect in its speech:

how do you know the moon
is moving: see the dry
casting of the beach worm
        dissolve at the
delicate rising touch:

that is the
        expression of sea level,
the talk of giants,
of ocean, moon, sun, of everything,
spoken in a dampened grain of sand.

SOUTH WIND[3]
Tu Fu
translated by Kenneth Rexroth

Kenneth Rexroth has called Chinese poet Tu Fu (713–770) the "greatest [lyric] poet who has survived in any language."[4] Tu Fu spent his early days at the brilliant court of Emperor Ming Huang but

[3]Kenneth Rexroth, *One Hundred Poems from the Chinese*. Copyright © 1971 by Kenneth Rexroth. All rights reserved. Reprinted by permission of New Directions Publishing Corporation.

[4]*One Hundred Poems from the Chinese*, p. 135. New Directions, New York, 1971.

lived much of his later life in exile for objecting to the emperor's
morals and foreign policy. Making a virtue of necessity, he learned to
love the simple pleasures of life.

The days grow long, the mountains
Beautiful. The south wind blows
Over blossoming meadows.
Newly arrived swallows dart
Over the steaming marshes.
Ducks in pairs drowse on the warm sand.

HARKENING TO THE CRYING CRANES[5]
Hung Tzu-Ch'eng
translated by Chao Tze-Chiang

Hung Tzu-Ch'eng was a sixteenth-century Chinese poet of
the Ming Dynasty.

Harkening to the crying cranes under a
frosty firmament or the crowing cocks on
a snowy night, one can catch the pure spirit
of Heaven and Earth. Beholding the flying
birds in the clear sky or the playful fishes
in the flowing water, one can understand the
life-force in the universe.

Sitting by a teapoy in a room bathed with pure
breezes and moonbeams, one can read the mind of
Heaven in every thing. Walking along a running
brook in the clouded mountain, one can observe
the mysteries of the Tao in every moment.

[5] Hung Tzu-Ch'eng "Harkening to the Crying Cranes___" translated by Chao Tze-
Chiang, *A Chinese Garden of Serenity*, Peter Pauper Press, Copyright © 1959.

NIGHT SOWING[6]
David Campbell

David Campbell (1915–) is an Australian poet. Campbell belongs to the group of poets who "take their chief strength from that contemplation of natural themes in which, during the 'forties, Australian poetry overcame its problem of adaptation to the Australian landscape."[7]

O gentle, gentle land
Where the green ear shall grow,
Now you are edged with light:
The moon has crisped the fallow,
The furrows run with night.

This is the season's hour:
While couples are in bed,
I sow the paddocks late,
Scatter like sparks the seed
And see the dark ignite.

THE MARSHES OF GLYNN
Sidney Lanier

Sidney Lanier (1842–1881) was a Georgia-born novelist, scholar, and poet. In his poetry, Lanier attempted to produce the sound patterns of music. The marshes of Glynn, along the east coast of Georgia, are being threatened by pollution from nearby pulp mills and by pressure from companies that want to stripmine for phosphate.

[6]"Night Sowing" by David Campbell. From *The Miracle of Mullion Hill*, Angus and Robertson, Ltd. © 1956. Reprinted by permission.

[7]Judith Wright, *A Book of Australian Verse*, Oxford University Press (Melbourne, 1968), p. 8.

Glooms of the live-oaks, beautiful-braided and woven
With intricate shades of the vines that myriad-cloven
    Clamber the forks of the multiform boughs,—
        Emerald twilights,—
        Virginal shy lights,
Wrought of the leaves to allure to the whisper of vows,
When lovers pace timidly down through the green colonnades
Of the dim sweet woods, of the dear dark woods,
    Of the heavenly woods and glades,
That run to the radiant marginal sand-beach within
      The wide sea-marshes of Glynn;—

Beautiful glooms, soft dusks in the noon-day fire,—
Wildwood privacies, closets of lone desire,
Chamber from chamber parted with wavering arras of leaves,—
Cells for the passionate pleasure of prayer to the soul that grieves,
Pure with a sense of the passing of saints through the wood,
Cool for the dutiful weighing of ill with good;—

O braided dusks of the oak and woven shades of the vine,
While the riotous noon-day sun of the June-day long did shine
Ye held me fast in your heart and I held you fast in mine;
But now when the noon is no more, and riot is rest,
And the sun is a-wait at the ponderous gate of the West,
And the slant yellow beam down the wood-aisle doth seem
Like a lane into heaven that leads from a dream,—
Ay, now, when my soul all day hath drunken the soul of the oak,
And my heart is at ease from men, and the wearisome sound of the stroke
    Of the scythe of time and the trowel of trade is low,
      And belief overmasters doubt, and I know that I know,
      And my spirit is grown to a lordly great compass within,
That the length and the breadth and the sweep of the marshes of Glynn
Will work me no fear like the fear they have wrought me of yore
When length was fatigue, and when breadth was but bitterness sore,
And when terror and shrinking and dreary unnamable pain
Drew over me out of the merciless miles of the plain,—

Oh, now, unafraid, I am fain to face
 The vast sweet visage of space.
To the edge of the wood I am drawn, I am drawn,
Where the gray beach glimmering runs, as a belt of the dawn,
 For a mete and a mark
 To the forest-dark: —
 So:
Affable live-oak, leaning low, —
Thus—with your favor—soft, with a reverent hand,
(Not lightly touching your person, Lord of the land!)
Bending your beauty aside, with a step I stand
On the firm-packed sand,
 Free
By a world of marsh that borders a world of sea.
 Sinuous southward and sinuous northward the shimmering band
Of the sand-beach fastens the fringe of the marsh to the folds of the land.
Inward and outward to northward and southward the beach-lines linger and
 curl
As a silver-wrought garment that clings to and follows the firm sweet limbs of a
 girl.

Vanishing, swerving, evermore curving again into sight,
Softly the sand-beach wavers away to a dim gray looping of light.
And what if behind me to westward the wall of the woods stands high?
The world lies east: how ample, the marsh and the sea and the sky!
A league and a league of marsh-grass, waist-high, broad in the blade,
Green, and all of a height, and unflecked with a light or a shade,
Stretch leisurely off, in a pleasant plain,
To the terminal blue of the main.

Oh, what is abroad in the marsh and the terminal sea?
 Somehow my soul seems suddenly free
From the weighing of fate and the sad discussion of sin,
By the length and the breadth and the sweep of the marshes of Glynn.

Ye marshes, how candid and simple and nothing-withholding and free
Ye publish yourselves to the sky and offer yourselves to the sea!
Tolerant plains, that suffer the sea and the rains and the sun,
Ye spread and span like the catholic man who hath mightily won
God out of knowledge and good out of infinite pain
And sight out of blindness and purity out of a stain.

As the marsh-hen secretly builds on the watery sod,
Behold I will build me a nest on the greatness of God:
I will fly in the greatness of God as the marsh-hen flies
In the freedom that fills all the space 'twixt the marsh and the skies:
By so many roots as the marsh-grass sends in the sod
I will heartily lay me a-hold on the greatness of God:
Oh, like to the greatness of God is the greatness within
The range of the marshes, the liberal marshes of Glynn.

And the sea lends large, as the marsh: lo, out of his plenty the sea
Pours fast: full soon the time of the flood-tide must be:
Look how the grace of the sea doth go
About and about through the intricate channels that flow
                    Here and there,
                              Everywhere,
Till his waters have flooded the uttermost creeks and the low-lying lanes,
And the marsh is meshed with a million veins,
That like as with rosy and silvery essences flow
              In the rose-and-silver evening glow.
                         Farewell, my lord Sun!
The creeks overflow: a thousand rivulets run
'Twixt the roots of the sod; the blades of the marsh-grass stir;
Passeth a hurrying sound of wings that westward whirr;
Passeth, and all is still; and the currents cease to run;
And the sea and the marsh are one.

How still the plains of the waters be!
The tide is in his ecstasy.
The tide is at his highest height:
                    And it is night.

And now from the Vast of the Lord will the waters of sleep
Roll in on the souls of men,
But who will reveal to our waking ken
The forms that swim and the shapes that creep
                    Under the waters of sleep?
And I would I could know what swimmeth below when the tide comes in
On the length and the breadth of the marvellous marshes of Glynn.

CHAPTER
FOUR
Man and Nature—
the Common Bond

We are nature; long have we been absent; but now we return.

Walt Whitman

MAN'S ANCIENT, POWERFUL LINK TO NATURE—
A SOURCE OF FEAR AND JOY[1]
Joseph Wood Krutch

Joseph Wood Krutch (1893–1970), scholar, critic, naturalist, essayist, philosopher, was one of the most versatile American thinkers of the twentieth century. He was not only an authority on the whole range of English and American literature (he published books on Samuel Johnson, Elizabethan criticism, modern drama, literary aesthetics, Edgar Allan Poe, and H. D. Thoreau), but also a naturalist of considerable abilities who did as much as any American to spark interest in ecology and to save the environment. "Man's Ancient Powerful Link to Nature" was written in 1961, well before the current ecology movement got under way.

What is "nature"? One standard reference devotes five columns to fifteen different—and legitimate—definitions of the word. But for the purposes of this article the meaning is simple. Nature is that part of the world which man did not make and which has not been fundamentally changed by him. It is the mountains, the woods, the rivers, the trees, the plants, and the animals which have continued to be very much what they would have been had he never existed.

In another sense man is, of course, himself a part of nature. But he is also in so many ways so unique that it is convenient to speak of man *and* nature, especially of man's relation to the rest of this nature of which he is also a part.

The relationship is something which he can never forget; but he responds to it in the most diverse ways. He regards nature sometimes as a friend and sometimes as an enemy. He loves it and he fears it. He uses it and destroys it. Nature is what he tries to get away from and then something he wishes to keep. He replaces it with his homes and factories, then wishes to return to it. He tries to impose on it human order and civilization, and then suddenly finds himself dreaming of a golden age when man and nature were one.

This paradox is as old as civilization itself. Though it is true that man never admired the more savage aspects of nature until life had become comparatively safe, it is equally true that he had scarcely built the first cities before he began to try to get away from them. In ancient Greece poets idealized the shepherd's life, and in imperial Rome the literary cult of the simple life had already reached the point where satirists ridiculed it. In our modern world the engineer, the industrialist, and the builder of skyscrapers moves his family to a country house in the suburbs. He plants trees and cultivates a garden. He acquires animals as pets, and perhaps he takes up bird watching—all of which reveals his unwillingness to let go of what, in theory at least, he has not valued.

Ancient as these paradoxes and conflicts are, there is today one supremely important respect in which they pose a problem that never existed in so acute a form before: now for the first time man can effectively act out his impulses and his decisions. He can, if he so desires, all but banish nature and the natural from the earth he has come to rule.

Until a few centuries ago man was not even a very numerous species. It has been an even shorter time since his technology became advanced to the point where he could upset seriously the ancient balances of the natural world. Formerly he might love nature or hate her, might attempt to preserve her or destroy her; but she was more powerful than he. Except over relatively small areas she remained in control. Now the balance has shifted. Man controls forces which at least rival and seem on the point of surpassing hers. He can decide as never before what part, if any, of the natural world will be permitted to exist. Thus the question "What is man's place in nature and what ought to be his relation to her?" is fateful as it never was before.

In its most abstract form this fundamental question was asked and opposing answers were given by the ancient religions. In the Hebraic tradition man was the child of God, and God was separate from, rather than a part of, nature. Greek paganism, on the other hand, worshiped gods who were themselves aspects of nature and it taught man to think of himself also as part of her. These gods were more at home in the woods and streams and mountains than in the temples built for them. Nature was the source of health, beauty, and joy, and to live in accord with nature's laws was wisdom. The Great God Pan, or nature god, was one of the most ancient and powerful of deities, so much so indeed that an early Christian tradition made the exclamation "Great Pan is dead" a cry of victory announcing the triumph for the new faith; and many centuries later, the neopagan poet Swinburne could turn it into a lament to Christ Himself: "Thou hast conquered, O pale Galilean; the world has grown grey from thy breath."

To Noah, unloading his animals after the flood, Jehovah said, "And the fear of you and the dread of you shall be upon every beast of the earth, and upon every fowl of the air, upon all that moveth upon the earth, and upon all the fishes of the sea; into your hand are they delivered." Throughout the Greek and Roman ascendencies and all through the Middle Ages the most admired aspects of nature were those which man had tamed, at least to a degree. It has often been said that the fourteenth-century Italian scholar Petrarch was the first man who ever confessed to climbing a mountain just for the sake of the view, and it is not so often added that, at the end of his description, he apologized for this eccentricity.

The conflicting attitudes which even today somehow relate "the natural" to "the divine" began to emerge some three centuries ago. The first great English biologist, the pious John Ray, in his enormously popular *The Wisdom of God Manifested in the Works of the Creation* (1691), maintained that God did not create the living world exclusively for man's use but that, on the contrary, He "takes pleasure that all His creatures enjoy themselves." And Ray urged that men should study nature as well as books because it was by such study that the greatness and goodness of God was most clearly revealed.

A bare generation later Alexander Pope, the most read English poet except Shakespeare, could put the same thing in epigrammatic couplets:

> *Has God, thou fool! work'd solely for thy good,*
> *Thy joy, thy pastime, thy attire, thy food? . . .*
> *Is it for thee the lark ascends and sings?*
> *Joy tunes his voice, joy elevates his wings.*
> *Is it for thee the linnet pours his throat?*
> *Loves of his own and raptures swell the note. . . .*
> *Know Nature's children all divide her care;*
> *The fur that warms a monarch warm'd a bear.*

Already we were halfway to Wordsworth's "the meanest flower that blows can give/Thoughts that do often lie too deep for tears" or Blake's "Kill not the moth nor butterfly/For the Last Judgment draweth nigh."

Out of such attitudes emerged the whole romantic glorification of nature which blossomed in the eighteenth century and continued almost unchecked to the middle of the nineteenth, when scientific objectivity began to struggle against it. By that time life had become comparatively secure and men increasingly were finding the somewhat terrifying spectacle of nature's savage grandeur thrillingly beautiful. Mountains, as modern scholarship has pointed out, were almost always called "sublime." The philosopher-statesman Edmund Burke devoted one of his earliest writings to distinguishing between "The Beautiful" (that which is soothing and reassuring) and "The Sublime" (that which strikes us with awe and with something almost like terror). Everywhere men were beginning to exclaim over thunderstorms, lashing seas, and icy peaks—over whatever suggested something grander and less comfortable than their own cities or, even, their own lawns and gardens.

In this period also the cult of nature as "the kind mother" or, in the words of Goethe, as "the living garment of God" grew. This wildly unrealistic view attributed to nature below the human level a consistent kindliness and benevolence which man himself to this day has by no means achieved. Nature is not always a kind mother; she is as often a stern, and sometimes a brutal one. Yet Burns spoke of "Man's inhumanity to man" and contrasted it with "Nature's social union" which, he said, man had so cruelly disturbed. Wordsworth's God had his dwelling in "the light of setting suns," and "Nature," he proclaimed, "never did betray the heart that loved her."

It was against such romantic idealism that the nineteenth century gradually rebelled until, just after the mid-century, Charles Darwin took a position at the opposite extreme and drew his picture of a natural world which assumed its form through the operation of mechanical processes, and which was devoid of anything which could be called moral values.

If few today doubt that Darwin's theory of "natural selection through the struggle for survival" explains much, there are many who insist that it does not explain everything. Some of the most primitive organisms have survived for many millions of years—far longer than other more advanced organisms and possibly longer than man himself will prevail. If only "the fittest survive," then the sea squirt is fitter than any mammal—including, perhaps, man. And "natural selection" cannot account for the intensification of man's consciousness or the value which he puts upon such ideals as justice, fair play and benevolence. It cannot account for them inasmuch as creatures in which these traits are not conspicuous are at least as successful in the "struggle for survival" as he is.

If nature herself has exhibited a tendency, if she seems to "want" anything, it is not merely to survive. She has tended to realize more and more completely the potentialities of protoplasm, and these include much that has no demonstrable "survival value." Evolution itself has spread before us the story of a striving toward "the higher," not merely toward that which enables an organism to survive.

If the romantic view of nature was mere wishful thinking, merely the projection upon nature of our own fully developed desires and ideals, then Darwinism generated a romanticism in reverse in which all is conflict, violence, and blood. But the fact is that animals do not spend all their time fighting for survival, though for the sake of excitement anti-romantic popular books and films do strive to give that impression. Animals also give tender love to their offspring as well as, sometimes, to their mates and the fellow members of their group. Those theories of human society which propose ruthless, devil-take-the-hindermost political and social systems sometimes claim that they are in accord with the laws of nature, but they are not.

There was a time not too long ago when orthodox science talked only of instincts, behavior patterns, chemical drives, and the like, while any tendency to see in the animal even faint analogies to the conscious processes, the intelligence, or the emotions of man was ridiculed as sentimental and "anthropomorphic"—*i.e.,* stated in terms appropriate to man only. But the tide has turned. So notable a student of animal behavior as Konrad Lorenz has protested against what he named "mechanomorphism"—the interpretation of animal behavior exclusively in terms of the mechanical—which he calls an error no less grave than anthropomorphism. Animals are not men, but neither are they machines. If they cannot think as man does in terms of abstract concepts, neither are they controlled entirely by push-button reflexes. To some extent they exhibit the beginnings of "the human." They can sometimes take in a situation and modify their behavior in the light of circumstances. They have individuality also; one does not behave exactly like another. Even insects, once thought to be the most automatic and invariable of creatures, seem to be able sometimes to change purposely the pattern of their conduct.

As a matter of fact, the life of the senses in some of the higher animals is possibly more vivid than ours, and in some of them the emotions may be more powerful also. As Sir Julian Huxley, one of the greatest living authorities on evolution, has said of the birds he has observed with scientific exactitude: "Their lives are often emotional, and their emotions are richly and finely expressed. . . . In birds the advance on the intellectual side has been less, on the emotional side greater: so that we can study in them a part of the single stream of life where emotion, untrammeled by much reason, has the upper hand."

Thus all the strange powers and potentialities of the living thing are diffused throughout animate nature—which remains mysterious, and our relation to it no less so. The universe is not the mere machine which early Darwinians tended to make it. The man who thinks of his dog as another human being is wrong, but no more so perhaps than his opposite who refuses to acknowledge any kinship. Yet an appreciation of this truth still leaves unanswered the question of man's own position. To what extent is he unique; to what extent is he not only "higher" than any other animal, but also radically different from, and discontinuous with, that great chain which connects by close links the humblest one-celled animal with the most intelligent of the apes?

The traditional answer, given by some philosophers and theologians, is that man is an animal to which something (a soul, if you like) has been added and that this something distinguishes him absolutely from all other living creatures. This answer is at least logically tenable, whether you accept it or not. If, on the other hand, you say, as some old-fashioned biologists did,'that though man has "evolved" by purely natural process, he is nevertheless endowed with capacities of which not a trace is to be found in any other animal, that is not logically tenable. "Evolution" implies the growing complexity of things previously existing in simpler form. Hence man's consciousness, thought, and sense of purpose must either have been added to his natural endowment by something outside nature, or they must have truly evolved from something in the "lower" forms of life.

William Morton Wheeler, the late great student of the social insects, once wrote that we can only guess why animals are as they are and can never know except very imperfectly how they came to be what they are. Nevertheless, he added, "[the fact] that organisms are as they are, that apart from members of our own species they are our only companions in an infinite and unsympathetic waste of electrons, planets, nebulae and stars, is a perennial joy and consolation." It is upon this "perennial joy and consolation" that the deepest and most rewarding "love of nature" must rest.

Even to say that we can and should know this joy and consolation is not to answer all the questions. How far should we not only enjoy nature but also follow her; to what extent should we take our cue, as it were, from the natural world? We are something more than merely part of it. However we came to be where we are, our position is, as an eighteenth-century poet put it, "on the isthmus of a middle state." We face back toward our primitive ancestors, perhaps even to the ape; but we also look forward to we know not what.

To what extent then should man, to what extent dare he, renounce nature; take over the management of the earth he lives on; and use it exclusively for what he sometimes regards as his higher purposes?

Extremists give and have always given extreme answers. Let us, say some, "return to nature," lead the simple life, try to become again that figment of the romantic imagination, "the noble savage." Henry David Thoreau, the greatest of American "nature lovers," is sometimes accused of having advocated just that. But he did not do so; he advocated only that we should live more simply and more aware of the earth which, he said with characteristic exaggeration, "is more wonderful than it is convenient; more beautiful than it is useful; it is more to be admired and enjoyed than used."

Others suggest a different extreme. They talk about "the biosphere" (loosely that which has been here defined as the natural world) as contrasted with "the noosphere" (translated as that portion of the earth upon which man has imposed his own will so successfully that whatever conditions prevail there do so because of his will). It appears that civilization, according to this notion, is to be completed only when the noosphere is the whole earth and the biosphere is completely subordinated to the human will.

Within the last one hundred years we have approached faster and closer to that condition than in all the preceding centuries of civilization. But would man, whose roots go so deep into nature, be happy should he achieve such a situation? Certainly he would become a creature very different from what he is, and the experience of living would be equally different from what it has always been. He would, indeed, have justified his boast that he can "conquer nature" but he would also have destroyed it. He would have used every spot of earth for homes, factories, and farms, or perhaps got rid of farms entirely, because by then he could synthesize food in the laboratory. But he would have no different companions in the adventures of living. The emotions which have inspired much of all poetry, music, and art would no longer be comprehensible. He would have all his dealings with things he alone has made. Would we then be, as some would imagine, men like gods? Or would we be only men like ants?

That we would not be satisfied with such a world is sufficiently evidenced by the fact that, to date at least, few do not want their country house, their country vacation, their camping or their fishing trip—even their seat in the park and their visit to the zoo. We need some contact with the things we spring from. We need nature at least as a part of the context of our lives. Though we are not satisfied with nature, neither are we happy without her. Without cities we cannot be civilized. Without nature, without wilderness even, we are compelled to renounce an important part of our heritage.

The late Aldo Leopold, who spent his life in forestry and conservation, once wrote: "For us of the minority, the opportunity to see geese is more important than television, and the chance to see a pasqueflower is a right as inalienable as free speech."

Many of us who share this conviction came to it only gradually. On some summer vacation or some country weekend we realize that what we are experiencing is more than merely a relief from the pressures of city life; that we have not merely escaped *from* something but also *into* something; that we have joined the greatest of all communities, which is not that of men alone but of everything which shares with us the great adventure of being alive.

This sense, mystical though it may seem, is no delusion. Throughout history some have felt it and many have found an explanation of it in their conviction that it arises out of the fact that all things owe their gift of life to God. But there is no reason why the most rationalistic of evolutionists should not find it equally inevitable. If man is only the most recent and the most complex of nature's children, then he must feel his kinship with them. If even his highest powers of consciousness, intellect, and conscience were evolved from simpler forms of the same realities, then his kinship with those who took the earlier steps is real and compelling. If nature produced him, and if she may someday produce something far less imperfect, then he may well hesitate to declare that she has done all she can for him and that henceforth he will renounce her to direct his own destiny.

In some ways man may seem wiser than she is, but it is not certain that he is wiser in all ways. He dare not trust her blindly, but neither does he dare turn his back upon her. He is in danger of relying too exclusively upon his own thoughts, to the entire neglect of her instincts; upon the dead machine he creates, while disregarding the living things of whose adventure he is a part.

We have heard much about "our natural resources" and of the necessity for conserving them, but these "resources" are not merely materially useful. They are also a great reservoir of the life from which we evolved, and they have both consolation to offer and lessons to each which are not alone those the biologist strives to learn. In their presence many of us experience a lifting of the heart for which mere fresh air and sunshine is not sufficient to account. We feel surging up in us the exuberant, vital urge which has kept evolution going but which tends to falter amid the complexities of a too civilized life. In our rise to the human state we have lost something, despite all we have gained.

Is it merely a sentimental delusion, a "pathetic fallacy," to think that one sees in the animal a capacity for joy which man himself is tending to lose? We have invented exercise, recreation, pleasure, amusement, and the rest. To "have fun" is a desire often expressed by those who live in this age of anxiety and most of us have at times actually "had fun." But recreation, pleasure, amusement, fun, and all the rest are poor substitutes for joy; and joy, I am convinced, has its roots in something from which civilization tends to cut us off.

Are at least some animals capable of teaching us this lesson of joy? Some biologists—but by no means all and by no means the best—deny categorically that animals feel it. The gift for real happiness and joy is not always proportionate to intelligence, as we understand it, even among the animals. As Professor N. J. Berrill has put it, "To be a bird is to be alive more intensively than any other living creature. . . . [Birds] live in a world that is always in the present, mostly full of joy." Similarly Sir Julian Huxley, no mere sentimental nature lover, wrote after watching the love play of herons: "I can only say that it seemed to bring such a pitch of emotion that I could have wished to be a Heron that I might experience it."

This does not mean that Sir Julian would desire, any more than you or I, to be permanently a bird. Perhaps some capacity for joy has been, must be, and should be sacrificed to other capacities. But some awareness of the world outside of man must exist if one is to experience the happiness and solace which some of us find in an awareness of nature and in our love for her manifestations.

Those who have never found either joy or solace in nature might begin by looking not for the *joy they can get,* but for the *joy that is there* amid those portions of the earth man has not yet entirely pre-empted for his own use. And perhaps when they have become aware of joy in other creatures they will achieve joy in themselves, by sharing it.

CHILDREN OF ADAM, *LEAVES OF GRASS*
Walt Whitman

With his first volume of verse, *Leaves of Grass,* Walt Whitman (1819–1892) introduced to America a new type of poetry, free verse, devoid of the traditional trappings of English poetry—rhyme, meter, and metaphor. Whitman is the great celebrator of nature, writing songs to the earth, celebrating its fecundity, wondrousness, and its ability to nurture and renew life.

We two, how long we were fool'd,
Now transmuted, we swiftly escape as Nature escapes,
We are Nature, long have we been absent, but now we return,
We become plants, trunks, foliage, roots, bark,
We are bedded in the ground, we are rocks,
We are oaks, we grow in the openings side by side,
We browse, we are two among the wild herds spontaneous as any,
We are two fishes swimming in the sea together,
We are what locust blossoms are, we drop scent around lanes mornings and
*   evenings,*

We are also the coarse smut of beasts, vegetables, minerals,
We are two predatory hawks, we soar above and look down,
We are two resplendent suns, we it is who balance ourselves orbic and stellar,
        we are as two comets,
We prowl fang'd and four-footed in the woods, we spring on prey,
We are two clouds forenoons and afternoons driving overhead,
We are seas mingling, we are two of those cheerful waves rolling over each
        other and interwetting each other,
We are what the atmosphere is, transparent, receptive, pervious, impervious,
We are snow, rain, cold, darkness, we are each product and influence of the
        globe,
We have circled and circled till we have arrived home again, we two,
We have voided all but freedom and all but our own joy.

SONGS OF PARTING, *LEAVES OF GRASS*
Walt Whitman

Song at Sunset

Splendor of ended day floating and filling me,
Hour prophetic, hour resuming the past,
Inflating my throat, you divine average,
You earth and life till the last ray gleams I sing.

Open mouth of my soul uttering gladness,
Eyes of my soul seeing perfection,
Natural life of me faithfully praising things,
Corroborating forever the triumph of things.

Illustrious every one!
Illustrious what we name space, sphere of unnumber'd spirits,
Illustrious the mystery of motion in all beings, even the tiniest insect,
Illustrious the attribute of speech, the senses, the body,
Illustrious the passing light—illustrious the pale reflection on the new moon in
        the western sky,
Illustrious whatever I see or hear or touch, to the last.

Good in all,
In the satisfaction and aplomb of animals,
In the annual return of the seasons,
In the hilarity of youth,
In the strength and flush of manhood,
In the grandeur and exquisiteness of old age,
In the superb vistas of death.

Wonderful to depart!
Wonderful to be here!
The heart, to jet the all-alike and innocent blood!
To breathe the air, how delicious!
To speak—to walk—to seize something by the hand!
To prepare for sleep, for bed, to look on my rose-color'd flesh!
To be conscious of my body, so satisfied, so large!
To be this incredible God I am!
To have gone forth among other Gods, these men and women I love.

Wonderful how I celebrate you and myself!
How my thoughts play subtly at the spectacles around!
How the clouds pass silently overhead!
How the earth darts on and on! and how the sun, moon, stars, dart on and on!
How the water sports and sings! (surely it is alive!)
How the trees rise and stand up, with strong trunks, with branches and leaves!
(Surely there is something more in each of the trees, some living soul.)

O amazement of things—even the least particle!
O spirituality of things!
O strain musical flowing through ages and continents, now reaching me and
         America!
I take your strong chords, intersperse them, and cheerfully pass them forward.

I too carol the sun, usher'd or at noon, or as now, setting,
I too throb to the brain and beauty of the earth and of all the growths of the
         earth,
I too have felt the resistless call of myself.

As I steam'd down the Mississippi,
As I wander'd over the prairies,
As I have lived, as I have look'd through my windows my eyes,
As I went forth in the morning, as I beheld the light breaking in the east,
As I bathed on the beach of the Eastern Sea, and again on the beach of the
                       Western Sea,
As I roam'd the streets of inland Chicago, whatever streets I have roam'd,
Or cities or silent woods, or even amid the sights of war,
Wherever I have been I have charged myself with contentment and triumph.

I sing to the last the equalities modern or old,
I sing the endless finales of things,
I say Nature continues, glory continues,
I praise with electric voice,
For I do not see one imperfection in the universe,
And I do not see one cause or result lamentable at last in the universe.

O setting sun! though the time has come,
I still warble under you, if none else does, unmitigated adoration.

AUTUMN RIVULETS, *LEAVES OF GRASS*
Walt Whitman

This Compost

1

Something startles me where I thought I was safest,
I withdraw from the still woods I loved,
I will not go now on the pastures to walk,
I will not strip the clothes from my body to meet my lover the sea,
I will not touch my flesh to the earth as to other flesh to renew me.

O how can it be that the ground itself does not sicken?
How can you be alive you growths of spring?
How can you furnish health you blood of herbs, roots, orchards, grain?
Are they not continually putting distemper'd corpses within you?
Is not every continent work'd over and over with sour dead?

Where have you disposed of their carcasses?
Those drunkards and gluttons of so many generations?
Where have you drawn off all the foul liquid and meat?
I do not see any of it upon you to-day, or perhaps I am deceiv'd,
I will run a furrow with my plough, I will press my spade through the sod and
    turn it up underneath,
I am sure I shall expose some of the foul meat.

2

Behold this compost! behold it well!
Perhaps every mite has once form'd part of a sick person —yet behold!
The grass of spring covers the prairies,
The bean bursts noiselessly through the mould in the garden,
The delicate spear of the onion pierces upward,
The apple-buds cluster together on the apple-branches,
The resurrection of the wheat appears with pale visage out of its graves,
The tinge awakes over the willow-tree and the mulberry-tree,
The he-birds carol mornings and evenings while the she-birds sit on their nests,
The young of the poultry break through the hatch'd eggs,
The new-born of animals appear, the calf is dropt from the cow, the colt from
    the mare,
Out of its little hill faithfully rise the potato's dark green leaves,
Out of its hill rises the yellow maize-stalk, the lilacs bloom in the dooryards,
The summer growth is innocent and disdainful above all those strata of
    sour dead.

What chemistry!
That the winds are really not infectious,
That this is no cheat, this transparent green-wash of the sea which is so
    amorous after me,
That it is safe to allow it to lick my naked body all over with its tongues,
That it will not endanger me with the fevers that have deposited themselves in it,
That all is clean forever and forever,
That the cool drink from the well tastes so good,
That blackberries are so flavorous and juicy,
That the fruits of the apple-orchard and the orange-orchard, that melons,
    grapes, peaches, plums, will none of them poison me,
That when I recline on the grass I do not catch any disease,
Though probably every spear of grass rises out of what was once a catching
    disease.

Now I am terrified at the Earth, it is that calm and patient,
It grows such sweet things out of such corruptions,
It turns harmless and stainless on its axis, with such endless successions of
       diseas'd corpses,
It distills such exquisite winds out of such infused fetor,
It renews with such unwitting looks its prodigal, annual, sumptuous
       crops,
It gives such divine materials to men, and accepts such leavings from them
       at last.

IF EVERYTHING HAPPENS THAT CAN'T BE DONE[2]
E. E. Cummings

      E. E. Cummings (1894–1962) was an American poet known for
stylistic experiment, concern with social issues, and originality of vision.

if everything happens that can't be done
(and anything's righter
than books
could plan)
the stupidest teacher will almost guess
(with a run
skip
around we go yes)
there's nothing as something as one

one hasn't a why or because or although
(and buds know better
than books
don't grow)
one's anything old being everything new
(with a what
which
around we come who)
one's everyanything so

so world is a leaf so tree is a bough
(and birds sing sweeter
than books
tell how)
so here is away and so your is a my
(with a down
up
around again fly)
forever was never till now

now I love you and you love me
(and books are shuter
than books
can be)
and deep in the high that does nothing but fall
(with a shout
each
around we go all)
there's somebody calling who's we

we're anything brighter than even the sun
(we're everything greater
than books
might mean)
we're everyanything more than believe
(with a spin
leap
alive we're alive)
we're wonderful one times one

RETURNING TO LIVE ON THE FARM, *SIX POEMS*[3]
T'ao Ch'ien
translated by Lily Pao-Hu Chang and Marjorie Sinclair

T'ao Ch'ien (c. 375–c. 475), Chinese poet, was born into an old
and distinguished family which had fallen onto hard times. In his

[3]From *The Poems of T'ao Ch'ien*, translated by Lily Pao-Hu Chang and Marjorie Sinclair.
Reprinted by permission of the University of Hawaii Press, © 1953.

twenties he took a position at court for a brief period, but he was unhappy there and left to return to the hard work and poverty of his farm, where he remained for the duration of his life.

[1]

When I was young, I was not fitted for a worldly rhythm.
By nature I loved the mountains and the hills.
I fell into the net of the world by mistake,
And I have stayed there for thirty years.
A bird in the cage longs for the old forest,
And a fish in the pond thinks of his former pool.
I cultivated rough land in the south,
And, keeping to simple ways, I returned to the field and garden.
I have over ten mu⁴ of land
And a thatched house of eight or nine rooms.
Birch and willow shade the back eaves;
Peach and plum spread their branches in the front courtyard.
Villages lie in the distance.
Smoke rises like mist from faraway fields.
Dogs bark in hidden lanes,
And roosters crow from the tops of mulberry trees.
Inside my house there is no worldly hubbub.
There is space, and I have leisure.
For a long time I was in a cage,
But now I am back with nature.

Reading the Classic MOUNTAINS AND SEAS⁵
THIRTEEN POEMS
T'ao Ch'ien
Translated by Lily Pao-Hu Chang and Marjorie Sinclair

[1]

In early summer, grass and trees grow,
And around the house, the sparse branches spread.

⁴A *mu* is about one-sixth of an acre.

⁵From *The Poems of T'ao Ch'ien*, translated by Lily Pao-Hu Chang and Marjorie Sinclair. Reprinted by permission of the University of Hawaii Press, © 1953.

All the birds are happy because they have shelter;
I, too, love my thatch.
The land is already tilled and planted with seed.
There is still time for my books.
In the lonely lane there are no deep worn tracks,
And the carts of old friends often turn back.
Happily we drink the spring wine,
And pick the greens from my garden.
A soft light rain comes from the east
And with it a good wind.
I turn carelessly through the record of Prince Chou,
Moving my eyes over the pictures in "Mountains and Seas."
Looking up and down I see the whole universe.
How can I but feel happy?

THE VALLEY WIND[6]
Lu Yun
translated by Arthur Waley

Lu Yun was a fourth-century Chinese poet.

Living in retirement beyond the World,
Silently enjoying isolation,
I pull the rope of my door tighter
And stuff my window with roots and ferns.
My spirit is tuned to the Spring-season:
At the fall of the year there is autumn in my heart.
Thus imitating cosmic changes
My cottage becomes a Universe.

[6]From *Translations from the Chinese*, by Arthur Waley. Copyright 1919, 1941 by Alfred A. Knopf, Inc. and renewed 1947 by Arthur Waley. Reprinted by permission of the publisher. *170 Chinese Poems* translated by Arthur Waley: Constable, London, 1918 (reprinted 1962).

WILLIE METCALF, *SPOON RIVER ANTHOLOGY*[7]
Edgar Lee Masters

    Edgar Lee Masters (1868–1950) was an American poet. His greatest work, *Spoon River Anthology*, consists of free-verse epitaphs in which the people buried in a Midwestern cemetery tell how they lived and died.

I was Willie Metcalf.
They used to call me "Doctor Meyers"
Because, they said, I looked like him.
And he was my father, according to Jack McGuire.
I lived in the livery stable,
Sleeping on the floor
Side by side with Roger Baughman's bulldog,
Or sometimes in a stall.
I could crawl between the legs of the wildest horses
Without getting kicked—we knew each other.
On spring days I tramped through the country
To get the feeling, which I sometimes lost,
That I was not a separate thing from the earth.
I used to lose myself, as if in sleep,
By lying with eyes half-open in the woods.
Sometimes I talked with animals—even toads and snakes—
Anything that had an eye to look into.
Once I saw a stone in the sunshine
Trying to turn into jelly.
In April days in this cemetery
The dead people gathered all about me,
And grew still, like a congregation in silent prayer.
I never knew whether I was a part of the earth
With flowers growing in me, or whether I walked—
Now I know.

[7] From *Spoon River Anthology*, by Edgar Lee Masters. Copyright © 1914, 1916, 1942, 1944. Reprinted with permission of Mrs. Ellen Masters.

BRING THE DAY[8]
Theodore Roethke

Theodore Roethke (1908–1963) combined a marvelous sense of humor with an extremely keen sensitivity and a unique way of looking at things and describing them. Brought up in northern Michigan, by a family who ran a greenhouse, Roethke had a strong feeling for nature.

1

Bees and lilies there were,
Bees and lilies there were,
Either to other,—
Which would you rather?
Bees and lilies were there.

The green grasses,—would they?
The green grasses?—
She asked her skin
To let me in:
The far leaves were for it.

Forever is easy, she said.
How many angels do you know?—
And over by Algy's
Something came by me,
It wasn't a goose,
It wasn't a poodle.

Everything's closer. Is this a cage?
The chill's gone from the moon.
Only the woods are alive.
I can't marry the dirt.

[8]"Bring the Day" copyright 1951 by Theodore Roethke, from *The Collected Poems of Theodore Roethke*. Reprinted by permission of Doubleday & Company, Inc. and Faber and Faber, Ltd.

I'm a biscuit. I'm melted already.
The white weather hates me.
Why is how I like it.
I can't catch a bush.

2

The herrings are awake.
What's all the singing between? —
Is it with whispers and kissing? —
I've listened into the least waves.
The grass says what the wind says:
Begin with the rock;
End with water.

When I stand, I'm almost a tree.
Leaves, do you like me any?
A swan needs a pond.
The worm and the rose
Both love
Rain.

3

O small bird wakening,
Light as a hand among blossoms,
Hardly any old angels are around any more.
The air's quiet under the small leaves.
The dust, the long dust, stays.
The spiders sail into summer.
It's time to begin!
To begin!

MELAMPUS
George Meredith

George Meredith (1828–1909) was a Victorian poet and novelist. Melampus, the subject of this poem, a figure from Greek mythology, acquired the power to understand birds and animals when he was licked by a brood of snakes; Homer tells his story in the Odyssey.

I

With love exceeding a simple love of the things
   That glide in grasses and rubble of woody wreck;
Or change their perch on a beat of quivering wings
   From branch to branch, only restful to pipe and peck;
Or, bristled, curl at a touch their snouts in a ball;
   Or cast their web between bramble and thorny hook;
The good physician Melampus, loving them all,
   Among them walked, as a scholar who reads a book.

II

For him the woods were a home and gave him the key
   Of knowledge, thirst for their treasures in herbs and flowers.
The secrets held by the creatures nearer than we
   To earth he sought, and the link of their life with ours:
And where alike we are, unlike where, and the veined
   Division, veined parallel, of a blood that flows
In them, in us, from the source by man unattained
   Save marks he well what the mystical woods disclose.

III

And this he deemed might be boon of love to a breast
   Embracing tenderly each little motive shape,
The prone, the flitting, who seek their food whither best
   Their wits direct, whither best from their foes escape:
For closer drawn to our mother's natural milk,
   As babes they learn where her motherly help is great:
They know the juice for the honey, juice for the silk,
   And need they medical antidotes find them straight.

IV

Of earth and sun they are wise, they nourish their broods,
　　　Weave, build, hive, burrow and battle, take joy and pain
Like swimmers varying billows: never in woods
　　　Runs white insanity fleeing itself: all sane
The woods revolve: as the tree its shadowing limns
　　　To some resemblance in motion, the rooted life
Restrains disorder: you hear the primitive hymns
　　　Of earth in woods issue wild of the web of strife.

V

Now sleeping once on a day of marvellous fire,
　　　A brood of snakes he had cherished in grave regret
That death his people had dealt their dam and their sire, .
　　　Through savage dread of them, crept to his neck, and set
Their tongues to lick him: the swift affectionate tongue
　　　Of each ran licking the slumberer: then his ears
A forked red tongue tickled shrewdly: sudden upsprung,
　　　He heard a voice piping: Ay, for he has no fears!

VI

A bird said that, in the notes of birds, and the speech
　　　Of men, it seemed: and another renewed: He moves
To learn and not to pursue, he gathers to teach;
　　　He feeds his young as do we, and as we love loves.
No fears have I of a man who goes with his head
　　　To earth, chance looking aloft at us, kind of hand:
I feel to him as to earth of whom we are fed;
　　　I pipe him much for his good could he understand.

VII

Melampus touched at his ears, laid finger on wrist:
　　　He was not dreaming, he sensibly felt and heard.
Above, through leaves, where the tree-twigs thick intertwist,
　　　He spied the bird and the bill of the speaking bird.
His cushion mosses in shades of various green,
　　　The lumped, the antlered, he pressed, while the sunny snake
Slipped under: draughts he had drunk of clear Hippocrene,
　　　It seemed, and sat with a gift of the Gods awake.

VIII

Divinely thrilled was the man, exultingly full,
    As quick well-waters that come of the heart of earth,
Ere yet they dart in a brook, are one bubble-pool
    To light and sound, wedding both at the leap of birth.
The soul of light vivid shone, a stream within stream;
    The soul of sound from a musical shell outflew;
Where others hear but a hum and see but a beam,
    The tongue and eye of the fountain of life he knew.

IX

He knew the Hours: they were round him, laden with seed
    Of hours bestrewn upon vapour, and one by one
They winged as ripened in fruit the burden decreed
    For each to scatter; they flushed like the buds in sun,
Bequeathing seed to successive similar rings,
    Their sisters, bearers to men of what men have earned:
He knew them, talked with the yet unreddened; the stings,
    The sweets, they warmed at their bosoms divined, discerned.

X

Not unsolicited, sought by diligent feet,
    By riddling fingers expanded, oft watched in growth
With brooding deep as the noon-ray's quickening wheat,
    Ere touch'd, the pendulous flower of the plants of sloth,
The plants of rigidness, answered question and squeeze,
    Revealing wherefore it bloomed uninviting, bent,
Yet making harmony breathe of life and disease,
    The deeper chord of a wonderful instrument.

XI

So passed he luminous-eyed for earth and the fates
    We arm to bruise or caress us: his ears were charged
With tones of love in a whirl of voluble hates,
    With music wrought of distraction his heart enlarged.
Celestial-shining, though mortal, singer, though mute,
    He drew the Master of harmonies, voiced or stilled,
To seek him; heard at the silent medicine-root
    A song, beheld in fulfilment the unfulfilled.

XII

Him Phoebus, lending to darkness colour and form
        Of light's excess, many lessons and counsels gave;
Showed Wisdom lord of the human intricate swarm,
        And whence prophetic it looks on the hives that rave;
And how acquired, of the zeal of love to acquire,
        And where it stands, in the centre of life a sphere;
And Measure, mood of the lyre, the rapturous lyre,
        He said was Wisdom, and struck him the notes to hear.

XIII

Sweet, sweet: 'twas glory of vision, honey, the breeze
        In heat, the run of the river on root and stone,
All senses joined, as the sister Pierides
        Are one, uplifting their chorus, the Nine, his own.
In stately order, evolved of sound into sight,
        From sight to sound intershifting, the man descried
The growths of earth, his adored, like day out of night,
        Ascend in song, seeing nature and song allied.

XIV

And there vitality, there, there solely in song,
        Resides, where earth and her uses to men, their needs,
Their forceful cravings, the theme are: there is it strong,
        The Master said: and the studious eye that reads
(Yea, even as earth to the crown of Gods on the mount)
        In links divine with the lyrical tongue is bound.
Pursue thy craft: it is music drawn of a fount
        To spring perennial; well-spring is common ground.

XV

Melampus dwelt among men: physician and sage,
        He served them, loving them, healing them; sick or maimed
Or them that frenzied in some delirious rage
        Outran the measure, his juice of the woods reclaimed.
He played on men, as his master, Phoebus, on strings
        Melodious: as the God did he drive and check,
Through love exceeding a simple love of the things
        That glide in grasses and rubble of woody wreck.

THE GARDEN
Andrew Marvell

Andrew Marvell (1621–1678), an English poet, is known for his masterpiece, "To His Coy Mistress," one of the most anthologized poems in English. Much of Marvell's best verse is pastoral, as is our selection. Critic Tucker Brooke called Marvell, aptly, "a poet of the virginal pleasures of the earth."[9]

How vainly men themselves amaze
To win the palm, the oak, or bays;
And their incessant labors see
Crowned from some single herb, or tree,
Whose short and narrow-verged shade
Does prudently their toils upbraid;
While all flowers and all trees do close
To weave the garlands of repose!

Fair Quiet, have I found thee here,
And Innocence, thy sister dear?
Mistaken long, I sought you then
In busy companies of men.
Your sacred plants, if here below,
Only among the plants will grow;
Society is all but rude
To this delicious solitude.

No white nor red was ever seen
So amorous as this lovely green.
Fond lovers, cruel as their flame,
Cut in these trees their mistress' name:
Little, alas! they know or heed
How far these beauties hers exceed!
Fair trees! wheres'e'er your barks I wound,
No name shall but your own be found.

[9] Albert C. Baugh, ed., *A Literary History of England* (Appleton-Century-Crofts, New York, 1948), p. 668.

When we have run our passion's heat,
Love hither makes his best retreat.
The gods, that mortal beauty chase,
Still in a tree did end their race;
Apollo hunted Daphne so,
Only that she might laurel grow;
And Pan did after Syrinx speed,
Not as a nymph, but for a reed.

What wondrous life in this I lead!
Ripe apples drop about my head;
The luscious clusters of the vine
Upon my mouth do crush their wine;
The nectarine, and curious peach,
Into my hands themselves do reach;
Stumbling on melons, as I pass,
Ensnared with flowers, I fall on grass.

Meanwhile the mind, from pleasure less,
Withdraws into its happiness;
The mind, that ocean where each kind
Does straight its own resemblance find;
Yet it creates, transcending these,
Far other worlds, and other seas,
Annihilating all that's made
To a green thought in a green shade.

Here at the fountain's sliding foot,
Or at some fruit-tree's mossy root,
Casting the body's vest aside,
My soul into the boughs does glide:
There, like a bird, it sits and sings,
Then whets and combs its silver wings,
And, till prepared for long flight,
Waves in its plums the various light.

Such was that happy garden state,
While man there walked without a mate:
After a place so pure and sweet,
What other help could yet be meet!
But 'twas beyond a mortal's share
To wander solitary there:
Two paradises 'twere in one,
To live in paradise alone.

How well the skilful gardener drew
Of flowers and herbs this dial new;
Where, from above, the milder sun
Does through a fragrant zodiac run,
And, as it works, th' industrious bee
Computes its time as well as we!
How could such sweet and wholesome hours
Be reckoned but with herbs and flowers!

SOLITUDE, *WALDEN*
Henry David Thoreau

Henry David Thoreau (1817–1862) was a New England poet, essayist, and naturalist. Like Emerson, his neighbor and patron, Thoreau was a Transcendentalist. Most of Thoreau's literary materials were provided by his feeling for social issues, and his belief in the unity of man and nature. His essay *Civil Disobedience* inspired Mahatma Gandhi and Martin Luther King, and became the basis for the modern concept of peaceful resistance. Thoreau's love of solitude, contemplation, and communion with nature resulted in his masterpiece, *Walden; or Life in the Woods,* from which our selection is taken.

This is a delicious evening, when the whole body is one sense, and imbibes delight through every pore. I go and come with a strange liberty in Nature, a part of herself. As I walk along the stony shore of the pond in my shirt sleeves, though it is cool as well as cloudy and windy, and I see nothing special to attract me, all the elements are unusually congenial to me. The bullfrogs trump to usher in the night, and the note of the whippoorwill is borne on the rippling wind from over the water. Sympathy with the fluttering alder and poplar leaves almost takes away my breath; yet, like the lake, my serenity is rippled but not ruffled. These small waves raised by the evening wind are as remote from storm as the smooth reflecting surface. Though it is now dark, the wind still blows and roars in the wood, the waves still dash, and some creatures lull the rest with their notes. The repose is never complete. The wildest animals do not repose, but seek their prey now; the fox, and skunk, and rabbit, now roam the fields and woods without fear. They are Nature's watchmen,—links which connect the days of animated life.

When I return to my house I find that visitors have been there and left their cards, either a bunch of flowers, or a wreath of evergreen, or a name in pencil on a yellow walnut leaf or a chip. They who come rarely to the woods take some little piece of the forest into their hands to play with by the way, which they leave, either intentionally or accidentally. One has peeled a willow wand, woven it into a ring, and dropped it on my table. I could always tell if visitors had called in my absence, either by the bended twigs or grass, or the print of their shoes, and generally of what sex or age or quality they were by some slight trace left, as a flower dropped, or a bunch of grass plucked and thrown away, even as far off as the railroad, half a mile distant, or by the lingering odor of a cigar or pipe. Nay, I was frequently notified of the passage of a traveller along the highway sixty rods off by the scent of his pipe.

There is commonly sufficient space about us. Our horizon is never quite at our elbows. The thick wood is not just at our door, nor the pond, but somewhat is always clearing, familiar and worn by us, appropriated and fenced in some way, and reclaimed from Nature. For what reason have I this vast range and circuit, some square miles of unfrequented forest, for my privacy, abandoned to me by men? My nearest neighbor is a mile distant, and no house is visible from any place but the hill tops within half a mile of my own. I have my horizon bounded by woods all to myself; a distant view of the railroad where it touches the pond on the one hand, and of the fence which skirts the woodland road on the other. But for the most part it is as solitary where I live as on the prairies. It is as much Asia or Africa as New England. I have, as it were, my own sun and moon and stars, and a little world all to myself. At night there was never a traveller passed my house, or knocked at my door, more than if I were the first or last man; unless it were in the spring, when at long intervals some came from the village to fish for pouts,—they plainly fished much more in the Walden Pond of their own natures, and baited their hooks with darkness,—but they soon retreated, usually with light baskets, and left "the world to darkness and to me," and the black kernel of the night was never profaned by any human neighborhood. I believe that men are generally still a little afraid of the dark, though the witches are all hung, and Christianity and candles have been introduced.

Yet I experienced sometimes that the most sweet and tender, the most innocent and encouraging society may be found in any natural object, even for the poor misanthrope and most melancholy man. There can be no very black melancholy to him who lives in the midst of Nature and has his senses still. There was never yet such a storm but it was Æolian music to a healthy and innocent ear. Nothing can rightly compel a simple and brave man to a vulgar sadness. While I enjoy the friendship of the seasons I trust that nothing can make life a burden to me. The gentle rain which waters my beans and keeps me in the house to-day is not drear and melancholy, but good for me, too. Though it prevents my hoeing them, it is of far more worth than my hoeing. If it should continue so long as to cause the seeds to rot in the ground and destroy the potatoes in the low lands, it would still be good for the grass on the uplands, and, being good for the grass, it would be good for me. Sometimes, when I compare myself with other men, it seems as if I were more favored by the gods than they, beyond any deserts that I am conscious of; as if I had a warrant and surety at their hands which my fellows have not, and were especially guided and guarded. I do not flatter myself, but if it be possible they flatter me. I have never felt lonesome, or in the least oppressed by a sense of solitude, but once, and that was a few weeks after I came to the woods, when, for an hour, I doubted if the near neighborhood of man was not essential to a serene and healthy life. To be alone was something unpleasant. But I was at the same time conscious of a slight insanity in my mood, and seemed to foresee my recovery. In the midst of a gentle rain while these thoughts prevailed, I was suddenly sensible of such sweet and beneficent society in Nature, in the very pattering of the drops, and in every sound and sight around my house, an infinite and unaccountable friendliness all at once like an atmosphere sustaining me, as made the fancied advantages of human neighborhood insignificant, and I have never thought of them since. Every little pine needle expanded and swelled with sympathy and befriended me. I was so distinctly made aware of the presence of something kindred to me, even in scenes which we are accustomed to call wild and dreary, and also that the nearest of blood to me and humanest was not a person nor a villager, that I thought no place could ever be strange to me again.—

> "*Mourning untimely consumes the sad;*
> *Few are their days in the land of the living,*
> *Beautiful daughter of Toscar.*"

Some of my pleasantest hours were during the long rain storms in the spring or fall, which confined me to the house for the afternoon as well as the forenoon, soothed by their ceaseless roar and pelting; when an early twilight ushered in a long evening in which many thoughts had time to take root and unfold themselves. In those driving northeast rains which tried the village houses so, when the maids stood ready with mop and pail in front entries to keep the deluge out, I sat behind my door in my little house, which was all entry, and thoroughly enjoyed its protection. In one heavy thunder shower the lightning struck a large pitch-pine across the pond, making a very conspicuous and perfectly regular spiral groove from top to bottom, an inch or more deep, and four or five inches wide, as you would groove a walking-stick. I passed it again the other day, and was struck with awe on looking up and beholding that mark, now more distinct than ever, where a terrific and resistless bolt came down out of the harmless sky eight years ago. Men frequently say to me, "I should think you would feel lonesome down there, and want to be nearer to folks, rainy and snowy days and nights especially." I am tempted to reply to such,—This whole earth which we inhabit is but a point in space. How far apart, think you, dwell the two most distant inhabitants of yonder star, the breadth of whose disk cannot be appreciated by our instruments? Why should I feel lonely? is not our planet in the Milky Way? This which you put seems to me not to be the most important question. What sort of space is that which separates a man from his fellows and makes him solitary? I have found that no exertion of the legs can bring two minds much nearer to one another. What do we want most to dwell near to? Not to many men surely, the depot, the post-office, the bar-room, the meeting-house, the school-house, the grocery, Beacon Hill, or the Five Points, where men most congregate, but to the perennial source of our life, whence in all our experience we have found that to issue, as the willow stands near the water and sends out its roots in that direction. This will vary with different natures, but this is the place where a wise man will dig his cellar. . . . I one evening overtook one of my townsmen, who has accumulated what is called "a handsome property,"—though I never got a *fair* view of it,—on the Walden road, driving a pair of cattle to market, who inquired of me how I could bring my mind to give up so many of the comforts of life. I answered that I was very sure I liked it passably well; I was not joking. And so I went home to my bed, and left him to pick his way through the darkness and the mud to Brighton,—or Brighttown,—which place he would reach sometime in the morning.

Any prospect of awakening or coming to life to a dead man makes indifferent all times and places. The place where that may occur is always the same, and indescribably pleasant to all our senses. For the most part we allow only outlying and transient circumstances to make our occasions. They are, in fact, the cause of our distraction. Nearest to all things is that power which fashions their being. *Next* to us the grandest laws are continually being executed. *Next* to us is not the workman whom we have hired, with whom we love so well to talk, but the workman whose work we are.

"How vast and profound is the influence of the subtile powers of Heaven and of Earth!"

"We seek to perceive them, and we do not see them; we seek to hear them, and we do not hear them; identified with the substance of things, they cannot be separated from them."

"They cause that in all the universe men purify and sanctify their hearts, and clothe themselves in their holiday garments to offer sacrifices and oblations to their ancestors. It is an ocean of subtile intelligences. They are everywhere, above us, on our left, on our right; they environ us on all sides."

We are the subjects of an experiment which is not a little interesting to me. Can we not do without the society of our gossips a little while under these circumstances,—have our own thoughts to cheer us? Confucius says truly, "Virtue does not remain as an abandoned orphan; it must of necessity have neighbors."

With thinking we may be beside ourselves in a sane sense. By a conscious effort of the mind we can stand aloof from actions and their consequences; and all things, good and bad, go by us like a torrent. We are not wholly involved in Nature. I may be either the driftwood in the stream, or Indra in the sky looking down on it. I *may* be affected by a theatrical exhibition; on the other hand, I *may not* be affected by an actual event which appears to concern me much more. I only know myself as a human entity; the scene, so to speak, of thoughts and affections; and am sensible of a certain doubleness by which I can stand as remote from myself as from another. However intense my experience, I am conscious of the presence of and criticism of a part of me, which, as it were, is not a part of me, but spectator, sharing no experience, but taking note of it; and that is no more I than it is you. When the play, it may be the tragedy, of life is over, the spectator goes his way. It was a kind of fiction, a work of the imagination only, so far as he was concerned. This doubleness may easily make us poor neighbors and friends sometimes.

I find it wholesome to be alone the greater part of the time. To be in company, even with the best, is soon wearisome and dissipating. I love to be alone. I never found the companion that was so companionable as solitude. We are for the most part more lonely when we go abroad among men than when we stay in our chambers. A man thinking or working is always alone, let him be where he will. Solitude is not measured by the miles of space that intervene between a man and his fellows. The really diligent student in one of the crowded hives of Cambridge College is as solitary as a dervish in the desert. The farmer can work alone in the field or the woods all day, hoeing or chopping, and not feel lonesome, because he is employed; but when he comes home at night he cannot sit down in a room alone, at the mercy of his thoughts, but must be where he can "see the folks," and recreate, and as he thinks remunerate, himself for his day's solitude; and hence he wonders how the student can sit alone in the house all night and most of the day without ennui and "the blues"; but he does not realize that the student, though in the house, is still at work in *his* field, and chopping in *his* woods, as the farmer in his, and in turn seeks the same recreation and society that the latter does, though it may be a more condensed form of it.

Society is commonly too cheap. We meet at very short intervals, not having had time to acquire any new value for each other. We meet at meals three times a day, and give each other a new taste of that old musty cheese that we are. We have to agree on a certain set of rules, called etiquette and politeness, to make this frequent meeting tolerable and that we need not come to open war. We meet at the post-office, and at the sociable, and about the fireside every night; we live thick and are in each other's way, and stumble over one another, and I think that we thus lose some respect for one another. Certainly less frequency would suffice for all important and hearty communications. Consider the girls in a factory,—never alone, hardly in their dreams. It would be better if there were but one inhabitant to a square mile, as where I live. The value of a man is not in his skin, that we should touch him.

I have heard of a man lost in the woods and dying of famine and exhaustion at the foot of a tree, whose loneliness was relieved by the grotesque visions with which, owing to bodily weakness, his diseased imagination surrounded him, and which he believed to be real. So also, owing to bodily and mental health and strength, we may be continually cheered by a like but more normal and natural society, and come to know that we are never alone.

I have a great deal of company in my house; especially in the morning, when nobody calls. Let me suggest a few comparisons, that some one may convey an idea of my situation. I am no more lonely than the loon in the pond that laughs so loud, or than Walden Pond itself. What company has that lonely lake, I pray? And yet it has not the blue devils, but the blue angels in it, in the azure tint of its waters. The sun is alone, except in thick weather, when there sometimes appear to be two, but one is a mock sun. God is alone,—but the devil, he is far from being alone; he sees a great deal of company; he is legion. I am no more lonely than a single mullein or dandelion in a pasture, or a bean leaf, or sorrel, or a horse-fly, or a humble-bee. I am no more lonely than the Mill Brook, or a weathercock, or the north star, or the south wind, or an April shower, or a January thaw, or the first spider in a new house.

I have occasional visits in the long winter evenings, when the snow falls fast and the wind howls in the wood, from an old settler and original proprietor, who is reported to have dug Walden Pond, and stoned it, and fringed it with pine woods; who tells me stories of old time and of new eternity; and between us we manage to pass a cheerful evening with social mirth and pleasant views of things, even without apples or cider,—a most wise and humorous friend, whom I love much, who keeps himself more secret than ever did Goffe or Whalley; and though he is thought to be dead, none can show where he is buried. An elderly dame, too, dwells in my neighborhood, invisible to most persons, in whose odorous herb garden I love to stroll sometimes, gathering simples and listening to her fables; for she has a genius of unequalled fertility, and her memory runs back farther than mythology, and she can tell me the original of every fable, and on what fact every one is founded, for the incidents occurred when she was young. A ruddy and lusty old dame, who delights in all weathers and seasons, and is likely to outlive all her children yet.

The indescribable innocence and beneficence of Nature,—of sun and wind and rain, of summer and winter,—such health, such cheer, they afford forever! and such sympathy have they ever with our race, that all Nature would be affected, and the sun's brightness fade, and the winds would sigh humanely, and the clouds rain tears, and the woods shed their leaves and put on mourning in midsummer, if any man should ever for a just cause grieve. Shall I not have intelligence with the earth? Am I not partly leaves and vegetable mould myself?

What is the pill which will keep us well, serene, contented? Not my or thy great-grandfather's, but our great-grandmother Nature's universal, vegetable, botanic medicines, by which she has kept herself young always, outlived so many old Parrs in her day, and fed her health with their decaying fatness. For my panacea, instead of one of those quack vials of a mixture dipped from Acheron and the Dead Sea, which come out of those long shallow black-schooner-looking wagons which we sometimes see made to carry bottles, let me have a draught of undiluted morning air. Morning air! If men will not drink of this at the fountain-head of the day, why, then, we must even bottle up some and sell it in the shops, for the benefit of those who have lost their subscription ticket to morning time in this world. But remember, it will not keep quite till noonday even in the coolest cellar, but drive out the stopples long ere that and follow westward the steps of Aurora. I am no worshipper of Hygeia, who was the daughter of that old herb-doctor Æsculapius, and who is represented on monuments holding a serpent in one hand, and in the other a cup out of which the serpent sometimes drinks; but rather of Hebe, cupbearer to Jupiter, who was the daughter of Juno and wild lettuce, and who had the power of restoring gods and men to the vigor of youth. She was probably the only thoroughly sound-conditioned, healthy, and robust young lady that ever walked the globe, and wherever she came it was spring.

JOURNALS
Henry David Thoreau

Aug. 17, 1851

This coolness comes to condense the dews and clear the atmosphere. The stillness seems more deep and significant. Each sound seems to come from out a greater thoughtfulness in nature, as if nature had acquired some character and mind. The cricket, the gurgling stream, the rushing wind amid the trees, all speak to me soberly yet encouragingly of the steady onward progress of the universe. My heart leaps into my mouth at the sound of the wind in the woods. I, whose life was but yesterday so desultory and shallow, suddenly recover my spirits, my spirituality, through my hearing. I see a goldfinch go twittering through the still, louring day, and am reminded of the peeping flocks which will soon herald the thoughtful season. Ah! if I could so live that there should be no desultory moment in all my life! that in the trivial season, when small fruits are ripe, my fruits might be ripe also! that I could match nature always with my moods! that in each season when some part of nature especially flourishes, then a corresponding part of me may not fail to flourish! Ah, I would walk, I would sit and sleep, with natural piety! What if I could pray aloud or to myself as I went along by the brook-sides a cheerful prayer like the birds! For joy I could embrace the earth; I shall delight to be buried in it. And then to think of those I love among men, who will know that I love them though I tell them not! I sometimes feel as if I were rewarded merely for expecting better hours. I did not despair of worthier moods, and now I have occasion to be grateful for the flood of life that is flowing over me. I am not so poor: I can smell the ripening apples; the very rills are deep; the autumnal flowers, the *Trichostema dichotomum*—not only its bright blue flower above the sand, but its strong wormwood scent which belongs to the season—feed my spirit, endear the earth to me, make me value myself and rejoice; the quivering of pigeons' wings reminds me of the tough fibre of the air which they rend. I thank you, God. I do not deserve anything, I am unworthy of the least regard; and yet I am made to rejoice. I am impure and worthless, and yet the world is gilded for my delight and holidays are prepared for me, and my path is strewn with flowers. But I cannot thank the Giver; I cannot even whisper my thanks to those human friends I have. It seems to me that I am more rewarded for my expectations than for anything I do or can do. Ah, I would not tread on a cricket in whose song is such a revelation, so soothing and cheering to my ear! Oh, keep my senses pure! And why should I speak to my friends? for how rarely is it that I am I; and are they, then, they? We will meet, then, far away. The seeds of the summer are getting dry and falling from a thousand nodding heads. If I did not know you through thick and thin, how should I know you at all? Ah, the very brooks seem fuller of reflections than they were! Ah, such provoking sibylline sentences they are! The shallowest is all at once unfathomable. How can that depth be fathomed where a man may see himself reflected? The rill I stopped to drink at I drink in more than I expected. I satisfy and still provoke the thirst of thirsts. Nut Meadow Brook where it crosses the road beyond Jenny Dugan's that was. I do not drink in vain. I mark that brook as if I had swallowed a water snake that would live in my stomach. I have swallowed something worth the while. The day is not what it was before I stooped to drink. Ah, I shall hear from that draught! It is not in vain that I have drunk. I have drunk an arrowhead. It flows from where all fountains rise.

Jan. 12, 1855

Perhaps what most moves us in winter is some reminiscence of far-off summer. How we leap by the side of the open brooks! What beauty in the running brooks! What life! What society! The cold is merely superficial; it is summer still at the core, far, far within. It is in the cawing of the crow, the crowing of the cock, the warmth of the sun on our backs. I hear faintly the cawing of a crow far, far away, echoing from some unseen wood-side, as if deadened by the springlike vapor which the sun is drawing from the ground. It mingles with the slight murmur of the village, the sound of children at play, as one stream empties gently into another, and the wild and tame are one. What a delicious sound! It is not merely crow calling to crow, for it speaks to me too. I am part of one great creature with him; if he has voice, I have ears. I can hear when he calls, and have engaged not to shoot nor stone him if he will caw to me each spring. On the one hand, it may be, is the sound of children at school saying their a, b, ab's, on the other, far in the wood-fringed horizon, the cawing of crows from their blessed eternal vacation, out at their long recess, children who have got dismissed! While the vaporous incense goes up from all the fields of the spring—if it were spring. Ah, bless the Lord, O my soul! bless him for wildness, for crows that will not alight within gunshot! and bless him for hens, too, that croak and cackle in the yard!

Feb. 7, 1841

The eaves are running on the south side of the house; the titmouse lisps in the poplar; the bells are ringing for church; while the sun presides over all and makes his simple warmth more obvious than all else. What shall I do with this hour, so like time and yet so fit for eternity? Where in me are these russet patches of ground, and scattered logs and chips in the yard? I do not feel cluttered. I have some notion what the John's-wort and life-everlasting may be thinking about when the sun shines on me as on them and turns my prompt thought into just such a seething shimmer. I lie out indistinct as a heath at noonday. I am evaporating and ascending into the sun.

ON THE SIU CHENG ROAD[10]
Su Tung P'o
translated by Kenneth Rexroth

Su Tung P'o (1036–1101) was a Chinese poet, painter, and
political official. Although he was born into a powerful family of
officials and scholars, the political turbulence of the times caused him
to alternate between periods of political influence and power and of
disgrace, exile, and imprisonment.

A gentle East wind is blowing.
I travel through the mountains.
White clouds rest on the peaks like
Caps of silk floss. Over
The tree tops the sun gleams like
A polished cymbal. Peach trees
Bloom beyond bamboo fences.
Along the streams, willows wave
Above the pools. The mountaineers
Of the West know how to be
Happy, full of melon soup
And fried bamboo shoots after
The spring sowing.

CLEAR EVENING AFTER RAIN[11]
Tu Fu
translated by Kenneth Rexroth

The sun sinks towards the horizon.
The light clouds are blown away.

A rainbow shines on the river.
The last raindrops spatter the rocks.
Cranes and herons soar in the sky.
Fat bears feed along the banks.
I wait here for the west wind
And enjoy the crescent moon
Shining through misty bamboos.

FISHING ON THE NINNESCAH[12]
Gar Bethel

Gar Bethel (1936–) was raised in Kansas and now teaches at the University of Oklahoma. He combines a keen eye for detail and sensitivity for language with a distinctly original way of viewing things.

As the old persimmon sun hung behind the trees,
we set trotlines across the river
where silt oozed in over our canvas shoes,
and the water was too cold for swimming
or knowing for sure we'd felt the current'
or a mudcat's rubbery whiskers.

We waited in the close darkness by the fire
that crackled brush like wrapping paper,
the beer bubbling gas to our noses,
and the bait on our hands smelled strangely ripe.

At dawn a light frost fringed the tangled bank,
and the naked trees made boney shadows
across the fields of flint and stubble.

[12]"Fishing on the Ninnescah" is reprinted by permission of Gar Bethel. Copyright © 1973 by Gar Bethel.

And when we crashed through the thicket of sumac,
the slick black bodies, dangling from the stringer,
clung to our pants drying the color of ash,
and going seemed as natural as coming
as everyday as being hungry in the morning.

SUWA-NO-SE ISLAND AND THE BANYAN ASHRAM[13]
Gary Snyder

Several years ago Nanao SAKAKI, the wanderer and poet, was traveling on a small interisland freighter between Kyushu and Amami Oshima and got into a conversation with a fellow passenger, an islander, who casually invited Nanao to come visit his island. Nanao did, another year, and just when a typhoon came; so he was holed up for over a week in a farmhouse waiting for the storm to blow over.

The island has only eight households—forty people—and, though the major part of the island is volcano and lavaflow, there is plenty of unoccupied land that is livable. Hence the islanders told Nanao that if he or his friends wished to come camp or live there, they'd be welcome.

Nanao's old circle of friends in Tokyo, the "Emerald Breeze" branch of the "Harijan" (formerly known as the Bum Academy) had already started a farm in the highlands of Nagano prefecture. They decided to add Suwa-no-se Island to their plans: In May, Nanao, Miko and Shinkai went down; Pon in June with several others; Franco, Naga, Masa, and me in July. You have to go to Kagoshima, the southernmost town of size in Kyushu. A boat leaves for the "Ten Islands" once a week. Unpredictably. So that we were hung up for five days in Kagoshima, a cheap waterfront inn, while the ship waited out a typhoon scare. Did our grocery shopping and walked out to the ends of breakwaters waiting.

The "Toshima Maru" left at six in the evening. A little diesel freighter of 250 tons. At daybreak coming in on Kuchi-no-erabu Island—silvery rainsqualls, green cliffs, flashings of seabirds. The

[13]Gary Snyder, *EARTH HOUSE HOLD.* Copyright © 1969 by Gary Snyder. Reprinted by permission of New Directions Publishing Corporation.

ship called at three islands through the day—anchoring beyond the edge of the coral reef, loading and unloading from tossing little unpainted island boats.

Late in the afternoon the ship was approaching Suwa-no-se, a violet mountain from afar, with cloudcaps and banners of mist. (The fishermen who come down from Miyazaki on Kyushu in their seaworthy little 3 ton fishing boats call it "Yake-jima"—Burning Island. Because much of the time the volcano is smoking.)

Anchoring offshore, the "Toshima Maru" blows its whistle and finally, down a steep trail through bamboo, a few men running. After half an hour a small boat puts out from behind a big boulder and cement breakwater at the base of the cliffs—steers through a path in the coral reef and comes alongside the freighter. The islanders brought out watermelons and wild goats. The goats go down to Amami Oshima where people like to eat them. Then, us, with our rucksacks and provisions, aboard the little boat, ashore through rough waves and getting wet, up on the rocky beach. Stepping over and through the lines and cables of several small fishing boats, nets, cables of the winch system for handling the boats in and out. Everybody waiting for us, almost black from being always in the sun. Packed all our groceries and rucksacks up the switchbacks and across a mile or so of trail through semijungle to the abandoned house and clearing they were using. Nanao and Shinkai had just finished a small extra shelter of bamboo; dome-shaped, with a thatch roof—so there was sleeping space for everyone. Fourteen people, almost half of them girls.

Suwa-no-se is latitude 29°36', which puts it on a level roughly with the Canary Islands, Cairo, Chihuahua, Persepolis and Lhasa. Almost halfway from Kyushu to Amami Oshima. The Amami group of islands continue into the Ryukyus and the culture is quite similar to the Okinawan but there are dialect differences. From Yoron Island you can see Okinawa they say. Yoron is part of Japan. Suwa-no-se was probably populated off and on for several thousand years, depending on the activity of the volcano. The "Ten Islands" are part of a steppingstone system of islands all the way from Taiwan to Kyushu, by which paleolithic voyagers worked their way up to Japan. So they must have stopped off. Suwa-no-se was abandoned after the great eruption of the 15th Century, and nobody returned until a century ago when some settlers came up from Amami to try again. Our villagers are thus of the Amami line, and speak Amami dialect; play the snake-head "jabisen" instead of the catskin-head "shamisen." They keep pigs, which is also an Amami custom. Mainland Japanese have never much taken to pigs. Also, they drink distilled sweet-potato liquor instead of sake; and sweet potatoes make a main part of the year's food—cheaper and easier to raise on the windy islands than rice.

The main part of the island is mountainous and uninhabited, but there is a kind of plateau about 400 feet above sea level that makes a southern extension, with several good streams running through it—an arable plateau may be two miles by three miles, and covered for the most part by bamboo and grasses. A great pasture of fifty or so acres toward the east, and some pine and *Tabu* forests on the flanks of the mountain. Banyan trees and other large subtropical plants follow in the watercourses.

Sweet-potato and watermelon fields are cut-out squares in the bamboo here and there. The houses are clustered toward the west, which is closest to the little harbor; each house separate and enclosed in a wall of bamboo. Even the trails are shadowy corridors through the bamboo jungle and under the limbs of the banyan.

In the open pasture twenty-three head of black beef cattle at large, and on the edge of.the pasture the abandoned farmhouse that became our headquarters. Up the meadow a way toward the mountain is a magnificent banyan on the edge of a ravine—we cleared out a meditation ground within its hanging roots—finally called our whole place "Banyan Ashram," or Pon calls it "Banyan Dream."

Daily work was clearing a new field for sweet-potato planting. We had to get all the bamboo root runners out, turning it over with hoes and grubbing the roots. Backbreaking work, and very slow. Because of midday heat it could only be done before 10:30 or after 4. In mid-day we napped in the shade of the banyan, or in the Bamboo House. Other work was fuel-gathering (dead pine underbranches; dead bamboo; or driftwood from the beaches loaded in a carrying basket and toted with a tumpline on the forehead) and cooking; done by turn in pairs in an open kitchen-shed with a thatch roof on an old brick campfire stove. Chinese style. (Our diet was basically brown rice and miso soup with potatoes and sweet potatoes and occasional water-melons or local bananas.) Also a lot of carpentry and construction work was continually going on, and a few hands every few days down to the village to join in on a village project, community trail-repair, or helping gut and flay an extra-large flying fish catch before it could spoil.

The ocean: every day except when the wind was too strong (fringe of a typhoon somewhere) most of us made it to the beach. There are three places to go: the eastern beach, forty minutes by trail, is wide and rough, with a good view of the volcano. The waves are very heavy. It looks across the Pacific toward Mexico. The coral reef goes out a long way, so it's not suitable for skindiving except when the weather is exceptionally calm. The beach has splendid driftwood and drift-lumber, and lots of seashells to gather. There's a cave toward one end within which thirty-six cows can stand in a rainstorm without getting wet. The southern beach is reached by a brushy trail also forty minutes—steep descent down the cliff but possible no-hands; it has a shorter coral ledge and a lovely natural cove within the coral which is deep and affords a passage into deep water under the breakers (i.e., you swim out to the gate and dive and glide underwater for thirty or forty feet and surface beyond the heavy pounding). There are strong tidal currents here, and we decided it was dangerous for anyone not an excellent swimmer and diver.

The western beach is the most sheltered and the best for fishing. We had vague ideas about spearfishing from the beginning and I brought a pocketful of steel harpoon heads (the smallest ones) with me—but it wasn't until Arikawa-san, the youngest family man of the islanders, showed us how to make a long bamboo spear with an iron rod in the end on which the spearhead sockets (attached to the main bamboo by leader) that we seriously began to think about adding fish to our diet. The spear is powered by inner-tube rubber, and is about nine feet long. Ito and I made three of these. With flippers and goggles, spent two fruitless days in the water 'til we began to understand the habits and feelings of the different species. Then we began to take them regularly. It became noticeably easier to do heavy work with more protein in the diet.

Most of us would be vegetarians by choice, but this was a real case of necessity and ecology. The volcanic soil of the island (and the volcanic ash fallout) makes it hard to raise many vegetables there; but the waters are rich in fish. We offered our respects and gratitude to the fish and the Sea Gods daily, and ate them with real love, admiring their extraordinarily beautiful, perfect little bodies.

Hundreds of varieties and thousands of individuals, all edible. Cobalt blue, shades of yellow and orange seemed the most common. None of the fish are really "tropical" and strange—but they are clearly subtropical with more variety than you'd find in colder waters. I became absorbed in the life of the sea. Without a fish book I came to recognize dozens of species and gradually came to know their habits and peculiarities and territories and emotions.

There is a great truth in the relationship established by hunting: like in love or art, you must become one with the other. (Which is why paleolithic hunting magic is so important historically: the necessities of identity, intuition, stillness, that go with hunting make it seem as though shamanism and yoga and meditation may have their roots in the requirements of the hunter—where a man learns to be motionless for a day, putting his mind in an open state so that his consciousness won't spook creatures that he knows will soon be approaching.)

In spearfishing we learned you must never choose a specific fish for a quarry: you must let the fish choose you, and be prepared to shoot the fish that will come into range. For some fish you must be one with the sea and consider yourself a fish among fish. But there was one large and unpredictable variety (cobalt with a crescent-shaped tail) that digs the strange. When one of those was around I would change my mind and consider myself a freak and be out of place; in which case he will come to look at you out of curiosity.

When you go down with the fishes minus your spear they treat you differently too. I got so I could go down to twenty-five or thirty feet fairly comfortably. An old man originally from Okinawa, Uaji-san, dives sixty feet. He's seventy years old, and has a wise, tough, beautiful young wife. He caught a sea turtle and gave most of it to the Ashram once.

Sometimes the islanders had special catches on their little boats; once we had all the shark meat we could eat; another time a giant feast of raw sawara; once a whole bucket of flying-fish eggs. A few times went on shellfish-gathering expeditions together. By next summer the Ashram plans to have a small boat, which will make fishing a regular and efficient operation.

The weather is breezy, the sun hot. The ocean sends up great squalls and sudden rainstorms which dry up in twenty minutes. The volcano goes grummmmmmmm and lots of purple smoke comes up, into the sky, to 15,000 feet.

Meals were served on the mat-floor of the farmhouse, everybody crosslegged, with Taku-chan the Gotos' two-year-old boy wandering stark naked through it all. After supper at night we generally sat almost totally silent around our two or three candles, sometimes humming mantras or folksongs; or went out in the cow pasture with a bottle of shochu and played the jew's-harp (which the Harijan all call a bigigi, the New Guinea name for it) and the Kenya drum (a present from Ginzap four years ago) to our patron star, Antares.

Those who rose very early went to meditate under the banyan—a lovely thing especially because of the song of the Akahige ("Redbeard" Temminck's Robin) which sings in the early-morning canyons with a remarkable trilling, falling song that drops three octaves and echoes across hills and meadows. Also the songs of the Hototo-gisu (Himalayan Cuckoo) and Blue Doves—filling up the whole morning world with song. While morning mists blow and curl around and the grass is all dewy and the Rising Sun of Japan comes up through the ocean and the fog like a big red rising sun flag.

After breakfast every morning there would be a quiet, natural discussion of the day's work; people would volunteer for various tasks—never any pressuring—somebody might say, "Let's be sure and put the tools back where we got them, I couldn't find the file yesterday" or something—but without acrimony; Westerners have much to learn from this easy cooperativeness and sense of getting the work done without fuss. The Banyan people had less ego-friction (none!) and difficulty over chores than any group I've ever seen.

Masa UEHARA and I were married on the island on August 6, the new moon. The whole Ashram stayed up late the night before, packing a breakfast for the morrow—and broiling a splendid pink tai that was a present from the village. (No marriage is complete if you don't eat tai afterwards, the noble, calm AUSPICIOUS FISH of Japan.) We got up at 4:30 and started up the brush trail in the dark. First dipping into a ravine and then winding up a jungly knife-edge ridge. By five we were out of the jungle and onto a bare lava slope. Following the long ridge to an older, extinct crater, and on to the crest of the main crater and the summit shortly after sunrise. The lip of the crater drops off into cloud; and out of the cloud comes a roaring like an airport full of jets: a billowing of steam upwards. The cloud and mist broke, and we could see 800 feet or so down into the crater—at least a mile across—and fumaroles and steam-jets; at the very center red molten lava in a little bubbly pond. The noise, according to the switch of the wind, sometimes deafening.

Standing on the edge of the crater, blowing the conch horn and chanting a mantra; offering shochu to the gods of the volcano, the ocean, and the sky; then Masa and I exchanged the traditional three sips—Pon and Nanao said a few words; Masa and I spoke; we recited the Four Vows together, and ended with three blasts on the conch. Got out of the wind and opened the rucksacks to eat the food made the night before, and drink the rest of the shochu. We descended from the summit and were down to the Banyan tree by eleven—went direct on out to the ocean and into the water; so that within one morning we passed from the windy volcanic summit to the warm coral waters. At four in the afternoon all the villagers came to the Ashram—we served saké and shochu—pretty soon everyone was singing Amami folksongs and doing traditional dances.

The sweet-potato field got cleared and planted; Franco left a bit early to be in San Luis Obispo by mid-September; we started clearing another patch of land and built a big outdoor table of driftwood; went around to the north side of the island in a small boat to investigate other possibilities of settlements and fishing.

Masa and I caught the "Toshima Maru" heading on south at the end of August and visited Cho in Koniya; with Shinkai checked on boatbuilders' prices; took another ship up to Kagoshima (all night on the deck sitting on matting watching the full moon).

And hitchhiked to Miyazaki for a three-day Harijan gathering and a look at the neolithic tumuli in the region; and back to Kyoto. Miko and Akibananda and others will be on the island all year; Pon and Nanao are back up in Nagano at the mountain Ashram now.

It is possible at last for Masa and me to imagine a little of what the ancient—archaic—mind and life of Japan were. And to see what could be restored to the life today. A lot of it is simply in being aware of clouds and wind.

Eighth Moon, 40067
(reckoning roughly from the earliest cave paintings)

EARTH HOUSE HOLD[14]
Gary Snyder

leaning in the doorway whistling
a chipmunk popped out
listening

[14]Gary Snyder, *EARTH HOUSE HOLD*. Copyright © 1969 by Gary Snyder. Reprinted by permission of New Directions Publishing Corporation.

Part
Two

Failures

They have sown the wind, and they shall reap the whirlwind.

Hosea 8:7

        While from Part One the list of men who manifest the ecological attitude may seem impressive, unfortunately they and those who share their views constitute a small minority of mankind. Throughout history man's relationship to his environment has been mainly destructive. Part Two treats some of man's chief failures—pollution of his environment, destruction of the wilderness, spread of urban blight, extermination of species, overpopulation. These failures may seem unpromising subjects for literature but, surprisingly, great poetry can be distilled from refuse. Twentieth-century poets sing of pollution: Federico Garcia Lorca of the Hudson "drunk upon oil," Robert Lowell of the "chemical air [which] sweeps in from New Jersey."

        John Steinbeck writes powerfully and angrily of the American tendency to bury ourselves in garbage:

> American cities are like badger holes, ringed with trash—all of them—surrounded by piles of wrecked and rusting automobiles, and almost smothered with rubbish.[1]

        Also of particular concern to many writers is the destruction of all vestiges of nature in our surroundings, and the substitution of an artificial environment. Carolyn Kizer's "The Suburbans" is an excellent example:

> *Forgetting sounds that we no longer hear—*
> *Nightingale, silent for a century:*
> *How touch that bubbling throat, let it touch us*
> *In cardboard-sided suburbs, where the glades*
> *And birds gave way to lawns, fake weathervanes*
> *Topping antennae, or a wrought-iron rooster*
> *Mutely presiding over third class mail.*[2]

Concern about the environment goes back at least a century and a half in America. One of the earliest protests against the destruction of the American wilderness is voiced by James Fenimore Cooper's hero, Natty Bumppo in *The Prairie*. Natty, known also as Deerslayer and Leatherstocking in Cooper's novels, decries the set tlers who "scourge the very 'arth with their axes."

Cooper, writing in the first half of the nineteenth century, was torn between conflicting attitudes towards the settling of the American continent. On the one hand he looked favorably on the spread of civilization to the untamed frontier. On the other, he deplored the destruction of the American wilderness. Natty Bumppo is the spokesman for the view favoring the preservation of the wilderness. Although he is a hunter and trapper, Leatherstocking takes only what he needs to support himself and lives in harmony with nature.

Cooper based Leatherstocking in large part on Daniel Boone, an ambivalent, mythical American hero even in his own lifetime. To some, Boone represented the scout who broke new ground in the wilderness, clearing the way for settlers to follow bringing civilization with them. To others, Boone was a noble savage, a white Indian who fled civilization and detested settlements, moving further west whenever he saw settlers' smoke on the eastern horizon. Cooper modeled Leatherstocking on Boone the noble savage and loner.

In our selection, Boone is more savage than noble. In an account that John James Audubon, the ornithologist, gives of sporting life in frontier Kentucky, Boone makes a game of killing squirrels—something that Leatherstocking, with his reverence for all that lives, would never do.

Another American folk hero who makes a game of killing is Buffalo Bill Cody. In this chapter he tells of a buffalo killing contest he had with Billy Comstock. The virtual extermination of the bison, in which Cody played so large a part, is one of the sorriest chapters in American history.

Americans also hunted the passenger pigeon to extinction. Aldo Leopold's essay, "On A Monument to the Pigeon," is an elegy to the departed species.

We conclude with Thomas Robert Malthus' powerful warning—now almost two centuries old—on overpopulation. Today Malthus' direst predictions seem to be coming true, and many ecologists fear that overpopulation, with its concomitant problems of starvation and destruction of the environment, may be the most serious problem we will face at the end of the twentieth century.

CHAPTER FIVE
The Vanishing Wilderness

ORANGE COUNTY PLAGUE[1]
Laurence Lieberman

Laurence Lieberman was born in Michigan in 1935 and currently teaches English at the University of Illinois. About Orange County, California, he has this to say: "The subject of all my recent poetry is Orange County, where I have been a kind of inmate and spy for the past four years. I will be released from the County in three days, but will never go scot free: I will always be a spiritual parolee.

[1] Reprinted with permission of The Macmillan Company from *The Unblinding* by Laurence Lieberman. Copyright © 1965, 1968 by Laurence Lieberman.

There is no place more suited to disaster. . . . In this John Birch capital of the world, the roots of the grass stick up like nails. To go barefoot is to risk permanent impalement, crucifixion to the earth."

SCENE I: Dislocations

In Orange, tree-plague has struck the mile-long groves. Greased
Chainsaws slide through trunks as knives slice butter.
Autos skid in the orangesap treejuice
Blend flooding the gutter.
Psychotic farmers hallucinate glues
To restore limbs slashed by sharktoothed steeljawed beasts.
If some of the screws are loose,
It doesn't matter.
At least,
Teenage lovers scatter
Back to the parks. They cruise
From bench to bench, and a few coolcats grow chaste
Perhaps. There is less temptation to bruise
Forbidden fruit—a daughter
Waits for her father's permission to choose
Her life. Blood-mistakes are small enough to blotter,
Like smudges of ink. Loss-of-faith is mended with library paste.

SCENE 2: Stump Fugue

In unison, hundreds of shovels vanish under stumps. They descend
By regular strokes, like oil-drills. Workmen's faces
Whiten; their bodies absent, statuesque.
White knuckles, weightless,
Glitter in the falling sun. Dusk
Attends the snapping of roots. Arms, self-moving, blend
With saws. The sun's disc
In the last oasis
Sinks. Send
Rain where the Human Race is
Still tree-loving, still able to risk
Life to preserve the beauty that lives. What sickens, mend!

Great fists of roots in trucks whisk
Up Coast Hi-way, menacing crisis:
WIDE LOAD marked in red. The clay-stuck
Upturned stumps, tree-corpses, bounce on the chassis
And sway . . . clotted hands, upcast, clutching madly at the wind.

SCENE 3: Freeway Skeletons

(a deserted grove: mostly dead trees, rotten fruit)

Near the freeway, the unburied dead raise delicate skeletons, brittle
Arms extending frail hands—mock-perch for birds.
In a light breeze the air is black
With falling fingers; words
From the dying lips of lynchees, their luck
Run out—the crackle of twigs; last drools of spittle—
Drops of sap that fleck
The bark, wood's
Blood. Ill
Winds rattle old boards
(Or bones) in America's (hush!) rack-
Negroes slaughterhouse. The passing motorists, cattle
Armed to butcher each other, slack
Their speed to loot. Rewards
Are few. But the thieves have a special knack
For sorting the stray good orange from the rotting hoards.
Listen for the moos. Chewing of the cud. The spirit's death-rattle.

SCENE 4: Tree Burning

At the center of a stump-studded field, a disordered pyre, strewn
With mangled tree-carcass, waits. Branches, at all
Angles, prevent neat piling of logs.
An indignity too subtle
For the influx of watchers (pyros) begs
Notice. For hours, blood-thirst in the air has grown.
Eyes, unwinking, glare. Legs
Stiffen into metal.

Night. No moon.
Lit match! Odd chanting. A riddle.
Burn, witch, burn! Crotchety old bags
Burn. Witch, burn, witch! Nigger-witch. Which nigger? One!
How spot a witch? Check for wigs,
Or black mustache. Telltale
Itch in the crotch, sticky lips: Nigger-stags!
Or check bold strut, briar tongue, fire in the eyes, mettle.
Guilt stinks under the arms and dons old rags. Nigger-witch, burn!

SCENE 5: Preservatives

Mid-day. A mammoth Redwood creeps on wheels. Four lanes of autos,
Reluctant, bestow reverence; the giant's funeral
Hearse shambles. The corpse, exposed,
Has not begun to smell.
Tree-flesh, unembalmed, won't rust
Or rot. Tree bodies outlast tree souls, Mulattos,
In America's death-in-life lust
Agony, grow beautiful
As trees. Bistros
Are mills where blackwhite people
Logs are cut to prayer size; kiss-Christ
Blues—a holy rage of buzzsaw jazz . . . sham Castros
Preach re-growth from severed roots. . .
Boogie-and-twist swivel
Hips roll—tree limbs in tornados tossed.
Battered Races, timbers that seem to rise as they fall,
Murderously blossom in the suffering and dancing country of ghettos.

SCENE 6: The American Halfway

Above, the farm and pasture—halfway—the metropolis below,
Smog in the eyes and throat, dung-stink in the nose,
Fordtruck in the front yard, moocow in back;
That's how you sing the halfway blues.
On the freeway, herded twelve-deep in dumptrucks,
Stooped on the warped floorboards of stalls (Jim Crow

In the Deep South, spics
Out West) braceros
Sing. Sow
Beanfields gold in the sunrise,
Half-frozen all night in pasteboard shacks!
Free country good for beez-ness. Amor in Meh-hee-koh.
(Slave labor don't mind the dirt wages: Mex
Eat crow.) They file through bean-rows,
Swift and frail as antelope. If anyone ask,
Why drudge all day in sun-fire, strings for clothes?
Ah-meh-ree-kuh ees work! eat! sleep! Amor in Meh-hee-koh!

SCENE 7: The Wire Forests

On their sides, resembling fallen timbers without rough
Barks—a hundred feet apart—lie power poles.
Just yesterday, this road was edged
With Eucalyptus; in aisles
Between rows of trees, seats for the aged.
Now tree-odors hover in the air, residues of life.
The poles are erected. The frigid
Passionless verticals
Strive
To fill the socket-shaped holes
Left by trees. Identical, cement-wedged
Below, parasitically fastened to live wires above—
Tree-impostors, never to be budged
From a telegraphic owl's
Knowitallness, they stand—rigid!
Sad children, wishing to climb, scan the miles
And miles of uninterrupted electric forests for leaves.

SCENE 8: Tree Praise

Beauty is poorness of posture, a studied unevenness of frame.
Trees have sex appeal, gnarled character, a stubborn
Knottiness: a refusal to grow one way;
Preference for curves, fork-turns
Over a sapling's uprightness; asymmetry

Of branches, leaf-shapes askew, imbalance of color-scheme.
The Eucalyptus, obsessed with nudity
Or eager for sunburn,
Sheds lame
Barks as snakes slough skins.
The leaning Birch, to hide its branchless purity
Of form, loves to dance in a blinding gale, and for shame
Of the drab whiteness of bark, for eternity
Would spring up and back—and burn
In the driving wind. I think of the sway-
Backed Oak, the lackadaisical Willow, the Juniper, Hawthorn—
And a preference for woods over human society, at last, I proclaim.

SCENE 9: The Sterilization

Hydra-trees survive the death of parts. Some trees
Dead at the top outlive bad weather, poisons.
Decapitation cures. My Pepper
Tree (a kind of treason?)
Has become a bush. Trees, like lepers,
Slough their rotten limbs. Gratuitous sprays,
"Weed-killers," infect the upper
Earth. Do those men
Who squeeze
Death spray suffer my vision?
They sterilize loam in fields. The deadly vapors
Spread to my backyard. Today, in the faintest breeze—
Like beautiful hanks of hair in the barber
Shop—fall dried stem-
Husks, brittle, bewildered to sever
From roots and lie in useless piles, my Bougain-
Villea withered to brown scrolls of leafage. . . No rose.

SCENE 10: The View from the Kitchen

Sides sheered off, the sand level on the bottom, this river-bed
Is dry. The parallel cyclone fences entice scores
Of children to enter; without risk, play
Is dull. Forbidden tours

Follow *KEEP OUT* signs as crime follows prey.
FLOOD CONTROL threats replace *NO FISHING. The mud*
Is moistened with sewage. Debris
And watercress lure
Vagrants, mutts,
Wildlife. An occasional horse
And horseman, cyclists, tractors pass by
Alongside the ditch. In my kitchen I watch, and the skid-
Row scum watch back. What can we say
To each other? Who is worse
Off? *In Winter, the fantastic rains wash away*
Tons of dirt from the banks. Nothing is safe in my house.
In Spring, I measure the narrowing margin of earth near my yard.

SCENE 11: *The Waves*

House-high waves envelop the pier with algae, brine,
Sea-scum. The roughest surf in years excites
Beach bums to risk their skins. Life
Guards, who lift weights
After hours, imbibe their fill of grief.
The deaths they swallow turn to cramps in the groin
Nightfall. High tides knife
Trenches in cliff-sides,
Undermine
Foundations of lavish estates.
Many slide downhill. One topples off
Into the sea, somersaulting over stilts, a falling crane
Or heron. Beach houses on a low bluff
Wash away like orangecrates.
Nothing slakes the hunger of the thief-
Pacific. Maddened by the tedium of days, he mates
With womanish earth. Anything human is chaff of the grain.

SCENE 12: *The Ice Phallus*

Frozen halibut is fresher than today's catch. Vacuum-packed
Bass in freezers grow purer than life. Time stops.

Ice crystals' skill competes with veteran
Seamen's. Fish essence sleeps
In Stiffened flesh. In our future, semen
Shall cease to flow. Ice-birth will men slacked
Morals and eliminate sin —
Love snarls and rapes,
Sex-locked.
An idle fisherman drops
Bait from the pier. Fish, like women
Immune, resist his hook. His rod is cracked,
His reel jammed with backlash, the line
snagged on a rock. Surfers' lips
Are mockeries below, the mouths green-
Blue, sea-numbed. The highest breaker snaps
Torso-whips. The brain's deepfreeze they love, wave-bucked.

SCENE 13: Afterlife of a War-jet

(at a children's park)

Fresh coats of paint disguise the emblems of war. Maggots
Restoring the flesh of dead wolves to life
In the elixir of gnashing jaws and gut:
Children swarming in the safe
Cockpit and fuselage of a killer-jet,
A surprise package of doom in the hands of bigots.
Stale blood and fresh snotspit
Mix in the mouth-strafe
Of play. Tots
On the wings rehearse tough
Battle lingo, or they regurgitate
Movie war poses: salute, the march, rigor mortis.
Both with and without honor they commit
War crimes, and forget. The chafe
Of rough surface on hands and face whets
The appetite for more. Morticians render grief
Therapy. Death-play opens all of the emotion spigots.

SCENE 14: *Mines and Missiles*

(Naval Munitions Station, Seal Beach)

In plain view from Coast Highway, thousands of steel balls,
Arranged neatly as cans on the grocer's shelf,
Lie dormant. In World War II, they guarded
The nation's bodies from Adolf
Hitler, Mussolini, Hirohito. In morbid
Idleness they rest, their monomaniacal death-wills,
By munitions-surgery, rendered
Sterile. A stray calf
Moos. Gulls
Swoop off the coast. *The gulf*
Between TNT and the Atom is underscored
By the Atlas ICBMs, the length of the battleships' hulls,
Maneuvering in highway traffic. Shrouded
With canvas, they exceed half
Of the road's six lanes in width. The livid
Faces of motorists sicken, as they mutter gruff
Curses at the traffic deadlock. Oblivious to mines or missiles.

SCENE 15: *Meditation Upon the Power House*

Most of the County's vital organs, exposed to all weathers
And the bomb of assassin, form the power house.
Vulnerable, it hums in the night,
Quivers with a queer pulse.
Visible for miles, it looms in the soot-
Dark fields of the coast—a meteoric glow—and gathers
The dark into arteries of light-
Alchemy. Small wills
Smother
In One—*encompassing* Else—
That engenders power as swiftly as thought
Flashes in the brain. In the Great Whole, parts wither
Into the truth. Daybreak. When Lot's
Wife looked back, the Gospels

Tell, she changed to a pillar of salt. . .
Such risk the listener takes when, in daylight, he mulls
Over the divinity of a dynamo that resembles a grain elevator.

SCENE 16: Spotlights

A pulsating three-hundred-sixty degree incandescent eye,
On the clubhouse roof, patrols my midnight walk.
The moon is a spotlight too. Lights
Guard and watch; they mock
My secret thoughts with telltale watts.
The sacred grasses glitter like a black-green sea.
This is no place for halfwits
Who treasure the dark.
Bats. I
Walk soft, but my shadow, a block
Long, jerks like hiccups in the epiglottis.
I hunt myself on the links, out-of-bounds, a bit loony.
I seek my moon's dark side. Light waits
In ambush, behind my back.
In love or art, the Beloved shuts
Her eyes and turns her face from glare of daybreak.
The beam of the watchman's flashlight squelches immortality.

SCENE 17: Interference

Tonight, strolling the hills overlooking the shore, I gasp
At the beauty of an electric storm. My radio's static
Muddles the up-to-the-minute news.
Punctual as a nervous tic,
The sea-and-skyscape, palpitant, glows.
Will the lovely pulse of the universe ever collapse?
How much there is to lose.
We forget. The cynic
Traps us
In ourselves, like a hypodermic.
I welcome tonight's interference: snows
On the TV screen, dimmer lights, an occasional lapse
In telephone service. Cut the wires. I refuse

To answer the door. *The clock*
Misses a tick. More than the wind blows.
In precious night, we touch. *I pray for the fantastic*
Messages one can learn to receive when the heartbeat skips.

THE PRAIRIE
James Fenimore Cooper

James Fenimore Cooper (1789–1851) was an American romantic novelist, renowned for the Leatherstocking Tales, especially *The Deerslayer, The Last of the Mohicans,* and *The Prairie*. This selection is from *The Prairie*. Natty Bumppo, Leatherstocking, is the speaker.

"There is then a better choice towards the other ocean?" demanded the squatter, pointing in the direction of the Pacific.

"There is, and I have seen it all," was the answer of the other, who dropped his rifle to the earth, and stood leaning on its barrel, like one who recalled the scenes he had witnessed with melancholy pleasure. "I have seen the waters of the two seas! On one of them was I born, and raised to be a lad like yonder tumbling boy. America has grown, my men, since the days of my youth, to be a country larger than I once had thought the world itself to be. Near seventy years I dwelt in York, province and State together: you've been in York, 't is like?"

"Not I—not I; I never visited the towns; but often have heard the place you speak of named. 'T is a wide clearing there, I reckon."

"Too wide! too wide! They scourge the vary 'arth with their axes. Such hills and hunting-grounds as I have seen stripped of the gifts of the Lord, without remorse or shame! I tarried till the mouths of my hounds were deafened by the blows of the chopper, and then I came West in search of quiet. It was a grievous journey that I made, a grievous toil to pass through falling timber, and to breathe the thick air of smoky clearings, week after week, as I did. 'T is a far country too, that State of York, from this!"

"It lies agin the outer edge of old Kentuck, I reckon, though what the distance may be I never knew."

"A gull would have to fan a thousand miles of air to find the eastern sea. And yet it is no mighty reach to hunt across, when shade and game are plenty! The time has been when I followed the deer in the mountains of the Delaware and Hudson, and took the beaver on the streams of the upper lakes, in the same season; but my eye was quick and certain at that day, and my limbs were like the legs of a moose! The dam of Hector," dropping his look kindly to the aged hound that crouched at his feet, "was then a pup, and apt to open on the game the moment she struck the scent. She gave a deal of trouble, that slut, she did!"

"Your hound is old, stranger, and a rap on the head would prove a mercy to the beast."

"The dog is like his master," returned the trapper, without appearing to heed the brutal advice the other gave, "and will number his days when his work amongst the game is over, and not before. To my eye things seem ordered to meet each other in this creation. 'T is not the swiftest running deer that always throws off the hounds, nor the biggest arm that holds the truest rifle. Look around you, men; what will the Yankee choppers say, when they have cut their path from the eastern to the western waters, and find that a hand, which can lay the 'arth bare at a blow, has been here and swept the country, in very mockery of their wickedness. They will turn on their tracks like a fox that doubles, and then the rank smell of their own footsteps will show them the madness of their waste. Howsomever, these are thoughts that are more likely to rise in him who has seen the folly of eighty seasons, than to teach wisdom to men still bent on the pleasures of their kind!"

BINSEY POPLARS
Gerard Manley Hopkins

felled 1879

> My aspens dear, whose airy cages quelled,
> Quelled or quenched in leaves the leaping sun,
> All felled, felled, are all felled;
>> Of a fresh and following folded rank
>> Not spared, not one
>> That dandled a sandalled
> Shadow that swam or sank
> On a meadow and river and wind-wandering weed-winding bank.

O if we but knew what we do
    When we delve or hew—
Hack and rack the growing green!
    Since country is so tender
    To touch, her being só slender,
    That, like this sleek and seeing ball
    But a prick will make no eye at all,
    Where we, even where we mean
        To mend her we end her,
    When we hew or delve:
After-comers cannot guess the beauty been.
    Ten or twelve, only ten or twelve
    Strokes of havoc únselve
        The sweet especial scene,
    Rural scene, a rural scene,
    Sweet especial rural scene.

THE CLEVELAND WRECKING YARD[2]
Richard Brautigan

Until recently my knowledge about the Cleveland Wrecking Yard had come from a couple of friends who'd bought things there. One of them bought a huge window: the frame, glass and everything for just a few dollars. It was a fine-looking window.

Then he chopped a hole in the side of his house up on Potrero Hill and put the window in. Now he has a panoramic view of the San Francisco County Hospital.

He can practically look right down into the wards and see old magazines eroded like the Grand Canyon from endless readings. He can practically hear the patients thinking about breakfast: *I hate milk,* and thinking about dinner: *I hate peas,* and then he can watch the hospital slowly drown at night, hopelessly entangled in huge bunches of brick seaweed.

He bought that window at the Cleveland Wrecking Yard.

My other friend bought an iron roof at the Cleveland Wrecking Yard and took the roof down to Big Sur in an old station wagon

[2] From *Trout Fishing in America* by Richard Brautigan. Copyright © 1967 by Richard Brautigan. A Seymour Lawrence Book/Delacorte Press. Reprinted by permission of the publisher.

and then he carried the iron roof on his back up the side of a mountain. He carried up half the roof on his back. It was no picnic. Then he bought a mule, George, from Pleasanton. George carried up the other half of the roof.

The mule didn't like what was happening at all. He lost a lot of weight because of the ticks, and the smell of the wildcats up on the plateau made him too nervous to graze there. My friend said jokingly that George had lost around two hundred pounds. The good wine country around Pleasanton in the Livermore Valley probably had looked a lot better to George than the wild side of the Santa Lucia Mountains.

My friend's place was a shack right beside a huge fireplace where there had once been a great mansion during the 1920s, built by a famous movie actor. The mansion was built before there was even a road down at Big Sur. The mansion had been brought over the mountains on the backs of mules, strung out like ants, bringing visions of the good life to the poison oak, the ticks, and the salmon.

The mansion was on a promontory, high over the Pacific. Money could see farther in the 1920s, and one could look out and see whales and the Hawaiian Islands and the Kuomintang in China.

The mansion burned down years ago.

The actor died.

His mules were made into soap.

His mistresses became bird nests of wrinkles.

Now only the fireplace remains as a sort of Carthaginian homage to Hollywood.

I was down there a few weeks ago to see my friend's roof. I wouldn't have passed up the chance for a million dollars, as they say. The roof looked like a colander to me. If that roof and the rain were running against each other at Bay Meadows, I'd bet on the rain and plan to spend my winnings at the World's Fair in Seattle.

My own experience with the Cleveland Wrecking Yard began two days ago when I heard about a used trout stream they had on sale out at the Yard. So I caught the Number 15 bus on Columbus Avenue and went out there for the first time.

There were two Negro boys sitting behind me on the bus. They were talking about Chubby Checker and the Twist. They thought that Chubby Checker was only fifteen years old because he didn't have a mustache. Then they talked about some other guy who did the twist forty-four hours in a row until he saw George Washington crossing the Delaware.

"Man, that's what I call twisting," one of the kids said.

"I don't think I could twist no forty-four hours in a row," the other kid said. "That's a lot of twisting."

I got off the bus right next to an abandoned Time Gasoline filling station and an abandoned fifty-cent self-service car wash. There was a long field on one side of the filling station. The field had once been covered with a housing project during the war, put there for the shipyard workers.

On the other side of the Time filling station was the Cleveland Wrecking Yard. I walked down there to have a look at the used trout stream. The Cleveland Wrecking Yard has a very long front window filled with signs and merchandise.

There was a sign in the window advertising a laundry marking machine for $65.00. The original cost of the machine was $175.00. Quite a saving.

There was another sign advertising new and used two and three ton hoists. I wondered how many hoists it would take to move a trout stream.

There was another sign that said:

THE FAMILY GIFT CENTER,
GIFT SUGGESTIONS FOR THE ENTIRE FAMILY

The window was filled with hundreds of items for the entire family. *Daddy, do you know what I want for Christmas? What, son? A bathroom. Mommy, do you know what I want for Christmas? What, Patricia? Some roofing material.*

There were jungle hammocks in the window for distant relatives and dollar-ten-cent gallons of earth-brown enamel paint for other loved ones.

There was also a big sign that said:

USED TROUT STREAM FOR SALE.
MUST BE SEEN TO BE APPRECIATED.

I went inside and looked at some ship's lanterns that were for sale next to the door. Then a salesman came up to me and said in a pleasant voice, "Can I help you?"

"Yes," I said. "I'm curious about the trout stream you have for sale. Can you tell me something about it? How are you selling it?"

"We're selling it by the foot length. You can buy as little as you want or you can buy all we've got left. A man came in here this morning and bought 563 feet. He's going to give it to his niece for a birthday present," the salesman said.

"We're selling the waterfalls separately of course, and the trees and birds, flowers, grass and ferns we're also selling extra. The insects we're giving away free with a minimum purchase of ten feet of stream."

"How much are you selling the stream for?" I asked.

"Six dollars and fifty-cents a foot," he said. "That's for the first hundred feet. After that it's five dollars a foot."

"How much are the birds?" I asked.

"Thirty-five cents apiece," he said. "But of course they're used. We can't guarantee anything."

"How wide is the stream?" I asked. "You said you were selling it by the length, didn't you?"

"Yes," he said. "We're selling it by the length. Its width runs between five and eleven feet. You don't have to pay anything extra for width. It's not a big stream, but it's very pleasant."

"What kinds of animals do you have?" I asked.

"We only have three deer left," he said.

"Oh . . . What about flowers?"

"By the dozen," he said.

"Is the stream clear?" I asked.

"Sir," the salesman said. "I wouldn't want you to think that we would ever sell a murky trout stream here. We always make sure they're running crystal clear before we even think about moving them."

"Where did the stream come from?" I asked.

"Colorado," he said. "We moved it with loving care. We've never damaged a trout stream yet. We treat them all as if they were china."

"You're probably asked this all the time, but how's fishing in the stream?" I asked.

"Very good," he said. "Mostly German browns, but there are a few rainbows."

"What do the trout cost?" I asked.

"They come with the stream," he said. "Of course it's all luck. You never know how many you're going to get or how big they are. But the fishing's very good, you might say it's excellent. Both bait and dry fly," he said smiling.

"Where's the stream at?" I asked. "I'd like to take a look at it."

"It's around in back," he said. "You go straight through that door and then turn right until you're outside. It's stacked in lengths. You can't miss it. The waterfalls are upstairs in the used plumbing department."

"What about the animals?"

"Well, what's left of the animals are straight back from the stream. You'll see a bunch of our trucks parked on a road by the railroad tracks. Turn right on the road and follow it down past the piles of lumber. The animal shed's right at the end of the lot."

"Thanks," I said. "I think I'll look at the waterfalls first. You don't have to come with me. Just tell me how to get there and I'll find my own way."

"All right," he said. "Go up those stairs. You'll see a bunch of doors and windows, turn left and you'll find the used plumbing department. Here's my card if you need any help."

"Okay," I said. "You've been a great help already. Thanks a lot. I'll take a look around."

"Good luck," he said.

I went upstairs and there were thousands of doors there. I'd never seen so many doors before in my life. You could have built an entire city out of those doors. Doorstown. And there were enough windows up there to build a little suburb entirely out of windows. Windowville.

I turned left and went back and saw the faint glow of pearl-colored light. The light got stronger and stronger as I went farther back, and then I was in the used plumbing department, surrounded by hundreds of toilets.

The toilets were stacked on shelves. They were stacked five toilets high. There was a skylight above the toilets that made them glow like the Great Taboo Pearl of the South Sea movies.

Stacked over against the wall were the waterfalls. There were about a dozen of them, ranging from a drop of a few feet to a drop of ten or fifteen feet.

There was one waterfall that was over sixty feet long. There were tags on the pieces of the big falls describing the correct order for putting the falls back together again.

The waterfalls all had price tags on them. They were more expensive than the stream. The waterfalls were selling for $19.00 a foot.

I went into another room where there were piles of sweet-smelling lumber, glowing a soft yellow from a different color skylight above the lumber. In the shadows at the edge of the room under the sloping roof of the building were many sinks and urinals covered with dust, and there was also another waterfall about seventeen feet long, lying there in two lengths and already beginning to gather dust.

I had seen all I wanted of the waterfalls, and now I was very curious about the trout stream, so I followed the salesman's directions and ended up outside the building.

O I had never in my life seen anything like that trout stream. It was stacked in piles of various lengths: ten, fifteen, twenty feet, etc. There was one pile of hundred-foot lengths. There was also a box of scraps. The scraps were in odd sizes ranging from six inches to a couple of feet.

There was a loudspeaker on the side of the building and soft music was coming out. It was a cloudy day and seagulls were circling high overhead.

Behind the stream were big bundles of trees and bushes. They were covered with sheets of patched canvas. You could see the tops and roots sticking out the ends of the bundles.

I went up close and looked at the lengths of stream. I could see some trout in them. I saw one good fish. I saw some crawdads crawling around the rocks at the bottom.

It looked like a fine stream. I put my hand in the water. It was cold and felt good.

I decided to go around to the side and look at the animals. I saw where the trucks were parked beside the railroad tracks. I followed the road down past the piles of lumber, back to the shed where the animals were.

The salesman had been right. They were practically out of animals. About the only thing they had left in any abundance were mice. There were hundreds of mice.

Beside the shed was a huge wire birdcage, maybe fifty feet high, filled with many kinds of birds. The top of the cage had a piece of canvas over it, so the birds wouldn't get wet when it rained. There were woodpeckers and wild canaries and sparrows.

On my way back to where the trout stream was piled, I found the insects. They were inside a prefabricated steel building that was selling for eighty-cents a square foot. There was a sign over the door. It said

INSECTS

JOURNALS
Henry David Thoreau

Dec. 30, 1851

This afternoon, being on Fair Haven Hill, I heard the sound of a saw, and soon after from the Cliff saw two men sawing down a noble pine beneath, about forty rods off. I resolved to watch it till it fell, the last of a dozen or more which were left when the forest was cut and for fifteen years have waved in solitary majesty over the sproutland. I saw them like beavers or insects gnawing at the trunk of this noble tree, the diminutive manikins with their cross-cut saw which could scarcely span it. It towered up a hundred feet as I afterward found by measurement, one of the tallest probably in the township and straight as an arrow, but slanting a little toward the hillside, its top seen against the frozen river and the hills of Conantum. I watch closely to see when it begins to move. Now the sawers stop, and with an axe open it a little on the side toward which it leans, that it may break the faster. And now their saw goes again. Now surely it is going; it is inclined one quarter of the quadrant, and, breathless, I expect its crashing fall. But no, I was mistaken; it has not moved an inch; it stands at the same angle as at first. It is fifteen minutes yet to its fall. Still its branches wave in the wind, as if it were destined to stand for a century, and the wind soughs through its needles as of yore; it is still a forest tree, the most majestic tree that waves over Musketaquid. The silvery sheen of the sunlight is reflected from its needles; it still affords an inaccessible crotch for the squirrel's nest; not a lichen has forsaken its mast-like stem, its raking mast—the hill is the hulk. Now, now's the moment! The manikins at its base are fleeing from their crime. They have dropped the guilty saw and axe. How slowly and majestically it starts! as if it were only swayed by a summer breeze, and would return without a sigh to its location in the air. And now it fans the hillside with its fall, and it lies down to its bed in the valley, from which it is never to rise, as softly as a feather, folding its green mantle about it like a warrior, as if, tired of standing, it embraced the earth with silent joy, returning its elements to the dust again. But hark! there you only saw, but did not hear. There now comes up a deafening crash to these rocks, advertising you that even trees do not die without a groan. It rushes to embrace the earth, and mingle its elements with the dust. And now all is still once more and forever, both to eye and ear.

WALDEN—JUNE 1939[3]
E. B. White

E. B. White (1899–) is an American humorist best known for *Stuart Little* and *Is Sex Necessary?* (written with James Thurber).

[June 1939]

Miss Nims, take a letter to Henry David Thoreau. Dear Henry: I thought of you the other afternoon as I was approaching Concord doing fifty on Route 62. That is a high speed at which to hold a philosopher in one's mind, but in this century we are a nimble bunch.

On one of the lawns in the outskirts of the village a woman was cutting the grass with a motorized lawn mower. What made me think of you was that the machine had rather got away from her, although she was game enough, and in the brief glimpse I had of the

---

[3]"Walden—June 1939" from *One Man's Meat* by E. B. White. Copyright 1939, by E. B. White. Reprinted by permission of Harper & Row, Publishers, Inc.

scene it appeared to me that the lawn was mowing the lady. She kept a tight grip on the handles, which throbbed violently with every explosion of the one-cylinder motor, and as she sheered around bushes and lurched along at a reluctant trot behind her impetuous servant, she looked like a puppy who had grabbed something that was too much for him. Concord hasn't changed much, Henry; the farm implements and the animals still have the upper hand.

I may as well admit that I was journeying to Concord with the deliberate intention of visiting your woods; for although I have never knelt at the grave of a philosopher nor placed wreaths on moldy poets, and have often gone a mile out of my way to avoid some place of historical interest, I have always wanted to see Walden Pond. The account which you left of your sojourn there is, you will be amused to learn, a document of increasing pertinence; each year it seems to gain a little headway, as the world loses ground. We may all be transcendental yet, whether we like it or not. As our common complexities increase, any tale of individual simplicity (and yours is the best written and the cockiest) acquires a new fascination; as our goods accumulate, but not our well-being, your report of an existence without material adornment takes on a certain awkward credibility.

My purpose in going to Walden Pond, like yours, was not to live cheaply or to live dearly there, but to transact some private business with the fewest obstacles. Approaching Concord, doing forty, doing forty-five, doing fifty, the steering wheel held snug in my palms, the highway held grimly in my vision, the crown of the road now serving me (on the righthand curves), now defeating me (on the lefthand curves), I began to rouse myself from the stupefaction which a day's motor journey induces. It was a delicious evening, Henry, when the whole body is one sense, and imbibes delight through every pore, if I may coin a phrase. Fields were richly brown where the harrow, drawn by the stripped Ford, had lately sunk its teeth; pastures were green; and overhead the sky had that same everlasting great look which you will find on Page 144 of the Oxford pocket edition. I could feel the road entering me, through tire, wheel, spring, and cushion; shall I not have intelligence with earth too? Am I not partly leaves and vegetable mold myself?—a man of infinite horsepower, yet partly leaves.

Stay with me on 62 and it will take you into Concord. As I say, it was a delicious evening. The snake had come forth to die in a bloody S on the highway, the wheel upon its head, its bowels flat now and exposed. The turtle had come up too to cross the road and die in the attempt, its hard shell smashed under the rubber blow, its intestinal yearning (for the other side of the road) forever squashed. There was a sign by the wayside which announced that the road had a "cotton surface." You wouldn't know what that is, but neither, for that matter, did I. There is a cryptic ingredient in many of our modern improvements—we are awed and pleased without knowing quite what we are enjoying. It is something to be traveling on a road with a cotton surface.

The civilization round Concord today is an odd distillation of city, village, farm, and manor. The houses, yards, fields look not quite suburban, not quite rural. Under the bronze beech and the blue spruce of the departed baron grazes the milch goat of the heirs. Under the porte-cochère stands the reconditioned station wagon; under the grape arbor sit the puppies for sale. (But why do men degenerate ever? What makes families run out?)

It was June and everywhere June was publishing her immemorial stanza; in the lilacs, in the syringa, in the freshly edged paths and the sweetness of moist beloved gardens, and the little wire wickets that preserve the tulips' front. Farmers were already moving the fruits of their toil into their yards, arranging the rhubarb, the asparagus, the strictly fresh eggs on the painted stands under the little shed roofs with the patent shingles. And though it was almost a hundred years since you had taken your ax and started cutting out your home on Walden Pond, I was interested to observe that the philosophical spirit was still alive in Massachusetts: in the center of a vacant lot some boys were assembling the framework of the rude shelter, their whole mind and skill concentrated in the rather inauspicious helter-skeleton of studs and rafters. They too were escaping from town, to live naturally, in a rich blend of savagery and philosophy.

That evening, after supper at the inn, I strolled out into the twilight to dream my shapeless transcendental dreams and see that the car was locked up for the night (first open the right front door, then reach over, straining, and pull up the handles of the left rear and the left front till you hear the click, then the handle of the right rear, then shut the right front but open it again, remembering that the key is still in the ignition switch, remove the key, shut the right front again with a bang, push the tiny keyhole cover to one side, insert key, turn, and withdraw). It is what we all do, Henry. It is called locking the car. It is said to confuse thieves and keep them from making off with the laprobe. Four doors to lock behind one robe. The driver himself never uses a laprobe, the free movement of his legs being vital to the operation of the vehicle; so that when he locks the car it is a pure and unselfish act. I have in my life gained very little essential heat from laprobes, yet I have ever been at pains to lock them up.

The evening was full of sounds, some of which would have stirred your memory. The robins still love the elms of New England villages at sundown. There is enough of the thrush in them to make song inevitable at the end of day, and enough of the tramp to make them hang round the dwellings of men. A robin, like many another American, dearly loves a white house with green blinds. Concord is still full of them.

Your fellow-townsmen were stirring abroad—not many afoot, most of them in their cars; and the sound which they made in Concord at evening was a rustling and a whispering. The sound lacks steadfastness and is wholly unlike that of a train. A train, as you know who lived so near the Fitchburg line, whistles once or twice sadly and is gone, trailing a memory in smoke, soothing to ear and mind. Automobiles, skirting a village green, are like flies that have gained the inner ear—they buzz, cease, pause, start, shift, stop, halt, brake, and the whole effect is a nervous polytone curiously disturbing.

As I wandered along, the toc toc of ping pong balls drifted from an attic window. In front of the Reuben Brown house a Buick was drawn up. At the wheel, motionless, his hat upon his head, a man sat, listening to Amos and Andy on the radio (it is a drama of many scenes and without an end). The deep voice of Andrew Brown, emerging from the car, although it originated more than two hundred miles away, was unstrained by distance. When you used to sit on the shore of your pond on Sunday morning, listening to the church bells of Acton and Concord, you were aware of the excellent filter of the intervening atmosphere. Science has attended to that, and sound now maintains its intensity without regard for distance. Properly sponsored, it goes on forever.

A fire engine, out for a trial spin, roared past Emerson's house, hot with readiness for public duty. Over the barn roofs the martins dipped and chittered. A swarthy daughter of an asparagus grower, in culottes, shirt, and bandanna, pedalled past on her bicycle. It was indeed a delicious evening, and I returned to the inn(I believe it was your house once) to rock with the old ladies on the concrete veranda.

Next morning early I started afoot for Walden, out Main Street and down Thoreau, past the depot and the Minuteman Chevrolet Company. The morning was fresh, and in a bean field along the way I flushed an agriculturalist, quietly studying his beans. Thoreau Street soon joined Number 126, an artery of the State. We number our highways nowadays, our speed being so great we can remember little of their quality or character and are lucky to remember their number. (Men have an indistinct notion that if they keep up this activity long enough all will at length ride somewhere, in next to no time.) Your pond is on 126.

I knew I must be nearing your woodland retreat when the Golden Pheasant lunchroom came into view—Sealtest ice cream, toasted sandwiches, hot frankfurters, waffles, tonics, and lunches. Were I the proprietor, I should add rice, Indian meal, and molasses—just for old time's sake. The Pheasant, incidentally, is for sale: a chance for some nature lover who wishes to set himself up beside a pond in the Concord atmosphere and live deliberately, fronting only the essential facts of life on Number 126. Beyond the Pheasant was a place called Walden Breezes, an oasis whose porch pillars were made of old green shutters sawed into lengths. On the porch was a distorting mirror, to give the traveler a comical image of himself, who had miraculously learned to gaze in an ordinary glass without smiling. Behind the Breezes, in a sun-parched clearing, dwelt your philosophical descendants in their trailers, each trailer the size of your hut, but all grouped together for the sake of congeniality. Trailer people leave the city, as you did, to discover solitude and in any weather, at any hour of the day or night, to improve the nick of time; but they soon collect in villages and get bogged deeper in the mud than ever. The camp behind Walden Breezes was just rousing itself to the morning. The ground was packed hard under the heel, and the sun came through the clearing to bake the soil and enlarge the wry smell of cramped housekeeping. Cushman's bakery truck had stopped to deliver an early basket of rolls. A camp dog, seeing me in the road, barked petulantly. A man emerged from one of the trailers and set forth with a bucket to draw water from some forest tap.

Leaving the highway I turned off into the woods toward the pond, which was apparent through the foliage. The floor of the forest was strewn with dried old oak leaves and *Transcripts*. From beneath the flattened popcorn wrapper *(granum explosum)* peeped the frail violet. I followed a footpath and descended to the water's edge. The pond lay clear and blue in the morning light, as you have seen it so many times. In the shallows a man's waterlogged shirt undulated gently. A few flies came out to greet me and convoy me to your cove, past the No Bathing signs on which the fellows and the girls had scrawled their names. I felt strangely excited suddenly to be snooping around your premises, tiptoeing along watchfully, as though not to tread by mistake upon the intervening century. Before I got to the cove I heard something which seemed to me quite wonderful: I heard your frog, a full, clear *troonk,* guiding me, still hoarse and solemn, bridging the years as the robins had bridged them in the sweetness of the village evening. But he soon quit, and I came on a couple of young boys throwing stones at him.

Your front yard is marked by a bronze tablet set in a stone. Four small granite posts, a few feet away, show where the house was. On top of the tablet was a pair of faded blue bathing trunks with a white stripe. Back of it is a pile of stones, a sort of cairn, left by your visitors as a tribute I suppose. It is a rather ugly little heap of stones, Henry. In fact the hillside itself seems faded, browbeaten; a few tall skinny pines, bare of lower limbs, a smattering of young maples in suitable green, some birches and oaks, and a number of trees felled by the last big wind. It was from the bole of one of these fallen pines, torn up by the roots, that I extracted the stone which I added to the cairn—a sentimental act in which I was interrupted by a small terrier from a nearby picnic group, who confronted me and wanted to know about the stone.

I sat down for a while on one of the posts of your house to listen to the bluebottles and the dragonflies. The invaded glade sprawled shabby and mean at my feet, but the flies were tuned to the old vibration. There were the remains of a fire in your ruins, but I doubt that it was yours; also two beer bottles trodden into the soil and become part of earth. A young oak had taken root in your house, and two or three ferns, unrolling like the ticklers at a banquet. The only other furnishings were a DuBarry pattern sheet, a page torn from a picture magazine, and some crusts in wax paper.

Before I quit I walked clear round the pond and found the place where you used to sit on the northeast side to get the sun in the fall, and the beach where you got sand for scrubbing your floor. On the eastern side of the pond, where the highway borders it, the State has built dressing rooms for swimmers, a float with diving towers, drinking fountains of porcelain, and rowboats for hire. The pond is in fact a State Preserve, and carries a twenty-dollar fine for picking wild flowers, a decree signed in all solemnity by your fellow-citizens Walter C. Wardwell, Erson B. Barlow, and Nathaniel I. Bowditch. There was a smell of creosote where they had been building a wide wooden stairway to the road and the parking area. Swimmers and boaters were arriving; bodies plunged vigorously into the water and emerged wet and beautiful in the bright air. As I left, a boatload of town boys were splashing about in mid-pond, kidding and fooling, the young fellows singing at the tops of their lungs in a wild chorus:

> *Amer-ica, Amer-ica, God shed his grace on thee,*
> *And crown thy good with brotherhood*
> *From sea to shi-ning sea!*

I walked back to town along the railroad, following your custom. The rails were expanding noisily in the hot sun, and on the slope of the roadbed the wild grape and the blackberry sent up their creepers to the track.

The expense of my brief sojourn in Concord was:

Canvas shoes $1.95		
Baseball bat .... .25	gifts to take back	
Left-handed fielder's glove 1.25	to a boy	
Hotel and meals .... <u>4.25</u>		
In all $7.70		

As you see, this amount was almost what you spent for food for eight months. I cannot defend the shoes or the expenditure for shelter and food: they reveal a meanness and grossness in my nature which you would find contemptible. The baseball equipment, however, is the kind of impediment with which you were never on even terms. You must remember that the house where you practiced the sort of economy which I respect was haunted only by mice and squirrels. You never had to cope with a shortstop.

STOVEWOOD[4]
Gary Snyder

two thousand years of fog and sucking minerals
*   from the soil,*
Russian river ox-team & small black train
*   haul to mill;*
fresh-sawed rough cut by wagon
*   and built into a barn;*
tear it down and split it up
*   and stick it in a stove.*

A BROOK IN THE CITY[5]
Robert Frost

The farmhouse lingers, though averse to square
With the new city street it has to wear
A number in. But what about the brook
That held the house as in an elbow-crook?
I ask as one who knew the brook, its strength
And impulse, having dipped a finger length
And made it leap my knuckle, having tossed
A flower to try its currents where they crossed.
The meadow grass could be cemented down
From growing under pavements of a town;
The apple trees be sent to hearthstone flame.
Is water wood to serve a brook the same?
How else dispose of an immortal force
No longer needed? Staunch it at its source
With cinder loads dumped down? The brook was thrown
Deep in a sewer dungeon under stone
In fetid darkness still to live and run —
And all for nothing it had ever done,
Except forget to go in fear perhaps.

[4]Gary Snyder, *Regarding Wave.* Copyright © 1970 by Gary Snyder. Reprinted by permission of New Directions Publishing Corporation.

[5]From *The Poetry of Robert Frost* edited by Edward Connery Lathem. Copyright 1916, 1923, © 1969 by Holt, Rinehart and Winston, Inc. Copyright © 1942, 1944, 1951 by Robert Frost. Copyright © 1970 by Lesley Frost Ballantine. Reprinted by permission of Holt, Rinehart and Winston, Inc.

No one would know except for ancient maps
That such a brook ran water. But I wonder
If from its being kept forever under,
The thoughts may not have risen that so keep
This new-built city from both work and sleep.

THE LINE-GANG[6]
Robert Frost

Here come the line-gang pioneering by.
They throw a forest down less cut than broken.
They plant dead trees for living, and the dead
They string together with a living thread.
They string an instrument against the sky
Wherein words whether beaten out or spoken
Will run as hushed as when they were a thought.
But in no hush they string it: they go past
With shouts afar to pull the cable taut,
To hold it hard until they make it fast,
To ease away—they have it. With a laugh,
An oath of towns that set the wild at naught,
They bring the telephone and telegraph.

[6]From *The Poetry of Robert Frost* edited by Edward Connery Lathem. Copyright 1916, 1923, © 1969 by Holt, Rinehart and Winston, Inc. Copyright © 1942, 1944, 1951 by Robert Frost. Copyright © 1970 by Lesley Frost Ballantine. Reprinted by permission of Holt, Rinehart and Winston, Inc.

CHAPTER SIX
Our Synthetic Environment

THE SUBURBANS[1]
Carolyn Kizer

Carolyn Kizer was born in Spokane, Washington, in 1925. Although too conservative stylistically to rate much attention from the hip circles in American poetry today, Miss Kizer is a major talent, ranking with such acknowledged figures as Robert Lowell and James Dickey.

[1]"The Suburbans" by Carolyn Kizer from the books *The Ungrateful Garden,* Copyright © 1961 by Indiana University Press and *Midnight Was My Cry*. Reprinted by permission of Doubleday & Company, Inc.

Forgetting sounds that we no longer hear—
Nightingale, silent for a century:
How touch that bubbling throat, let it touch us
In cardboard-sided suburbs, where the glades
And birds gave way to lawns, fake weathervanes
Topping antennae, or a wrought-iron rooster
Mutely presiding over third class mail?—
We live on ironed land like cemeteries,
Those famous levelers of human contours.

But cemeteries are a green relief;
Used-car and drive-in movie lots alike
Enaisle and regulate the gaudy junk
That runs us, in a "Park" that is no park.
Our greens kept up for doomed Executives;
Though golf embalms its land, as libraries
Preserve an acre for the mind to play
When, laboring at its trash, the trapped eye leaps,
Beholding greensward or the written word.

What common symbols dominate our work?
"Perpetual care;" the library steps with lions
More free than moving kinsmen in the zoos;
The seagull is our bird, who eats our loot,
Adores our garbage, but can rise above it—
Clean scavenger, picks clean, gets clean away!—
Past bays and rivers of industrial waste,
Infected oysters, fish-bloat, belly up
In sloughs of sewage, to the open sea.

So much for Nature, carved and animate!
Step in, a minute. . . . But our ankles, brushed
With that swift, intimate electric shock,
Signal the muse: the passing of a cat—
All that remains of tygers, mystery,
Eye-gleam at night, synecdoche for jungle;
We catch her ancient freedom in a cage
Of tidy rhyme. Page the anthologies!
A bridge between our Nature and our Time.

Easily she moves from outer life to inner,
While we, nailed to our domesticity
Like Van Gogh to the wall, wild in his frame,
Double in mirrors, that the sinister self
Who moves along with us may own at least
His own reverses, duck behind his molding
When our phones jerk us on a leash of noise.
Hence mirror poems, Alice, The Looking Glass,
Those dull and partial couplings with ourselves.

Our gold-fish gazes, our transparent nerves!
As we weave above these little colored stones—
Fish-furniture—bob up for dusty food:
"Just heat and serve;" our empty pear-shaped tones!
Home is a picture window, and our globes
Are mirrors too: we see ourselves outside.
Afraid to become our neighbors, we revolt
In verse: "This proves I'm not the average man."
Only the average poet, which is worse.

The drooping 19th-century bard in weeds
On his stone bench, beside a weedy grave,
Might attitudinize, but his tears were free
And easy. He heard authentic birds.
Nobody hid recordings in his woods,
Or draped his waterfalls with neon gauze.
No sign disturbed his orisons, commanding,
"Go to Church this Sunday!" or be damned!
He was comfortably damned when he was born.

But we are saved, from the boring Hell of churches;
We run to graves for picnics or for peace:
Beer cans on headstones, eggshells in the grass,
"Deposit Trash in Baskets." For release
From hells of public and domestic noise,
We sprawl, although we neither pose nor pray,
Compose our stanzas here, like that dead bard,
But writing poems on poems. Gravely gay,
Our limited salvation is the word.

BIG YELLOW TAXI[2]
Joni Mitchell

Joni Mitchell is a Canadian-born singer and composer of rock songs. Her lyrics, especially "Marcie," "Songs to Aging Children Come," and "Both Sides Now," reveal her to be an excellent poet as well as a talented performer.

They paved paradise
And put up a parking lot,
With a pink hotel
A boutique and a swinging hot spot.

Don't it always seem to go
That you don't know what you've got till it's gone?

They took all the trees
And put them in a tree museum,
And they charged all the people
A dollar and a half just to see 'em.

Don't it always seem to go
That you don't know what you've got till it's gone?

Hey, farmer, farmer,
Put away that D.D.T. now,
Give me spots on my apples
But leave me the birds and the bees.
Please!

Don't it always seem to go
That you don't know what you've got till it's gone?

Late last night
I heard the screen door slam,
And a big yellow taxi
Took away my old man.

Don't it always seem to go
That you don't know what you've got till it's gone?

TRAVELS WITH CHARLEY[3]
John Steinbeck

John Steinbeck (1902–1968) was an American novelist, best known for his novel of the Great Depression, *The Grapes of Wrath*. This selection is from *Travels with Charley*, a travel memoir of a trip across America that Steinbeck took with his poodle, Charley, in 1960.

From the beginning of my journey, I had avoided the great high-speed slashes of concrete and tar called "thruways," or "super-highways." Various states have different names for them, but I had dawdled in New England, the winter grew apace, and I had visions of being snowbound in North Dakota. I sought out U. S. 90, a wide gash of a super-highway, multiple-lane carrier of the nation's goods. Rocinante[4] bucketed along. The minimum speed on this road was greater than any I had previously driven. I drove into a wind quartering in from my starboard bow and felt the buffeting, sometimes staggering blows of the gale I helped to make. I could hear the sough of it on the square surfaces of my camper top. Instructions screamed at me from the road once: "Do not stop! No stopping. Maintain speed." Trucks as long as freighters went roaring by, delivering a wind like the blow of a fist. These great roads are wonderful for moving goods but not for inspection of a countryside. You are bound to the wheel and your eyes to the car ahead and to the rear-view mirror for the car behind and the side mirror for the car or truck about to pass, and at the same time you must read all the signs for fear you may miss some instructions or orders. No roadside stands selling squash juice, no antique stores, no farm products or factory outlets. When we get these thruways across the whole country, as we will and must, it will be possible to drive from New York to California without seeing a single thing.

At intervals there are places of rest and recreation, food, fuel and oil, postcards, steam-table food, picnic tables, garbage cans all fresh and newly painted, rest rooms and lavatories so spotless, so

[3]From *Travels with Charley: In Search of America*, by John Steinbeck. Copyright © 1961, 1962 by The Curtis Publishing Company, Inc. Copyright © 1962 by John Steinbeck. Reprinted by permission of The Viking Press, Inc.

[4]Steinbeck's pickup truck, named for Don Quixote's horse.

incensed with deodorants and with detergents that it takes a time to get your sense of smell back. For deodorants are not quite correctly named; they substitute one smell for another, and the substitute must be much stronger and more penetrating than the odor it conquers. I had neglected my own country too long. Civilization had made great strides in my absence. I remember when a coin in a slot would get you a stick of gum or a candy bar, but in these dining palaces were vending machines where various coins could deliver handkerchiefs, comb-and-nail-file sets, hair conditioners and cosmetics, first-aid kits, minor drugs such as aspirin, mild physics, pills to keep you awake. I found myself entranced with these gadgets. Suppose you want a soft drink; you pick your kind—Sungrape or Cooly Cola—press a button, insert the coin, and stand back. A paper cup drops into place, the drink pours out and stops a quarter of an inch from the brim—a cold, refreshing drink guaranteed synthetic. Coffee is even more interesting, for when the hot black fluid has ceased, a squirt of milk comes down and an envelope of sugar drops beside the cup. But of all, the hot-soup machine is the triumph. Choose among ten—pea, chicken noodle, beef and veg., insert the coin. A rumbling hum comes from the giant and a sign lights up that reads "Heating." After a minute a red light flashes on and off until you open a little door and remove the paper cup of boiling-hot soup.

It is life at a peak of some kind of civilization. The restaurant accommodations, great scallops of counters with simulated leather stools, are as spotless as and not unlike the lavatories. Everything that can be captured and held down is sealed in clear plastic. The food is oven-fresh, spotless and tasteless: untouched by human hands. I remembered with an ache certain dishes in France and Italy touched by innumerable human hands.

CHAPTER SEVEN
Man and Beast

INTIMATIONS OF IMMORTALITY[1]
W. H. Hudson

Notwithstanding all this, the fear of death came back to me in a little while, and for a long time disquieted me, especially when the fact of death was brought sharply before me. These reminders were all too frequent; there was seldom a day on which I did not see something killed. When the killing was instantaneous, as when a bird

[1] From "Far Away and Long Ago" in *Idle Days in Patagonia* by W. H. Hudson. Reprinted by permission of E. P. Dutton & Co., Inc.

was shot and dropped dead like a stone, I was not disturbed; it was nothing but a strange, exciting spectacle, but failed to bring the fact of death home to me. It was chiefly when cattle were slaughtered that the terror returned in its full force. And no wonder! The native manner of killing a cow or bullock at that time was peculiarly painful. Occasionally it would be slaughtered out of sight on the plain, and the hide and flesh brought in by the men, but, as a rule, the beast would be driven up close to the house to save trouble. One of the two or three mounted men engaged in the operation would throw his lasso over the horns, and, galloping off, pull the rope taut; a second man would then drop from his horse, and running up to the animal behind, pluck out his big knife and with two lightning-quick blows sever the tendons of both hind legs. Instantly the beast would go down on his haunches, and the same man, knife in hand, would flit round to its front or side, and, watching his opportunity, presently thrust the long blade into its throat just above the chest, driving it in to the hilt and working it round; then when it was withdrawn a great torrent of blood would pour out from the tortured beast, still standing on his fore-legs, bellowing all the time with agony. At this point the slaughterer would often leap lightly on to its back, stick his spurs in its sides, and, using the flat of his long knife as a whip, pretend to be riding a race, yelling with fiendish glee. The bellowing would subside into deep, awful, sob-like sounds and chokings; then the rider, seeing the animal about to collapse, would fling himself nimbly off. The beast down, they would all run to it, and throwing themselves on its quivering side as on a couch, begin making and lighting their cigarettes.

Slaughtering a cow was grand sport for them, and the more active and dangerous the animal, the more prolonged the fight, the better they liked it; they were as joyfully excited as at a fight with knives or an ostrich hunt. To me it was an awful object-lesson, and held me fascinated with horror. For this was death! The crimson torrents of blood, the deep, human-like cries, made the beast appear like some huge, powerful man caught in a snare by small, weak, but cunning adversaries, who tortured him for their delight and mocked him in his agony.

ALONE, YET NOT ALONE[2]
W. H. Hudson

Close to the mouth of the river there is a low flat island, about half a mile in length, covered in most part by a dense growth of coarse grass and rushes. It is inhabited by a herd of swine; and although these animals do not increase, they have been able to maintain their existence for a long period without diminishing in number, in spite of the occasional great tides that flood the whole island, and of multitudes of hungry eagles and caranchos always on the look-out for stray sucklings. Many years ago, while some gauchos were driving a troop of half-wild cows near the shore on the neighbouring mainland, a heifer took to the water and succeeded in swimming to the island, where she was lost to her owner. About a year later this animal was seen by a man who had gone to the island to cut rushes for thatching purposes. The cow and the pigs, to the number of about twenty-five or twenty-six, were lying fast asleep in a small grassy hollow where he found them, the cow stretched out at full length on the ground, and the pigs grouped or rather heaped around her; for they were all apparently ambitious to rest with their heads pillowed on her, so that she was almost concealed under them. Presently one of the drove, more wakeful than his fellows, became aware of his presence and gave the alarm, whereupon they started up like one animal and vanished into a rush-bed. The cow, thus doomed to live "alone, yet not alone," was subsequently seen on several occasions by the rush-cutters, always with her fierce followers grouped round her like a bodyguard. This continued for some years, and the fame of the cow that had become the leader and queen of the wild island pigs was spread abroad in the valley; then a human being, who was not a "sentimentalist," betook himself to her little kingdom with a musket loaded with ball, and succeeded in finding and shooting her.

In spite of what we have been taught, it is sometimes borne in on us that man is a little lower than the brutes.

After hearing this incident one does not at once sit down with a good appetite to roast beef or swine's flesh.

[2] From *Idle Days in Patagonia* by W. H. Hudson. Reprinted by permission of E. P. Dutton & Co., Inc.

KENTUCKY SPORTS, *DELINEATIONS OF AMERICAN SCENERY AND CHARACTER*
John James Audubon

John James Audubon (1785–1851), Haitian-born ornithologist and artist, was a man of remarkable talents. He was not only a great naturalist but also an extremely good painter, trained by French artist Jacques David. The selections, here and in chapter 10, are from his book *Delineations of American Scenery and Character.*

Surprisingly, despite his abilities as a naturalist, Audubon was curiously unfeeling toward the animals and birds he studied. In his account of Kentucky sports he seems not to find Boone's game with the squirrels cruel and inhumane. Far more shocking, however, is his account of the slaughter of hundreds of cormorants so that he could get one specimen ("The Florida Keys," chapter 12).

It may not be amiss, before I attempt to give some idea of the pleasures experienced by the sportsmen of Kentucky, to introduce the subject with a slight description of that State.

Kentucky was formerly attached to Virginia, but in those days the Indians looked upon that portion of the western wilds as their own, and abandoned the district only when forced to do so, moving with disconsolate hearts farther into the recesses of the unexplored forests. Doubtless the richness of its soil, and the beauty of its borders, situated as they are along one of the most beautiful rivers in the world, contributed as much to attract the Old Virginians, as the desire so generally experienced in America, of spreading over the uncultivated tracts, and bringing into cultivation lands that have for unknown ages teemed with the wild luxuriance of untamed nature. The conquest of Kentucky was not performed without many difficulties. The warfare that long existed between the intruders and the Redskins was sanguinary and protracted; but the former at length made good their footing, and the latter drew off their shattered bands, dismayed by the mental superiority and indomitable courage of the white men.

This region was probably discovered by a daring hunter, the renowned Daniel Boon. The richness of its soul, its magnificent forests, its numberless navigable streams, its salt springs and licks, its saltpetre caves, its coal strata, and the vast herds of buffaloes and deer that browsed on its hills and amidst its charming valleys, afforded ample inducements to the new settler, who pushed forward with a spirit far above that of the most undaunted tribes, which for ages had been the sole possessors of the soil.

The Virginians thronged towards the Ohio. An axe, a couple of horses, and a heavy rifle, with store of ammunition, were all that were considered necessary for the equipment of the man, who, with his family, removed to the new State, assured that, in that land of exuberant fertility, he could not fail to provide amply for all his wants. To have witnessed the industry and perseverance of these emigrants must at once have proved the vigour of their minds. Regardless of the fatigue attending every movement which they made, they pushed through an unexplored region of dark and tangled forests, guiding themselves by the sun alone, and reposing at night on the bare ground. They had to cross numberless streams on rafts, with their wives and children, their cattle and their luggage, often drifting to considerable distances before they could effect a landing on the opposite shores. Their cattle would often stray amid the rice pasturage of these shores, and occasion a delay of several days. To these troubles add the constantly impending danger of being murdered, while asleep in their encampments, by the prowling and ruthless Indians; while they had before them a distance of hundreds of miles to be traversed, before they could reach certain places of rendezvous called *stations*. To encounter difficulties like these must have required energies of no ordinary kind; and the reward which these veteran settlers enjoy was doubtless well merited.

Some removed from the Atlantic shores to those of the Ohio in more comfort and security. They had their wagons, their Negroes, and their families. Their way was cut through the woods by their own axemen, the day before their advance, and when night overtook them, the hunters attached to the party came to the place pitched upon for encamping, loaded with the dainties of which the forest yielded an abundant supply, the blazing light of a huge fire guiding their steps as they approached, and the sounds of merriment that saluted their ears assuring them that all was well. The flesh of the buffalo, the bear, and the deer, soon hung in large and delicious steaks, in front of the embers; the cakes already prepared were deposited in their proper places, and under the rich drippings of the juicy roasts, were quickly baked. The wagons contained the bedding, and whilst the horses which had drawn them were turned loose to feed on the luxuriant undergrowth of the woods, some perhaps hobbled, but the greater number merely with a light bell hung to their neck, to guide their owners in the morning to the spot where they might have rambled, the party were enjoying themselves after the fatigues of the day.

In anticipation all is pleasure; and these migrating bands feasted in joyous sociality, unapprehensive of any greater difficulties than those to be encountered in forcing their way through the pathless woods to the land of abundance; and although it took months to accomplish the journey, and a skirmish now and then took place between them and the Indians, who sometimes crept unperceived into their very camp, still did the Virginians cheerfully proceed towards the western horizon, until the various groups all reached the Ohio, when, struck with the beauty of that magnificent stream, they at once commenced the task of clearing land, for the purpose of establishing a permanent residence.

Others, perhaps encumbered with too much luggage, preferred descending the stream. They prepared *arks* pierced with port-holes, and glided on the gentle current, more annoyed, however, than those who marched by land, by the attacks of the Indians, who watched their motions. Many travellers have described these boats, formerly called *arks*, but now named *flat-boats*. But have they told you, reader, that in those times a boat thirty or forty feet in length, by ten or twelve in breadth, was considered a stupendous fabric; that this boat contained men, women and children, huddled together, with horses, cattle, hogs and poultry for their companions, while the remaining portion was crammed with vegetables and packages of seeds? The roof or deck of the boat was not unlike a farm-yard, being covered with hay, ploughs, carts, wagons, and various agricultural implements, together with numerous others among which the spinning-wheels of the matrons were conspicuous. Even the sides of the floating mass were loaded with the wheels of the different vehicles, which themselves lay on the roof. Have they told you that these boats contained the little all of each family of venturous emigrants, who, fearful of being discovered by the Indians, under night moved in darkness, groping their way from one part to another of these floating habitations, denying themselves the comfort of fire or light, lest the foe that watched them from the shore should rush upon them and destroy them? Have they told you that this boat was used, after the tedious voyage was ended, as the first dwelling of these new settlers? No, such things have not been related to you before. The travellers who have visited our country have had other objects in view.

I shall not describe the many massacres which took place among the different parties of White and Red men, as the former moved down the Ohio; because I have never been very fond of battles, and indeed have always wished that the world were more peaceably inclined than it is; and shall merely add, that, in one way or other, Kentucky was wrested from the original owners of the soil. Let us, therefore, turn our attention to the sports still enjoyed in that now happy portion of the United States.

We have individuals in Kentucky, that even there are considered wonderful adepts in the management of the rifle. To *drive a nail* is a common feat, not more thought of by the Kentuckians than to cut off a wild turkey's head, at a distance of a hundred yards. Others will *bark* off squirrels one after another, until satisfied with the number procured. Some, less intent on destroying game, may be seen under night *snuffing a candle* at the distance of fifty yards, offhand, without extinguishing it. I have been told that some have proved so expert and cool, as to make choice of the eye of a foe at a wonderful distance, boasting beforehand of the sureness of their piece, which has afterwards been fully proved when the enemy's head has been examined!

Having resided some years in Kentucky, and having more than once been witness of rifle sport, I will present you with the results of my observation, leaving you to judge how far rifle-shooting is understood in that State.

Several individuals who conceive themselves expert in the management of the gun, are often seen to meet for the purpose of displaying their skill, and betting a trifling sum, put up a target, in the centre of which a common-sized nail is hammered for about two-thirds of its length. The marksmen make choice of what they consider a proper distance, which may be forty paces. Each man cleans the interior of his tube, which is called *wiping* it, places a ball in the palm of his hand, pouring as much powder from his horn upon it as will cover it. This quantity is supposed to be sufficient for any distance within a hundred yards. A shot which comes very close to the nail is considered as that of an indifferent marksman; the bending of the nail is, of course, somewhat better; but nothing less than hitting it right on the head is satisfactory. Well, kind reader, one out of three shots generally hits the nail, and should the shooters amount to half a dozen, two nails are frequently needed before each can have a shot. Those who drive the nail have a further trial amongst themselves, and the two best shots of these generally settle the affair, when all the sportsmen adjourn to some house, and spend an hour or two in friendly intercourse, appointing, before they part, a day for another trial. This is technically termed *Driving the Nail*.

Barking off squirrels is delightful sport, and in my opinion requires a greater degree of accuracy than any other. I first witnessed this manner of procuring squirrels whilst near the town of Frankfort. The performer was the celebrated Daniel Boon. We walked out together, and followed the rocky margins of the Kentucky River, until we reached a piece of flat land thickly covered with black walnuts, oaks and hickories. As the general mast was a good one that year, squirrels were seen gambolling on every tree around us. My companion, a stout, hale, and athletic man, dressed in a homespun hunting-shirt, bare-legged and moccasined, carried a long and heavy rifle, which, as he was loading it, he said had proved efficient in all his former undertakings, and which he hoped would not fail on this occasion, as he felt proud to show me his skill. The gun was wiped, the powder measured, the ball patched with six-hundred-thread linen, and the charge sent home with a hickory rod. We moved not a step from the place, for the squirrels were so numerous that it was unnecessary to go after them. Boon pointed to one of these animals which had observed us, and was crouched on a branch about fifty paces distant, and bade me mark well the spot where the ball should hit. He raised his piece gradually, until the *bead* (that being the name given by the Kentuckians to the *sight*) of the barrel was brought to a line with the spot which he intended to hit. The whip-like report resounded through the woods and along the hills in repeated echoes. Judge of my surprise, when I perceived that the ball had hit the piece of the bark immediately beneath the squirrel, and shivered it into splinters, the concussion produced by which had killed the animal, and sent it whirling through the air, as if it had been blown up by explosion of a powder magazine. Boon kept up his firing, and before many hours had elapsed, we had procured as many squirrels as we wished; for you must know, that to load a rifle requires only a moment, and that if it is wiped once after each shot, it will do duty for hours. Since that first interview with our veteran Boon, I have seen many other individuals perform the same feat.

The *snuffing of a candle* with a ball, I first had an opportunity of seeing near the banks of Green River, not far from a large pigeon-roost, to which I had previously made a visit. I heard many reports of guns during the early part of a dark night, and knowing them to be those of rifles, I went towards the spot to ascertain the cause. On reaching the place, I was welcomed by a dozen of tall stout men, who told me they were exercising, for the purpose of enabling them to shoot under night at the reflected light from the eyes of a deer or wolf, by torch-light, of which I shall give you an account somewhere else. A fire was blazing near, the smoke of which rose curling among the thick foliage of the trees. At a distance which rendered it scarcely distinguishable, stood a burning candle, as if intended for an offering to the goddess of night, but which in reality was only fifty yards from the spot on which we all stood. One man was within a few yards of it, to watch the effects of the shots, as well as to light the candle should it chance to go out, or to replace it should the shot cut it across. Each marksman shot in his turn. Some never hit either the snuff or the candle, and were congratulated with a loud laugh; while others actually snuffed the candle without putting it out, and were recompensed for their dexterity by numerous hurrahs. One of them, who was particularly expert, was very fortunate, and snuffed the candle three times out of seven, whilst all the other shots either put out the candle, or cut it immediately under the light.

Of the feats performed by the Kentuckians with the rifle, I could say more than might be expedient on the present occasion. In every thinly peopled portion of the State, it is rare to meet one without a gun of that description, as well as a tomahawk. By way of recreation they often cut off a piece of the bark of a tree, make a target of it, using a little powder wetted with water or saliva for the bull's eye, and shoot into the mark all the balls they have about them, picking them out of the wood again.

After what I have said, you may easily imagine with what ease a Kentuckian procures game, or dispatches an enemy, more especially when I tell you that every one in the State is accustomed to handle the rifle from the time when he is first able to shoulder it until near the close of his career. That murderous weapon is the means of procuring them subsistence during all their wild and extensive rambles, and is the source of their principal sports and pleasures.

THE SALT CREEK COYOTES[3]
Richard Brautigan

High and lonesome and steady, it's the smell of sheep down in the valley that has done it to them. Here all afternoon in the rain I've been listening to the sound of the coyotes up on Salt Creek.

The smell of the sheep grazing in the valley has done it to them. Their voices water and come down the canyon, past the summer homes. Their voices are a creek, running down the mountain, over the bones of sheep, living and dead.

O, THERE ARE COYOTES UP ON SALT CREEK so the sign on the trail says, and it also says, WATCH OUT FOR CYANIDE CAPSULES PUT ALONG THE CREEK TO KILL COYOTES. DON'T PICK THEM UP AND EAT THEM. NOT UNLESS YOU'RE A COYOTE. THEY'LL KILL YOU. LEAVE THEM ALONE.

Then the sign says this all over again in Spanish. ¡AH! HAY COYOTES EN SALT CREEK, TAMBIEN. CUIDADO CON LAS CAPSULAS DE CIANURO: MATAN. NO LAS COMA; A MENOS QUE SEA VD. UN COYOTE. MATAN. NO LAS TOQUE.

It does not say it in Russian.

I asked an old guy in a bar about those cyanide capsules up on Salt Creek and he told me that they were a kind of pistol. They put a pleasing coyote scent on the trigger (probably the smell of a coyote snatch) and then a coyote comes along and gives it a good sniff, a fast feel and BLAM! That's all, brother.

I went fishing up on Salt Creek and caught a nice little Dolly Varden trout, spotted and slender as a snake you'd expect to find in a jewelry store, but after a while I could think only of the gas chamber at San Quentin.

O Caryl Chessman and Alexander Robillard Vistas! as if they were names for tracts of three-bedroom houses with wall-to-wall carpets and plumbing that defies the imagination.

Then it came to me up there on Salt Creek, capital punishment being what it is, an act of state business with no song down the

[3]From *Trout Fishing in America* by Richard Brautigan. Copyright © 1967 by Richard Brautigan. A Seymour Lawrence/Delacorte Press. Reprinted by permission of the publisher.

railroad track after the train has gone and no vibration on the rails, that they should take the head of a coyote killed by one of those God-damn cyanide things up on Salt Creek and hollow it out and dry it in the sun and then make it into a crown with the teeth running in a circle around the top of it and a nice green light coming off the teeth.

Then the witnesses and newspapermen and gas chamber flunkies would have to watch a king wearing a coyote crown die there in front of them, the gas rising in the chamber like a rain mist drifting down the mountain from Salt Creek. It has been raining here now for two days, and through the trees, the heart stops beating.

THE RABBIT-HUNTER[4]
Robert Frost

Careless and still
The hunter lurks
With gun depressed,
Facing alone
The alder swamps
Ghastly snow-white.
And his hound works
In the offing there
Like one possessed,
And yelps delight
And sings and romps,
Bringing him on
The shadowy hare
For him to rend
And deal a death
That he nor it
(Nor I) have wit
To comprehend.

[4]From *The Poetry of Robert Frost* edited by Edward Connery Lathem. Copyright 1916, 1923, © 1969 by Holt, Rinehart and Winston, Inc. Copyright 1942, 1944, 1951 by Robert Frost. Copyright © 1970 by Lesley Frost Ballantine. Reprinted by permission of Holt, Rinehart and Winston, Inc.

SHEEP[5]
W. H. Davies

William Henry Davies (1871–1940) spent his early life as an itinerant peddler, panhandler, and tramp in England and America. At the age of thirty-four he became a poet and shortly afterward was adopted and patronized by London society. Critic Samuel Chew says of Davies, "He could be odd or grim, but he had found the secret of happiness in a fresh contact with the natural of hills, woodlands, flowers, birds, and small four-footed creatures."[6]

When I was once in Baltimore,
    A man came up to me and cried,
'Come, I have eighteen hundred sheep,
    And we will sail on Tuesday's tide.

'If you will sail with me, young man,
    I'll pay you fifty shillings down;
These eighteen hundred sheep I take
    From Baltimore to Glasgow town.'

He paid me fifty shillings down,
    I sailed with eighteen hundred sheep;
We soon had cleared the harbour's mouth,
    We soon were in the salt sea deep.

The first night we were out at sea
    Those sheep were quiet in their mind;
The second night they cried with fear—
    They smelt no pastures in the wind.

They sniffed, poor things, for their green fields,
    They cried so loud I could not sleep:
For fifty thousand shillings down
    I would not sail again with sheep.

---

[5]Copyright © 1963 by Jonathan Cape Ltd. Reprinted from *The Complete Poems of W. H. Davies*, by permission of Wesleyan University Press.

[6]Albert C. Baugh et. al., *A Literary History of England* (New York: Appleton-Century-Crofts, 1948), p. 1577.

IT'S NOT THE SAME WITHOUT PELICANS[7]
Henry Gibson

Henry Gibson was the house poet of Rowan and Martin's "Laugh-In."

It's not the same without pelicans,
You know?
I mean, dinosaurs . . .
Well, they're too big to miss . . .
And besides, it was their own fault.
But we all grew up with pelicans!
I hope the ducks hold out.

ON A MONUMENT TO THE PIGEON[8]
Aldo Leopold

Aldo Leopold (1887–1948) was an American naturalist, member of the U.S. Forest Service, one of the founders of the Wilderness Society. Leopold established the profession of game management and wrote the first major book on the subject. *A Sand County Almanac* begins with an account of Leopold's life on a Wisconsin farm, and includes a series of essays on other ecological topics. Our selection is taken from Part Two, "The Quality of the Landscape."

We have erected a monument to commemorate the funeral of a species.[9] It symbolizes our sorrow. We grieve because no living man will see again the onrushing phalanx of victorious birds, sweeping a

[7] Posters 403, 404 by Henry Gibson. Reprinted by permission of Synergisms. © 1970.

[8] From *A Sand County Almanac with Other Essays on Conservation from Round River* by Aldo Leopold. Copyright © 1949, 1953, 1966 by Oxford University Press, Inc. Reprinted by permission.

[9] The monument to the Passenger Pigeon, placed in Wyalusing State Park, Wisconsin, by the Wisconsin Society for Ornithology. Dedicated 11 May 1947.

path for spring across the March skies, chasing the defeated winter from all the woods and prairies of Wisconsin.

Men still live who, in their youth, remember pigeons. Trees still live who, in their youth, were shaken by a living wind. But a decade hence only the oldest oaks will remember, and at long last only the hills will know.

There will always be pigeons in books and in museums, but these are effigies and images, dead to all hardships and to all delights. Book-pigeons cannot dive out of a cloud to make the deer run for cover, or clap their wings in thunderous applause of mast-laden woods. Book-pigeons cannot breakfast on new-mown wheat in Minnesota, and dine on blueberries in Canada. They know no urge of seasons; they feel no kiss of sun, no lash of wind and weather. They live forever by not living at all.

Our grandfathers were less well-housed, well-fed, well-clothed than we are. The strivings by which they bettered their lot are also those which deprived us of pigeons. Perhaps we now grieve because we are not sure, in our hearts, that we have gained by the exchange. The gadgets of industry bring us more comforts than the pigeons did, but do they add as much to the glory of the spring?

It is a century now since Darwin gave us the first glimpse of the origin of species. We know now what was unknown to all the preceding caravan of generations: that men are only fellow-voyagers with other creatures in the odyssey of evolution. This new knowledge should have given us, by this time, a sense of kinship with fellow-creatures; a wish to live and let live; a sense of wonder over the magnitude and duration of the biotic enterprise.

Above all we should, in the century since Darwin, have come to know that man, while now captain of the adventuring ship, is hardly the sole object of its quest, and that his prior assumptions to this effect arose from the simple necessity of whistling in the dark.

These things, I say, should have come to us. I fear they have not come to many.

For one species to mourn the death of another is a new thing under the sun. The Cro-Magnon who slew the last mammoth thought only of steaks. The sportsman who shot the last pigeon thought only of his prowess. The sailor who clubbed the last auk thought of nothing at all. But we, who have lost our pigeons, mourn the loss. Had the funeral been ours, the pigeons would hardly have mourned us. In this fact, rather than in Mr. DuPont's nylons or Mr. Vannevar Bush's bombs, lies objective evidence of our superiority over the beasts.

This monument, perched like a duckhawk on this cliff, will scan this wide valley, watching through the days and years. For many a March it will watch the geese go by, telling the river about clearer, colder, lonelier waters on the tundra. For many an April it will see the redbuds come and go, and for many a May the flush of oak-blooms on a thousand hills. Questing wood ducks will search these basswoods for hollow limbs; golden prothonotaries will shake golden pollen from the river willows, Egrets will pose on these sloughs in August; plovers will whistle from September skies. Hickory nuts will plop into October leaves, and hail will rattle in November woods. But no pigeons will pass, for there are no pigeons, save only this flightless one, graven in bronze on this rock. Tourists will read this inscription, but their thoughts will not take wing.

We are told by economic moralists that to mourn the pigeon is mere nostalgia; that if the pigeoners had not done away with him, the farmers would ultimately have been obliged, in self-defense, to do so.

This is one of those peculiar truths that are valid, but not for the reasons alleged.

The pigeon was a biological storm. He was the lightning that played between two opposing potentials of intolerable intensity: the fat of the land and the oxygen of the air. Yearly the feathered tempest roared up, down, and across the continent, sucking up the laden fruits of forest and prairie, burning them in a traveling blast of life. Like any other chain reaction, the pigeon could survive no diminution of his own furious intensity. When the pigeoners subtracted from his numbers, and the pioneers chopped gaps in the continuity of his fuel, his flame guttered out with hardly a sputter or even a wisp of smoke.

Today the oaks still flaunt their burden at the sky, but the feathered lightning is no more. Worm and weevil must now perform slowly and silently the biological task that once drew thunder from the firmament.

The wonder is not that the pigeon went out, but that he ever survived through all the millennia of pre-Babbittian time.

The pigeon loved his land: he lived by the intensity of his desire for clustered grape and bursting beechnut, and by his contempt of miles and seasons. Whatever Wisconsin did not offer him gratis today, he sought and found tomorrow in Michigan, or Labrador, or Tennessee. His love was for present things, and these things were present somewhere; to find them required only the free sky, and the will to ply his wings.

To love what *was* is a new thing under the sun, unknown to most people and to all pigeons. To see America as history, to conceive of destiny as a becoming, to smell a hickory tree through the still lapse of ages—all these things are possible for us, and to achieve them takes only the free sky, and the will to ply our wings. In these things, and not in Mr. Bush's bombs and Mr. DuPont's nylons, lies objective evidence of our superiority over the beasts.

THE LIFE OF BUFFALO BILL
William Cody

William Cody (1846–1917), better known as Buffalo Bill, was a frontier scout, Indian fighter, and the proprietor of a wild west show. In our selection, from his autobiography, he is doing what he is most famous for—killing buffaloes. He boasts of being the killer of most of the buffaloes whose heads are in "prominent positions at the leading hotels, depots, and other public buildings."

Chapter XV. Champion Buffalo Killer

Shortly after the adventures mentioned in the preceding chapter, I had my celebrated buffalo hunt with Billy Comstock, a noted scout, guide and interpreter, who was then chief of scouts at Fort Wallace, Kansas. Comstock had the reputation, for a long time, of being a most successful buffalo hunter, and the officers in particular, who had seen him kill buffaloes, were very desirous of backing him in a match against me. It was accordingly arranged that I should shoot him a buffalo-killing match, and the preliminaries were easily and satisfactorily agreed upon. We were to hunt one day of eight hours, beginning at eight o'clock in the morning, and closing at four o'clock in the afternoon. The wager was five hundred dollars a side, and the man who should kill the greater number of buffaloes from on horseback was to be declared the winner.

The hunt took place about twenty miles east of Sheridan, and as it had been pretty well advertised and noised abroad, a large crowd witnessed the interesting and exciting scene. An excursion party, mostly from St. Louis, consisting of about a hundred gentlemen and ladies, came out on a special train to view the sport, and among the number was my wife, with little baby Arta, who had come to remain with me for a while.

The buffaloes were quite plenty, and it was agreed that we should go into the same herd at the same time and "make a run," as we called it, each one killing as many as possible. A referee was to follow each of us on horseback when we entered the herd, and count the buffaloes killed by each man. The St. Louis excursionists, as well as the other spectators, rode out to the vicinity of the hunting grounds in wagons and on horseback, keeping well out of sight of the buffaloes, so as not to frighten them, until the time came for us to dash into the herd; when they were to come up as near they pleased and witness the chase.

We were fortunate in the first run in getting good ground. Comstock was mounted on one of his favorite horses, while I rode old Brigham. I felt confident that I had the advantage of Comstock in two things—first , I had the best buffalo horse that ever made a track; and second, I was using what was known at that time as the needle-gun, a breech-loading Springfield rifle—calibre 50,—it was my favorite old "Lucretia," which has already been introduced to the notice of the reader; while Comstock was armed with a Henry rifle, and although he could fire a few shots quicker than I could, yet I was pretty certain that it did not carry powder and lead enough to do execution equal to my calibre 50.

At last the time came to begin the match. Comstock and I dashed into a herd, followed by the referees. The buffaloes separated; Comstock took the left bunch and I the right. My great *forte* in killing buffaloes from horseback was to get them circling by riding my horse at the head of the herd, shooting the leaders, thus crowding their followers to the left, till they would finally circle round and round.

On this morning the buffaloes were very accommodating, and I soon had them running in a beautiful circle, when I dropped them thick and fast, until I had killed thirty-eight; which finished my run.

Comstock began shooting at the rear of the herd, which he was chasing, and they kept straight on. He succeeded, however, in killing twenty-three, but they were scattered over a distance of three miles, while mine lay close together. I had "nursed" my buffaloes, as a billiard-player does the balls when he makes a big run.

After the result of the first run had been duly announced, our St. Louis excursion friends—who had approached to the place where we had stopped—set out a lot of champagne, which they had brought with them, and which proved a good drink on a Kansas prairie, and a buffalo hunter was a good man to get away with it.

While taking a short rest, we suddenly spied another herd of buffaloes coming toward us. It was only a small drove, and we at once prepared to give the animals a lively reception. They proved to be a herd of cows and calves—which, by the way, are quicker in their movements than the bulls. We charged in among them, and I concluded my run with a score of eighteen, while Comstock killed fourteen. The score now stood fifty-six to thirty-seven, in my favor.

Again the excursion party approached, and once more the champagne was tapped. After we had eaten a lunch which was spread for us, we resumed the hunt. Striking out for a distance of three miles, we came up close to another herd. As I was so far ahead of my competitor in the number killed, I thought I could afford to give an extra exhibition of my skill. I had told the ladies that I would, on the next run, ride my horse without saddle or bridle. This had raised the excitement to fever heat among the excursionists, and I remember one fair lady who endeavored to prevail upon me not to attempt it.

"That's nothing at all," said I; "I have done it many a time, and old Brigham knows as well as I what I am doing, and sometimes a great deal better."

So, leaving my saddle and bridle with the wagons, we rode to the windward of the buffaloes, as usual, and when within a few hundred yards of them we dashed into the herd. I soon had thirteen laid out on the ground, the last one of which I had driven down close to the wagons, where the ladies were. It frightened some of the tender creatures to see the buffalo coming at full speed directly toward them;

but when he had got within fifty yards of one of the wagons, I shot him dead in his tracks. This made my sixty-ninth buffalo, and finished my third and last run, Comstock having killed forty-six.

As it was now late in the afternoon, Comstock and his backers gave up the idea that he could beat me, and thereupon the referees declared me the winner of the match, as well as the champion buffalo-hunter of the plains.[10]

On our way back to camp, we took with us some of the choice meat and finest heads. In this connection it will not be out of place to state that during the time I was hunting for the Kansas Pacific, I always brought into camp the best buffalo heads, and turned them over to the company, who found a very good use for them. They had them mounted in the best possible manner, and sent them to all the principal cities and railroad centers in the country, having them placed in prominent positions at the leading hotels, depots, and other public buildings, as a sort of trade-mark, or advertisement, of the Kansas Pacific Railroad; and to-day they attract the attention of the traveler almost everywhere. Whenever I am traveling over the country and see one of these trade-marks, I feel pretty certain that I was the cause of the death of the old fellow whose body it once ornamented, and many a wild and exciting hunt is thus called to mind.

[10]Poor Billy Comstock was afterwards treacherously murdered by the Indians. He and Sharpe Grover visited a village of Indians, supposed to be peaceably inclined, near Big Spring Station, in Western Kansas; and after spending several hours with the redskins in friendly conversation, they prepared to depart, having declined an invitation to pass the night there. It appears that Comstock's beautiful white-handled revolver had attracted the attention of the Indians, who overtook him and his companion when they had gone about half a mile. After surrounding the two men they suddenly attacked them. They killed, scalped and robbed Comstock; but Grover, although severely wounded, made his escape, owing to the fleetness of the excellent horse which he was riding. This sad event occurred August 27, 1868.

CHAPTER EIGHT
The Perils of Pollution

A FABLE FOR TOMORROW[1]
Rachel Carson

Rachel Carson (1907–1964) was an American biologist and author. *Silent Spring* (1962), about the dangers of pesticides, probably did more than any other single work to wake up Americans to the ecological crisis.

There was once a town in the heart of America where all life seemed to live in harmony with its surroundings. The town lay in the midst of a checkerboard of prosperous farms, with fields of grain and

[1]"A Fable for Tomorrow" from *Silent Spring* by Rachel Carson. Copyright © 1962 by Rachel L. Carson. Reprinted by permission of Houghton Mifflin Company.

hillsides of orchards where, in spring, white clouds of bloom drifted above the green fields. In autumn, oak and maple and birch set up a blaze of color that flamed and flickered across a backdrop of pines. Then foxes barked in the hills and deer silently crossed the fields, half hidden in the mists of the fall mornings.

Along the roads, laurel, viburnum and alder, great ferns and wildflowers delighted the traveler's eye through much of the year. Even in winter the roadsides were places of beauty, where countless birds came to feed on the berries and on the seed heads of the dried weeds rising above the snow. The countryside was, in fact, famous for the abundance and variety of its bird life, and when the flood of migrants was pouring through in spring and fall people traveled from great distances to observe them. Others came to fish the streams, which flowed clear and cold out of the hills and contained shady pools where trout lay. So it had been from the days many years ago when the first settlers raised their houses, sank their wells, and built their barns.

Then a strange blight crept over the area and everything began to change. Some evil spell had settled on the community: mysterious maladies swept the flocks of chickens; the cattle and sheep sickened and died. Everywhere was a shadow of death. The farmers spoke of much illness among their families. In the town the doctors had become more and more puzzled by new kinds of sickness appearing among their patients. There had been several sudden and unexplained deaths, not only among adults but even among children, who would be stricken suddenly while at play and die within a few hours.

There was a strange stillness. The birds, for example—where had they gone? Many people spoke of them, puzzled and disturbed. The feeding stations in the backyards were deserted. The few birds seen anywhere were moribund; they trembled violently and could not fly. It was a spring without voices. On the mornings that had once throbbed with the dawn chorus of robins, catbirds, doves, jays, wrens, and scores of other bird voices there was now no sound; only silence lay over the fields and woods and marsh.

On the farms the hens brooded, but no chicks hatched. The farmers complained that they were unable to raise any pigs—the litters were small and the young survived only a few days. The apple trees were coming into bloom but no bees droned among the blossoms, so there was no pollination and there would be no fruit.

The roadsides, once so attractive, were now lined with browned and withered vegetation as though swept by fire. These, too, were silent, deserted by all living things. Even the streams were now lifeless. Anglers no longer visited them, for all the fish had died.

In the gutters under the eaves and between the shingles of the roofs, a white granular powder still showed a few patches; some weeks before it had fallen like snow upon the roofs and the lawns, the fields and streams.

No witchcraft, no enemy action had silenced the rebirth of new life in this stricken world. The people had done it themselves.

This town does not actually exist, but it might easily have a thousand counterparts in America or elsewhere in the world. I know of no community that has experienced all the misfortunes I describe. Yet every one of these disasters has actually happened somewhere, and many real communities have already suffered a substantial number of them. A grim specter has crept upon us almost unnoticed, and this imagined tragedy may easily become a stark reality we all shall know.

What has already silenced the voices of spring in countless towns in America? This book is an attempt to explain.

ECO-CATASTROPHE![2]
Dr. Paul Ehrlich

Paul Ehrlich is professor of biology at Stanford and author of *The Population Bomb.* The article "Eco-Catastrophe" first appeared in *Ramparts,* September, 1969.

[I.]

The end of the ocean came late in the summer of 1979, and it came even more rapidly than the biologists had expected. There had been signs for more than a decade, commencing with the discovery in

[2]"Eco-Catastrophe," by Paul Ehrlich. Copyright Paul Ehrlich. Reprinted with permission of the author.

1968 that DDT slows down photosynthesis in marine plant life. It was announced in a short paper in the technical journal, Science, but to ecologists it smacked of doomsday. They knew that all life in the sea depends on photosynthesis, the chemical process by which green plants bind the sun's energy and make it available to living things. And they knew that DDT and similar chlorinated hydrocarbons had polluted the entire surface of the earth, including the sea.

But that was only the first of many signs. There had been the final gasp of the whaling industry in 1973, and the end of the Peruvian anchovy fishery in 1975. Indeed, a score of other fisheries had disappeared quietly from over-exploitation and various eco-catastrophes by 1977. The term "eco-catastrophe" was coined by a California ecologist in 1969 to describe the most spectacular of man's attacks on the systems which sustain his life. He drew his inspiration from the Santa Barbara offshore oil disaster of that year, and from the news which spread among naturalists that virtually all of the Golden State's seashore bird life was doomed because of chlorinated hydrocarbon interference with its reproduction. Eco-catastrophes in the sea became increasingly common in the early 1970s. Mysterious "blooms" of previously rare microorganisms began to appear in offshore waters. Red tides—killer outbreaks of a minute single-celled plant—returned to the Florida Gulf coast and were sometimes accompanied by tides of other exotic hues.

It was clear by 1975 that the entire ecology of the ocean was changing. A few types of phytoplankton were becoming resistant to chlorinated hydrocarbons and were gaining the upper hand. Changes in the phytoplankton community led inevitably to changes in the community of zooplankton, the tiny animals which eat the phytoplankton. These changes were passed on up the chains of life in the ocean to the herring, plaice, cod and tuna. As the diversity of life in the ocean diminished, its stability also decreased.

Other changes had taken place by 1975. Most ocean fishes that returned to fresh water to breed, like the salmon, had become extinct, their breeding streams so dammed up and polluted that their powerful homing instinct only resulted in suicide. Many fishes and shellfishes that bred in restricted areas along the coasts followed them as onshore pollution escalated.

By 1977 the annual yield of fish from the sea was down to 30 million metric tons, less than one-half the per capita catch of a decade earlier. This helped malnutrition to escalate sharply in a world where an estimated 50 million people per year were already dying of starvation. The United Nations attempted to get all chlorinated hydrocarbon insecticides banned on a worldwide basis, but the move was defeated by the United States. This opposition was generated primarily by the American petrochemical industry, operating hand in glove with its subsidiary, the United States Department of Agriculture. Together they persuaded the government to oppose the U.N. move—which was not difficult since most Americans believed that Russia and China were more in need of fish products than was the United States. The United Nations also attempted to get fishing nations to adopt strict and enforced catch limits to preserve dwindling stocks. This move was blocked by Russia, who, with the most modern electronic equipment, was in the best position to glean what was left in the sea. It was, curiously, on the very day in 1977 when the Soviet Union announced its refusal that another ominous article appeared in Science. It announced that incident solar radiation had been so reduced by worldwide air pollution that serious effects on the world's vegetation could be expected.

[**II.**]

Apparently it was a combination of ecosystem destabilization, sunlight reduction, and a rapid escalation in chlorinated hydrocarbon pollution from massive Thanodrin applications which triggered the ultimate catastrophe. Seventeen huge Soviet-financed Thanodrin plants were operating in underdeveloped countries by 1978. They had been part of a massive Russian "aid offensive" designed to fill the gap caused by the collapse of America's ballyhooed "Green Revolution."

It became apparent in the early '70s that the "Green Revolution" was more talk than substance. Distribution of high yield "miracle" grain seeds had caused temporary local spurts in agricultural production. Simultaneously, excellent weather had produced record harvests. The combination permitted bureaucrats, especially in the

United States Department of Agriculture and the Agency for International Development (AID), to reverse their previous pessimism and indulge in an outburst of optimistic propaganda about staving off famine. They raved about the approaching transformation of agriculture in the underdeveloped countries (UDCs). The reason for the propaganda reversal was never made clear. Most historians agree that a combination of utter ignorance of ecology, a desire to justify past errors, and pressure from agro-industry (which was eager to sell pesticides, fertilizers, and farm machinery to the UDCs and agencies helping the UDCs) was behind the campaign. Whatever the motivation, the results were clear. Many concerned people, lacking the expertise to see through the Green Revolution drivel, relaxed. The population-food crisis was "solved."

But reality was not long in showing itself. Local famine persisted in northern India even after good weather brought an end to the ghastly Bihar famine of the mid-'60s. East Pakistan was next, followed by a resurgence of general famine in northern India. Other foci of famine rapidly developed in Indonesia, the Philippines, Malawi, the Congo, Egypt, Colombia, Ecuador, Honduras, the Dominican Republic, and Mexico.

Everywhere hard realities destroyed the illusion of the Green Revolution. Yields dropped as the progressive farmers who had first accepted the new seeds found that their higher yields brought lower prices—effective demand (hunger plus cash) was not sufficient in poor countries to keep prices up. Less progressive farmers, observing this, refused to make the extra effort required to cultivate the "miracle" grains. Transport systems proved inadequate to bring the necessary fertilizer to the fields where the new and extremely fertilizer-sensitive grains were being grown. The same systems were also inadequate to move produce to markets. Fertilizer plants were not built fast enough, and most of the underdeveloped countries could not scrape together funds to purchase supplies, even on concessional terms. Finally, the inevitable happened, and pests began to reduce yields in even the most carefully cultivated fields. Among the first were the famous "miracle rats" which invaded Philippine "miracle rice" fields early in 1969. They were quickly followed by many insects and viruses, thriving on the relatively pest-susceptible new grains, encouraged by the vast and dense plantings, and rapidly acquiring resistance to the chemicals used against them. As chaos spread until even the most obtuse agriculturists and economists realized that the Green Revolution had turned brown, the Russians stepped in.

In retrospect it seems incredible that the Russians, with the American mistakes known to them, could launch an even more incompetent program of aid to the underdeveloped world. Indeed, in the early 1970s there were cynics in the United States who claimed that outdoing the stupidity of American foreign aid would be physically impossible. Those critics were, however, obviously unaware that the Russians had been busily destroying their own environment for many years. The virtual disappearance of sturgeon from Russian rivers caused a great shortage of caviar by 1970. A standard joke among Russian scientists at that time was that they had created an artificial caviar which was indistinguishable from the real thing—except by taste. At any rate the Soviet Union, observing with interest the progressive deterioration of relations between the UDCs and the United States, came up with a solution. It had recently developed what it claimed was the ideal insecticide, a highly lethal chlorinated hydrocarbon complexed with a special agent for penetrating the external skeletal armor of insects. Announcing that the new pesticide, called Thanodrin, would truly produce a Green Revolution, the Soviets entered into negotiations with various UDCs for the construction of massive Thanodrin factories. The USSR would bear all the costs; all it wanted in return were certain trade and military concessions.

It is interesting now, with the perspective of years, to examine in some detail the reasons why the UDCs welcomed the Thanodrin plan with such open arms. Government officials in these countries ignored the protests of their own scientists that Thanodrin would not solve the problems which plagued them. The governments now knew that the basic cause of their problems was overpopulation, and that these problems had been exacerbated by the dullness, daydreaming, and cupidity endemic to all governments. They knew that only population control and limited development aimed primarily at agriculture could have spared them the horrors they now faced. They knew it, but they were not about to admit it. How much easier it was simply to accuse the Americans of failing to give them proper aid; how much simpler to accept the Russian panacea.

And then there was the general worsening of relations between the United States and the UDCs. Many things had contributed to this. The situation in America in the first half of the 1970s deserves our close scrutiny. Being more dependent on imports for raw materials than the Soviet Union, the United States had, in the early 1970s, adopted more and more heavy-handed policies in order to insure continuing supplies. Military adventures in Asia and Latin America had further lessened the international credibility of the United States as a great defender of freedom—an image which had begun to deteriorate rapidly during the pointless and fruitless Viet-Nam conflict. At home, acceptance of the carefully manufactured image lessened dramatically, as even the more romantic and chauvinistic citizens began to understand the role of the military and the industrial system in what John Kenneth Galbraith had aptly named "The New Industrial State."

At home in the USA the early '70s were traumatic times. Racial violence grew and the habitability of the cities diminished, as nothing substantial was done to ameliorate either racial inequities or urban blight. Welfare rolls grew as automation and general technological progress forced more and more people into the category of "unemployable." Simultaneously a taxpayers' revolt occurred. Although there was not enough money to build the schools, roads, water systems, sewage systems, jails, hospitals, urban transit lines, and all the other amenities needed to support a burgeoning population. Americans refused to tax themselves more heavily. Starting in Youngstown, Ohio in 1969 and followed closely by Richmond, California, community after community was forced to close its schools or curtail educational operations for lack of funds. Water supplies, already marginal in quality and quantity in many places by 1970, deteriorated quickly. Water rationing occurred in 1723 municipalities in the summer of 1974, and hepatitis and epidemic dysentery rates climbed about 500 per cent between 1970-1974.

[III.]

Air pollution continued to be the most obvious manifestation of environmental deterioration. It was, by 1972, quite literally in the eyes of all Americans. The year 1973 saw not only the New York and Los Angeles smog disasters, but also the publication of the Surgeon

General's massive report on air pollution and health. The public had been partially prepared for the worst by the publicity given to the U. N. pollution conference held in 1972. Deaths in the late '60s caused by smog were well known to scientists, but the public had ignored them because they mostly involved the early demise of the old and sick rather than people dropping dead on the freeways. But suddenly our citizens were faced with nearly 200,000 corpses and massive documentation that they could be the next to die from respiratory disease. They were not ready for that scale of disaster. After all, the U. N. conference had not predicted that accumulated air pollution would make the planet uninhabitable until almost 1990. The population was terrorized as TV screens became filled with scenes of horror from the disaster areas. Especially vivid was NBC's coverage of hundreds of unattended people choking out their lives outside of New York's hospitals. Terms like nitrogen oxide, acute bronchitis and cardiac arrest began to have real meaning for most Americans.

The ultimate horror was the announcement that chlorinated hydrocarbons were now a major constituent of air pollution in all American cities. Autopsies of smog disaster victims revealed an average chlorinated hydrocarbon load in fatty tissue equivalent to 26 parts per million of DDT. In October, 1973, the Department of Health, Education and Welfare announced studies which showed unequivocally that increasing death rates from hypertension, cirrhosis of the liver, liver cancer and a series of other diseases had resulted from the chlorinated hydrocarbon load. They estimated that Americans born since 1946 (when DDT usage began) now had a life expectancy of only 49 years, and predicted that if current patterns continued, this expectancy would reach 42 years by 1980, when it might level out. Plunging insurance stocks triggered a stock market panic. The president of Velsicol, Inc., a major pesticide producer, went on television to "publicly eat a teaspoonful of DDT" (it was really powdered milk) and announce that HEW had been infiltrated by Communists. Other giants of the petrochemical industry, attempting to dispute the indisputable evidence, launched a massive pressure campaign on Congress to force HEW to "get out of agriculture's business." They were aided by the agro-chemical journals, which had decades of experience in misleading the public about the benefits and dangers of pesticides. But by now the public realized that it had been duped. The Nobel Prize for medicine and physiology was given to Drs. J. L. Radomski and W. B. Deichmann, who in the late 1960s had pioneered in the documentation of the long-term lethal effects of chlorinated hydrocarbons. A Presidential Commission with unimpeachable credentials directly accused the agro-chemical complex of "condemning many millions of Americans to an early death." The year 1973 was the year in which Americans finally came to understand the direct threat to their existence posed by environmental deterioration.

And 1973 was also the year in which most people finally comprehended the indirect threat. Even the president of Union Oil Company and several other industrialists publicly stated their concern over the reduction of bird populations which had resulted from pollution by DDT and other chlorinated hydrocarbons. Insect populations boomed because they were resistant to most pesticides and had been freed, by the incompetent use of those pesticides, from most of their natural enemies. Rodents swarmed over crops, multiplying rapidly in the absence of predatory birds. The effect of pests on the wheat crop was especially disastrous in the summer of 1973, since that was also the year of the great drought. Most of us can remember the shock which greeted the announcement by atmospheric physicists that the shift of the jet stream which had caused the drought was probably permanent. It signalled the birth of the Midwestern desert. Man's air-polluting activities had by then caused gross changes in climatic patterns. The news, of course, played hell with commodity and stock markets. Food prices skyrocketed, as savings were poured into hoarded canned goods. Official assurances that food supplies would remain ample fell on deaf ears, and even the government showed signs of nervousness when California migrant field workers went out on strike again in protest against the continued use of pesticides by growers. The strike burgeoned into farm burning and riots. The workers, calling themselves "The Walking Dead," demanded immediate compensation for their shortened lives, and crash research programs to attempt to lengthen them.

It was in the same speech in which President Edward Kennedy, after much delay, finally declared a national emergency and called out the National Guard to harvest California's crops, that the first mention of population control was made. Kennedy pointed out that the United States would no longer be able to offer any food aid to other nations and was likely to suffer food shortages herself. He suggested that, in view of the manifest failure of the Green Revolution, the only hope of the UDCs lay in population control. His statement, you will recall, created an uproar in the underdeveloped countries. Newspaper editorials accused the United States of wishing to prevent small countries from becoming large nations and thus threatening American hegemony. Politicians asserted that President Kennedy was a "creature of the giant drug combine" that wished to shove its pills down every woman's throat.

Among Americans, religious opposition to population control was very slight. Industry in general also backed the idea. Increasing poverty in the UDCs was both destroying markets and threatening supplies of raw materials. The seriousness of the raw material situation had been brought home during the Congressional Hard Resources hearings in 1971. The exposure of the ignorance of the cornucopian economists had been quite a spectacle—a spectacle brought into virtually every American's home in living color. Few would forget the distinguished geologist from the University of California who suggested that economists be legally required to learn at least the most elementary facts of geology. Fewer still would forget that an equally distinguished Harvard economist added that they might be required to learn some economics, too. The overall message was clear: America's resource situation was bad and bound to get worse. The hearings had led to a bill requiring the Departments of State, Interior, and Commerce to set up a joint resource procurement council with the express purpose of "insuring that proper consideration of American resource needs be an integral part of American foreign policy."

Suddenly the United States discovered that it had a national consensus: population control was the only possible salvation of the underdeveloped world. But that same consensus led to heated debate. How could the UDCs be persuaded to limit their populations, and should not the United States lead the way by limiting its own? Members of the intellectual community wanted America to set an example. They pointed out that the United States was in the midst of a new baby boom: her birth rate, well over 20 per thousand per year, and her growth rate of over one per cent per annum were among the very highest of the developed countries. They detailed the deterioration of the American physical and psychic environments, the growing health threats, the impending food shortages, and the insufficiency of funds for desperately needed public works. They contended that the nation was clearly unable or unwilling to properly care for the people it already had. What possible reason could there be, they queried, for adding any more? Besides, who would listen to requests by the United States for population control when that nation did not control her own profligate reproduction?

Those who opposed population controls for the U. S. were equally vociferous. The military-industrial complex, with its all-too-human mixture of ignorance and avarice, still saw strength and prosperity in numbers. Baby food magnates, already worried by the growing nitrate pollution of their products, saw their market disappearing. Steel manufacturers saw a decrease in aggregate demand and slippage for that holy of holies, the Gross National Product. And military men saw, in the growing population-food-environment crisis, a serious threat to their carefully nurtured Cold War. In the end, of course, economic arguments held sway, and the "inalienable right of every American couple to determine the size of its family," a freedom invented for the occasion in the early '70s, was not compromised.

The population control bill, which was passed by Congress early in 1974, was quite a document, nevertheless. On the domestic front, it authorized an increase from 100 to 150 million dollars in funds for "family planning" activities. This was made possible by a general feeling in the country that the growing army on welfare needed family planning. But the gist of the bill was a series of measures designed to impress the need for population control on the UDCs. All American aid to countries with overpopulation problems was required by law to consist in part of population control assistance. In order to receive any assistance each nation was required not only to accept the population control aid, but also to match it according to a complex formula. "Overpopulation" itself was defined by a formula based on U. N. statistics, and the UDCs were required not only to accept aid, but also to show progress in reducing birth rates. Every five years the status of the aid program for each nation was to be re-evaluated.

The reaction to the announcement of this program dwarfed the response to President Kennedy's speech. A coalition of UDCs attempted to get the U. N. General Assembly to condemn the United

States as a "genetic aggressor." Most damaging of all to the American cause was the famous "25 Indians and a dog" speech by Mr. Shankarnarayan, Indian Ambassador to the U. N. Shankarnarayan pointed out that for several decades the United States, with less than six per cent of the people of the world had consumed roughly 50 per cent of the raw materials used every year. He described vividly America's contribution to worldwide environmental deterioration, and he scathingly denounced the miserly record of United States foreign aid as "unworthy of a fourth-rate power, let alone the most powerful nation on earth."

It was the climax of his speech, however, which most historians claim once and for all destroyed the image of the United States. Shankarnarayan informed the assembly that the average American family dog was fed more animal protein per week than the average Indian got in a month. "How do you justify taking fish from protein-starved Peruvians and feeding them to your animals?" he asked. "I contend," he concluded, "that the birth of an American baby is a greater disaster for the world than that of 25 Indian babies." When the applause had died away, Mr. Sorensen, the American representative, made a speech which said essentially that "other countries look after their own self-interest, too." When the vote came, the United States was condemned.

[IV.]

This condemnation set the tone of U. S.-UDC relations at the time the Russian Thanodrin proposal was made. The proposal seemed to offer the masses in the UDCs an opportunity to save themselves and humiliate the United States at the same time; and in human affairs, as we all know, biological realities could never interfere with such an opportunity. The scientists were silenced, the politicians said yes, the Thanodrin plants were built, and the results were what any beginning ecology student could have predicted. At first Thanodrin seemed to offer excellent control of many pests. True, there was a rash of human fatalities from improper use of the lethal chemical, but, as Russian technical advisors were prone to note, these were more than compensated for by increased yields. Thanodrin use skyrocketed throughout the underdeveloped world. The Mikoyan design group developed a dependable, cheap agricultural aircraft which the Soviets donated to the effort in large numbers. MIG sprayers became even more common in UDCs than MIG interceptors.

Then the troubles began. Insect strains with cuticles resistant to Thanodrin penetration began to appear. And as streams, rivers, fish culture ponds and onshore waters became rich in Thanodrin, more fisheries began to disappear. Bird populations were decimated. The sequence of events was standard for broadcast use of a synthetic pesticide: great success at first, followed by removal of natural enemies and development of resistance by the pest. Populations of crop-eating insects in areas treated with Thanodrin made steady comebacks and soon became more abundant than ever. Yields plunged, while farmers in their desperation increased the Thanodrin dose and shortened the time between treatments. Death from Thanodrin poisoning became common. The first violent incident occurred in the Canete Valley of Peru, where farmers had suffered a similar chlorinated hydrocarbon disaster in the mid-'50s. A Russian advisor serving as an agricultural pilot was assaulted and killed by a mob of enraged farmers in January, 1978. Trouble spread rapidly during 1978, especially after the word got out that two years earlier Russia herself had banned the use of Thanodrin at home because of its serious effects on ecological systems. Suddenly Russia, and not the United States, was the *bête noir* in the UDCs. "Thanodrin parties" became epidemic, with farmers, in their ignorance, dumping carloads of Thanodrin concentrate into the sea. Russian advisors fled, and four of the Thanodrin plants were leveled to the ground. Destruction of the plants in Rio and Calcutta led to hundreds of thousands of gallons of Thanodrin concentrate being dumped directly into the sea.

Mr. Shankarnarayan again rose to address the U. N., but this time it was Mr. Potemkin, representative of the Soviet Union, who was on the hot seat. Mr. Potemkin heard his nation described as the greatest mass killer of all time as Shankarnarayan predicted at least 30 million deaths from crop failures due to overdependence on Thanodrin. Russia was accused of "chemical aggression," and the General Assembly, after a weak reply by Potemkin, passed a vote of censure.

It was in January, 1979, that huge blooms of a previously unknown variety of diatom were reported off the coast of Peru. The blooms were accompanied by a massive die-off of sea life and of the pathetic remainder of the birds which had once feasted on the anchovies of the area. Almost immediately another huge bloom was reported in the Indian ocean, centering around the Seychelles, and then a third in the South Atlantic off the African coast. Both of these were accompanied by spectacular die-offs of marine animals. Even more ominous were growing reports of fish and bird kills at oceanic points where there were no spectacular blooms: Biologists were soon able to explain the phenomena: the diatom had evolved an enzyme which broke down Thanodrin; that enzyme also produced a breakdown product which interfered with the transmission of nerve impulses, and was therefore lethal to animals. Unfortunately, the biologists could suggest no way of repressing the poisonous diatom bloom in time. By September, 1979, all important animal life in the sea was extinct. Large areas of coastline had to be evacuated, as windrows of dead fish created a monumental stench.

But stench was the least of man's problems. Japan and China were faced with almost instant starvation from a total loss of the seafood on which they were so dependent. Both blamed Russia for their situation and demanded immediate mass shipments of food. Russia had none to send. On October 13, Chinese armies attacked Russia on a broad front. . . .

[V.]

A pretty grim scenario. Unfortunately, we're a long way into it already. Everything mentioned as happening before 1970 has actually occurred; much of the rest is based on projections of trends already appearing. Evidence that pesticides have long-term lethal effects on human beings has started to accumulate, and recently Robert Finch, Secretary of the Department of Health, Education and Welfare expressed his extreme apprehension about the pesticide situation. Simultaneously the petrochemical industry continues its unconscionable poison-peddling. For instance, Shell Chemical has been carrying on a high-pressure campaign to sell the insecticide Azodrin to farmers as a killer of cotton pests. They continue their program even though they know that Azodrin is not only ineffective, but often *increases* the pest density. They've covered themselves nicely in an advertisement which states, "Even if an overpowering migration [sic] develops, the flexibility of Azodrin lets you regain control fast. Just increase the dosage according to label recommendations." It's a great game—get people to apply the poison and kill the natural enemies of the pests. Then blame the increased pests on "migration" and sell even more pesticide!

Right now fisheries are being wiped out by over-exploitation, made easy by modern electronic equipment. The companies producing the equipment know this. They even boast in advertising that only their equipment will keep fishermen in business until the final kill. Profits must obviously be maximized in the short run. Indeed, Western society is in the process of completing the rape and murder of the planet for economic gain. And, sadly, most of the rest of the world is eager for the opportunity to emulate our behavior. But the underdeveloped peoples will be denied that opportunity—the days of plunder are drawing inexorably to a close.

Most of the people who are going to die in the greatest cataclysm in the history of man have already been born. More than three and a half billion people already populate our moribund globe, and about half of them are hungry. Some 10 to 20 million will starve to death *this year.* In spite of this, the population of the earth will increase by 70 million souls in 1969. For mankind has artificially lowered the death rate of the human population, while in general birth rates have remained high. With the input side of the population system in high gear and the output side slowed down, our fragile planet has filled with people at an incredible rate. It took several million years for the population to reach a total of two billion people in 1930, while a *second two billion will have been added by 1975!* By that time some experts feel that food shortages will have escalated the present level of world hunger and starvation into famines of unbelievable proportions. Other experts, more optimistic, think the ultimate food-population collision will not occur until the decade of the 1980s. Of course more massive famine may be avoided if other events cause a prior rise in the human death rate.

Both worldwide plague and thermonuclear war are made more probable as population growth continues. These, along with famine, make up the trio of potential "death rate solutions" to the population problem—solutions in which the birth rate–death rate imbalance is redressed by a rise in the death rate rather than by a lowering of the birth rate. Make no mistake about it, *the imbalance will be redressed.* The shape of the population growth curve is one familiar to the biologist. It is the outbreak part of an outbreak-crash sequence. A population grows rapidly in the presence of abundant resources, finally runs out of food or some other necessity, and crashes to a low level or extinction. Man is not only running out of food, he is also destroying the life support systems of the Spaceship Earth. The situation was recently summarized very succinctly: "It is the top of the ninth inning. Man, always a threat at the plate, has been hitting Nature hard. It is important to remember, however, that NATURE BATS LAST."

TRAVELS WITH CHARLEY[3]
John Steinbeck

American cities are like badger holes, ringed with trash—all of them—surrounded by piles of wrecked and rusting automobiles, and almost smothered with rubbish. Everything we use comes in boxes, cartons, bins, the so-called packaging we love so much. The mountains of things we throw away are much greater than the things we use. In this, if in no other way, we can see the wild and reckless exuberance of our production, and waste seems to be the index. Driving along I thought how in France or Italy every item of these thrown-out things would have been saved and used for something. This is not said in criticism of one system or the other but I do wonder whether there will come a time when we can no longer afford our wastefulness—chemical wastes in the rivers, metal wastes everywhere, and atomic wastes buried deep in the earth or sunk in the sea. When an Indian village became too deep in its own filth, the inhabitants moved. And we have no place to which to move.

The new American finds his challenge and his love in traffic-choked streets, skies nested in smog, choking with the acids of industry, the screech of rubber and houses leashed in against one another while the townlets wither a time and die. And this, as I found, is as true in Texas as in Maine. Clarendon yields to Amarillo just as surely as Stacyville, Maine, bleeds its substance into Millinocket, where the logs are ground up, the air smells of chemicals, the rivers are choked and poisoned, and the streets swarm with this happy, hurrying breed. This is not offered in criticism but only as observation. And I am sure that, as all pendulums reverse their swing, so eventually will the swollen cities rupture like dehiscent wombs and disperse their children back to the countryside. This prophecy is underwritten by the tendency of the rich to do this already. Where the rich lead, the poor will follow, or try to.

IN THE PARK WITH LAO-TSE[4]
Bert Almon

reading in the grass, asphalt-bounded pastoral
green simplicity with buried sprinklers
bombers climb from a nearby field
trailing the thunder of a collapsing tunnel

Samson's temple grown into a world
with no wilderness safe for sages
just a park with shaking roof
sonic booms hammer a hard proverb:

Bend a bow until it bends no more
and you'll wish you'd stopped before.

MOUTH OF THE HUDSON[5]
Robert Lowell

Robert Lowell (1917–) was born in Boston, the descendant of New England's earliest colonists. His collection of verse, *Lord Weary's Castle*, received the Pulitzer Prize in 1947. During World

---

War II he refused to register for the draft, and served five months in prison. He was active in the Vietnam Peace Movement as well, traveling extensively with Eugene McCarthy during the 1968 presidential primaries, and participating in the March on the Pentagon memorialized in Norman Mailer's *Armies of the Night*.

A single man stands like a bird-watcher,
and scuffles the pepper and salt snow
from a discarded, gray
Westinghouse Electric cable drum.
He cannot discover America by counting
the chains of condemned freight-trains
from thirty states. They jolt and jar
and junk in the siding below him.
He has trouble with his balance.
His eyes drop,
and he drifts with the wild ice
ticking seaward down the Hudson,
like the blank sides of a jig-saw puzzle.

The ice ticks seaward like a clock.
A negro toasts
wheat-seeds over the coke-fumes
in a punctured barrel.
Chemical air
creeps in from New Jersey,
and smells of coffee.

CHAPTER NINE
Urban Blight

MARTIN CHUZZLEWIT
Charles Dickens

Charles Dickens (1812–1870) was one of England's greatest novelists. The strangulation of urban life and the horrors of industrialization were repeated themes in Dickens's work. His novels did a great deal to bring social reforms. *Martin Chuzzlewit* is chiefly of interest to American readers for its fascinating, if highly negative, picture of the United States in the mid-nineteenth century. *The Old Curiosity Shop,* a sentimental novel about the trials of saintly Little Nell, shows the horrors of city life. *Little Dorrit* depicts the degradation of debtor's prison.

Chapter IX   Town and Todgers's

Surely there never was, in any other borough, city, or hamlet in the world, such a singular sort of a place as Todgers's. And surely London, to judge from that part of it which hemmed Todgers's round, and hustled it, and crushed it, and stuck its brick-and-mortar elbows into it, and kept the air from it, and stood perpetually between it and the light, was worthy of Todgers's, and qualified to be on terms of close relationship and alliance with hundreds and thousands of the odd family to which Todgers's belonged.

You couldn't walk about in Todgers's neighbourhood, as you could in any other neighbourhood. You groped your way for an hour through lanes and bye-ways, and court-yards, and passages; and you never once emerged upon anything that might be reasonably called a street. A kind of resigned distraction came over the stranger as he trod those devious mazes, and, giving himself up for lost, went in and out and round about and quietly turned back again when he came to a dead wall or was stopped by an iron railing, and felt that the means of escape might possibly present themselves in their own good time, but that to anticipate them was hopeless. Instances were known of people who, being asked to dine at Todgers's, had travelled round and round for a weary time, with its very chimney-pots in view; and finding it, at last, impossible of attainment, had gone home again with a gentle melancholy on their spirits, tranquil and uncomplaining. Nobody had ever found Todgers's on a verbal direction, though given within a minute's walk of it. Cautious emigrants from Scotland or the North of England had been known to reach it safely, by impressing a charity-boy, town-bred, and bringing him along with them; or by clinging tenaciously to the postman; but these were rare exceptions, and only went to prove the rule that Todgers's was in a labyrinth, whereof the mystery was known but to a chosen few.

Several fruit-brokers had their marts near Todgers's; and one of the first impressions wrought upon the stranger's senses was of oranges—of damaged oranges, with blue and green bruises on them, festering in boxes, or mouldering away in cellars. All day long, a stream of porters from the wharves beside the river, each bearing on his back a bursting chest of oranges, poured slowly through the narrow passages; while underneath the archway by the public-house, the knots of those who rested and regaled within, were piled from morning until night. Strange solitary pumps were found near Todgers's hiding themselves for the most part in blind alleys, and keeping company with fire-ladders. There were churches also by dozens, with many a ghostly little churchyard, all overgrown with such straggling vegetation as springs up spontaneously from damp, and graves, and rubbish. In some of these dingy resting-places, which bore much the same analogy to green churchyards, as the pots of earth for mignonette and wall-flower in the windows overlooking them, did to rustic gardens, there were trees; tall trees; still putting forth their leaves in each succeeding year, with such a languishing remembrance of their kind (so one might fancy, looking on their sickly boughs) as birds in cages have of theirs. Here, paralysed old watchmen guarded the bodies of the dead at night, year after year, until at last they joined that solemn brotherhood; and, saving that they slept below the ground a sounder sleep than even they had ever known above it, and were shut up in another kind of box, their condition can hardly be said to have undergone any material change when they in turn were watched themselves.

Among the narrow thoroughfares at hand, there lingered, here and there, an ancient doorway of carved oak, from which, of old, the sounds of revelry and feasting often came; but now these mansions, only used for storehouses, were dark and dull, and, being filled with wool, and cotton, and the like—such heavy merchandise as stifles sound and stops the throat of echo—had an air of palpable deadness about them which, added to their silence and desertion, made them very grim. In like manner, there were gloomy court-yards in these parts, into which few but belated wayfarers ever strayed, and where vast bags and packs of goods, upward or downward bound, were for ever dangling between heaven and earth from lofty cranes. There were more trucks near Todgers's than you would suppose a whole city could ever need; not active trucks, but a vagabond race, for ever lounging in the narrow lanes before their masters' doors and stopping up the pass; so that when a stray hackney-coach or lumbering waggon came that way, they were the cause of such an uproar as enlivened the whole neighbourhood, and made the bells in the next church-tower vibrate again. In the throats and maws of dark no-thoroughfares near Todgers's, individual wine-merchants and wholesale dealers in grocery-ware had perfect little towns of their own; and, deep among the foundations of these buildings, the ground was undermined and burrowed out into stables, where cart-horses, troubled by rats, might be heard on a quiet Sunday rattling their halters, as disturbed spirits in tales of haunted houses are said to clank their chains.

To tell of half the queer old taverns that had a drowsy and secret existence near Todgers's, would fill a goodly book; while a second volume no less capacious might be devoted to an account of the quaint old guests who frequented their dimly-lighted parlours. These were, in general, ancient inhabitants of that region; born, and bred there from boyhood; who had long since become wheezy and asthmatical, and short of breath, except in the article of story-telling: in which respect they were still marvellously long-winded. These gentry were much opposed to steam and all new-fangled ways, and held ballooning to be sinful, and deplored the degeneracy of the times; which that particular member of each little club who kept the keys of the nearest church professionally, always attributed to the prevalence of dissent and irreligion: though the major part of the company inclined to the belief that virtue went out with hair-powder, and that Old England's greatness had decayed amain with barbers.

As to Todgers's itself—speaking of it only as a house in that neighbourhood, and making no reference to its merits as a commercial boarding establishment—it was worthy to stand where it did. There was one staircase-window in it: at the side of the house, on the ground-floor: which tradition said had not been opened for a hundred years at least, and which, abutting on an always dirty lane, was so begrimed and coated with a century's mud, that no one pane of glass could possibly fall out, though all were cracked and broken twenty times. But the grand mystery of Todgers's was the cellarage, approachable only by a little back door and a rusty grating: which cellarage within the memory of man had had no connexion with the house, but had always been the freehold property of somebody else, and was reported to be full of wealth: though in what shape—whether in silver, brass, or gold, or butts of wine, or casks of gunpowder—was matter of profound uncertainty and supreme indifference to Todgers's, and all its inmates.

The top of the house was worthy of notice. There was a sort of terrace on the roof, with posts and fragments of rotten lines, once intended to dry clothes upon; and there were two or three tea-chests out there, full of earth, with forgotten plants in them, like old walking-sticks. Whoever climbed to this observatory, was stunned at first from having knocked his head against the little door in coming out; and after that, was for the moment choked from having looked, perforce, straight down the kitchen chimney; but these two stages over, there were things to gaze at from the top of Todgers's, well worth your seeing too. For first and foremost, if the day were bright, you observed upon the house-tops, stretching far away, a long dark path: the shadow of the Monument: and turning round, the tall original was close beside you, with every hair erect upon his golden head, as if the doings of the city frightened him. Then there were steeples, towers, belfries, shining vanes, and masts of ships: a very forest. Gables, housetops, garret-windows, wilderness upon wilderness. Smoke and noise enough for all the world at once.

After the first glance, there were slight features in the midst of this crowd of objects, which sprung out from the mass without any reason, as it were, and took hold of the attention whether the spectator would or no. Thus, the revolving chimney-pots on one great stack of buildings, seemed to be turning gravely to each other every now and then, and whispering the result of their separate observation of what was going on below. Others, of a crook-backed shape, appeared to be maliciously holding themselves askew, that they might shut the prospect out and baffle Todgers's. The man who was mending a pen at an upper window over the way, became of paramount importance in the scene, and made a blank in it, ridiculously disproportionate in its extent, when he retired. The gambols of a piece of cloth upon the dyer's pole had far more interest for the moment than all the changing motion of the crowd. Yet even while the looker-on felt angry with himself for this, and wondered how it was, the tumult swelled into a roar; the hosts of objects seemed to thicken and expand a hundredfold; and after gazing round him, quite scared, he turned into Todgers's again, much more rapidly than he came out; and ten to one he told M. Todgers afterwards that if he hadn't done so, he would certainly have come into the street by the shortest cut: that is to say, headforemost.

LITTLE DORRIT
Charles Dickens

Chapter III   Home

It was a Sunday evening in London, gloomy, close and stale. Maddening church bells of all degrees of dissonance, sharp and flat, cracked and clear, fast and slow, made the brick-and-mortar echoes hideous. Melancholy streets in a penitential garb of soot, steeped the souls of the people who were condemned to look at them out of windows, in dire despondency. In every thoroughfare, up almost every alley, and down almost every turning, some doleful bell was throbbing, jerking, tolling, as if the Plague were in the city and the dead-carts were going round. Everything was bolted and barred that could by possibility furnish relief to an overworked people. No pictures, no unfamiliar animals, no rare plants or flowers, no natural or artificial wonders of the ancient world—all *taboo* with that enlightened strictness, that the ugly South Sea gods in the British Museum might have supposed themselves at home again. Nothing to see but streets, streets, streets. Nothing to breathe but streets, streets, streets. Nothing to change the brooding mind, or raise it up. Nothing for the spent toiler to do, but to compare the monotony of his seventh day with the monotony of his six days, think what a weary life he led, and make the best of it—or the worst, according to the probabilities.

At such a happy time, so propitious to the interests of religion and morality, Mr. Arthur Clennam, newly arrived from Marseilles by way of Dover, and by Dover coach the Blue-eyed Maid, sat in the window of a coffee-house on Ludgate Hill. Ten thousand responsible houses surrounded him, frowning as heavily on the streets they composed, as if they were every one inhabited by the ten young men of the Calendar's story, who blackened their faces and bemoaned their miseries every night. Fifty thousand lairs surrounded him where people lived so unwholesomely, that fair water put into their crowded rooms on Saturday night, would be corrupt on Sunday morning; albeit my lord, their county member, was amazed that they failed to sleep in company with their butcher's meat. Miles of close wells and pits of houses, where the inhabitants gasped for air, stretched far away towards every point of the compass. Through the heart of the town a deadly sewer ebbed and flowed, in the place of a fine fresh river. What secular want could the million or so of human beings whose daily labour, six days in the week, lay among these Arcadian objects, from the sweet sameness of which they had no escape between the cradle and the grave—what secular want could they possibly have upon their seventh day? Clearly they could want nothing but a stringent policeman.

Mr. Arthur Clennam sat in the window of the coffee-house on Ludgate Hill, counting one of the neighbouring bells, making sentences and burdens of songs out of it in spite of himself, and wondering how many sick people it might be the death of in the course of the year. As the hour approached, its changes of measure made it more and more exasperating. At the quarter, it went off into a condition of deadly-lively importunity, urging the populace in a voluble manner to Come to church, Come to church, Come to church! At the ten minutes, it became aware that the congregation would be scanty, and slowly hammered out in low spirits, They *won't* come, they *won't* come, they *won't* come! At the five minutes, it abandoned hope, and shook every house in the neighbourhood for three hundred seconds, with one dismal swing per second, as a groan of despair.

THE OLD CURIOSITY SHOP
Charles Dickens

Chapter XLV

In all their journeying, they[1] had never longed so ardently, they had never so pined and wearied, for the freedom of pure air and open country, as now. No, not even on that memorable morning, when, deserting their old home, they abandoned themselves to the mercies of a strange world, and left all the dumb and senseless things they had known and loved, behind—not even then, had they so yearned for the fresh solitudes of wood, hillside, and field, as now, when the noise and dirt and vapour of the great manufacturing town, reeking with lean misery and hungry wretchedness, hemmed them in on every side, and seemed to shut out hope, and render escape impossible.

[1] Nell Trent (Little Nell, the heroine), and her grandfather are traveling on foot from London towards western Europe.

"Two days and nights!" thought the child. "He said two days and nights we should have to spend among such scenes as these. Oh! if we live to reach the country once again, if we get clear of these dreadful places, though it is only to lie down and die, with what a grateful heart I shall thank God for so much mercy!"

With thoughts like this, and with some vague design of travelling to a great distance among streams and mountains, where only very poor and simple people lived, and where they might maintain themselves by very humble helping work in farms, free from such terrors as that from which they fled,—the child, with no resource but the poor man's gift, and no encouragement but that which flowed from her own heart, and its sense of the truth and right of what she did, nerved herself to this last journey and boldly pursued her task.

"We shall be very slow to-day, dear," she said, as they toiled painfully through the streets; "my feet are sore, and I have pains in all my limbs from the wet of yesterday. I saw that he looked at us and thought of that, when he said how long we should be upon the road."

"It was a dreary way he told us of," returned her grandfather, piteously. "Is there no other road? Will you not let me go some other way than this?"

"Places lie beyond these," said the child, firmly, "where we may live in peace, and be tempted to do no harm. We will take the road that promises to have that end, and we would not turn out of it, if it were a hundred times worse than our fears lead us to expect. We would not, dear, would we?"

"No," replied the old man, wavering in his voice, no less than in his manner. "No. Let us go on. I am ready. I am quite ready, Nell."

The child walked with more difficulty than she had led her companion to expect, for the pains that racked her joints were of no common severity, and every exertion increased them. But they wrung from her no complaint, or look of suffering: and, though the two travellers proceeded very slowly, they did proceed. Clearing the town in course of time, they began to feel that they were fairly on their way.

A long suburb of red-brick houses,—some with patches of garden-ground, where coal-dust and factory smoke darkened the shrinking leaves, and coarse rank flowers, and where the struggling vegetation sickened and sank under the hot breath of kiln and furnace, making them by its presence seem yet more blighting and unwholesome than in the town itself,—a long, flat, straggling suburb passed, they came, by slow degrees, upon a cheerless region, where not a blade of grass was seen to grow, where not a bud put forth its promise in the spring, where nothing green could live but on the surface of the stagnant pools, which here and there lay idly sweltering by the black roadside.

Advancing more and more into the shadow of this mournful place, its dark depressing influence stole upon their spirits, and filled them with a dismal gloom. On every side, and far as the eye could see into the heavy distance, tall chimneys, crowding on each other, and presenting that endless repetition of the same dull, ugly, form, which is the horror of oppressive dreams, poured out their plague of smoke, obscured the light, and made foul the melancholy air. On mounds of ashes by the wayside, sheltered only by a few rough boards, or rotten pent-house roofs, strange engines spun and writhed like tortured creatures; clanking their iron chains, shrieking in their rapid whirl from time to time as though in torment unendurable, and making the ground tremble with their agonies. Dismantled houses here and there appeared, tottering to the earth, propped up by fragments of others that had fallen down, unroofed, windowless, blackened, desolate, but yet inhabited. Men, women, children, wan in their looks and ragged in attire, tended the engines, fed their tributary fire, begged upon the road, or scowled half-naked from the doorless houses. Then came more of the wrathful monsters, whose like they almost seemed to be in their wildness and their untamed air, screeching and turning round and round again; and still, before, behind, and to the right and left, was the same interminable perspective of brick towers, never ceasing in their black vomit, blasting all things living or inanimate, shutting out the face of day, and closing in on all these horrors with a dense dark cloud.

But, night-time in this dreadful spot!—night, when the smoke was changed to fire; when every chimney spirted up its flame; and places, that had been dark vaults all day, now shone red-hot, with figures moving to and fro within their blazing jaws, and calling to one another with hoarse cries—night, when the noise of every strange machine was aggravated by the darkness; when the people near them looked wilder and more savage; when bands of unemployed labourers paraded the roads, or clustered by torch-light round their leaders, who told them, in stern language, of their wrongs, and urged them on to frightful cries and threats; when maddened men, armed with sword and firebrand, spurning the tears and prayers of women who would restrain them, rushed forth on errands of terror and destruction, to work no ruin half so surely as their own—night, when carts came rumbling by, filled with rude coffins (for contagious disease and death had been busy with the living crops); when orphans cried, and distracted women shrieked and followed in their wake—night, when some called for bread, and some for drink to drown their cares, and some with tears, and some with staggering feet, and some with blood-shot eyes, went brooding home—night, which, unlike the night that Heaven sends on earth, brought with it no peace, nor quiet, nor signs of blessed sleep—who shall tell the terrors of the night to the young wandering child!

POET IN NEW YORK²
Federico Garcia Lorca
translated by Ben Belitt

Federico Garcia Lorca (1898–1935), a Spanish poet and dramatist, is remembered in this country for his surrealistic collection of poems *Poet in New York* and for his plays *Blood Wedding, Yerma,* and *The House of Bernarda Alba.*

New York
(Office and Denunciation)

Under the multiplications
is a drop of duck's blood.
Beneath the divisions,
the sailor's blood-drop.
Under the sums, a river of delicate blood;
a river flows singing
by suburb and dormitory;
is sea-breeze, silver, cement,
in the counterfeit dawn of New York.
The mountains exist; I know that.

² Federico Garcia Lorca, *Poet in New York*, translated by Ben Belitt. Copyright © 1955 by Ben Belitt. Reprinted by permission of New Directions Publishing Corporation.

And the oracle's eye-glasses;
I know it. But I have not come here to ogle the sky.
Am here to look upon blood, the silt
in the blood that delivers the engines over the waterfalls
and our souls to the fang of the cobra.
They butcher each day in New York
four million ducks,
five million hogs,
two thousand doves, to a dying man's pleasure;
one million cows,
one million lambs,
two million roosters
that splinter all heaven to rubble.
Better sob while we strop down the razor
or murder the dogs in the blaze of the chase,
than oppose in the dawn
the interminable milk trains,
the blood trains, interminable,
the trains of the manacled roses, chained
by the drummers of perfume.
The ducks and the doves,
and the hogs and the lambs
shed their blood-drops
under the multiplications;
and the terrible babel of cattle, stampeding,
fills all the valley with weeping
where the Hudson flows, drunk upon oil.
I accuse all the living
who have put out of mind all those others,
the unregenerate half
who pile up the mountains of asphalt
where the hearts
of the little, unmemoried creatures beat on;
and we all shall go down
in the ultimate feasts of the drill.
I spit in your face: see.
The other half hears me,
they who feed themselves, fly, and make water, undefiled,

like the gatekeeper's children
who carry the breakable straw
to the pot-holes where rust
all the insect antennae.
This is not hell, but a street.
Not death, but a fruit-stand.
Here is the world of the sundering rivers, the infinite distances
in a cat's paw smashed by the motorist.
I hear out the song of the worm
in the manifold heart of the children.
Rust, fermentation, earth tremors.
Earthen yourself, who float on the office's numerals.
What shall I do now? Align all the landscapes?
Muster the lovers who turn into photographs
and later are splinters of wood, and mouthfuls of blood?
No, never; I accuse!
I accuse the conspiracy
of untenable offices
whose agonies never ray forth;
that efface the design of the forest;
and I offer myself to be eaten by cattle, the rabble
whose outcries have filled all the valley
where the Hudson flows, drunk upon oil.

ON POPULATION
Thomas Robert Malthus

Thomas Robert Malthus (1766–1834) was an English econ-
omist and clergyman. His *Essay on the Principle of Population*, first published in 1798, sounded an early warning on what has come to be one
of today's most serious problems, overpopulation.

Chapter I

The great and unlooked for discoveries that have taken place
of late years in natural philosophy, the increasing diffusion of general
knowledge from the extension of the art of printing, the ardent and
unshackled spirit of inquiry that prevails throughout the lettered and
even unlettered world, the new and extraordinary lights that have

been thrown on political subjects which dazzle and astonish the understanding, and particularly that tremendous phenomenon in the political horizon, the French revolution, which, like a blazing comet, seems destined either to inspire with fresh life and vigour, or to scorch up and destroy the shrinking inhabitants of the earth, have all concurred to lead able men into the opinion that we were touching on a period big with the most important changes, changes that would in some measure be decisive of the future fate of mankind.

It has been said that the great question is now at issue, whether man shall henceforth start forwards with accelerated velocity towards illimitable, and hitherto unconceived improvement, or be condemned to a perpetual oscillation between happiness and misery, and after every effort remain still at an immeasurable distance from the wished-for goal.

Yet, anxiously as every friend of mankind must look forwards to the termination of this painful suspense, and eagerly as the inquiring mind would hail every ray of light that might assist its view into futurity, it is much to be lamented that the writers on each side of this momentous question still keep aloof from each other. Their mutual arguments do not meet with a candid examination. The question is not brought to rest on fewer points, and even in theory scarcely seems to be approaching to a decision.

The advocate for the present order of things is apt to treat the sect of speculative philosophers either as a set of artful and designing knaves who preach up ardent benevolence and draw captivating pictures of a happier state of society only the better to enable them to destroy the present establishments and to forward their own deep-laid schemes of ambition, or as wild and mad-headed enthusiasts whose silly speculations and absurd paradoxes are not worthy the attention of any reasonable man.

The advocate for the perfectibility of man, and of society, retorts on the defender of establishments a more than equal contempt. He brands him as the slave of the most miserable and narrow prejudices; or, as the defender of the abuses of civil society, only because he profits by them. He paints him either as a character who prostitutes his understanding to his interest, or as one whose powers of mind are not of a size to grasp any thing great and noble, who cannot see above five yards before him, and who must therefore be utterly unable to take in the views of the enlightened benefactor of mankind.

In this unamicable contest the cause of truth cannot but suffer. The really good arguments on each side of the question are not allowed to have their proper weight. Each pursues his own theory, little solicitous to correct or improve it by an attention to what is advanced by his opponents.

The friend of the present order of things condemns all political speculations in the gross. He will not even condescend to examine the grounds from which the perfectibility of society is inferred. Much less will he give himself the trouble in a fair and candid manner to attempt an exposition of their fallacy.

The speculative philosopher equally offends against the cause of truth. With eyes fixed on a happier state of society, the blessings of which he paints in the most captivating colours, he allows himself to indulge in the most bitter invectives against every present establishment, without applying his talents to consider the best and safest means of removing abuses and without seeming to be aware of the tremendous obstacles that threaten, even in theory, to oppose the progress of man towards perfection.

It is an acknowledged truth in philosophy that a just theory will always be confirmed by experiment. Yet so much friction, and so many minute circumstances occur in practice, which it is next to impossible for the most enlarged and penetrating mind to forsee, that on few subjects can any theory be pronounced just, that has not stood the test of experience. But an untried theory cannot fairly be advanced as probable, much less as just, till all the arguments against it have been maturely weighed and clearly and consistently refuted.

I have read some of the speculations on the perfectibility of man and of society with great pleasure. I have been warmed and delighted with the enchanting picture which they hold forth. I ardently wish for such happy improvements. But I see great, and, to my understanding, unconquerable difficulties in the way to them. These difficulties it is my present purpose to state, declaring, at the same time, that so far from exulting in them, as a cause of triumph over the friends of innovation, nothing would give me greater pleasure than to see them completely removed.

The most important argument that I shall adduce is certainly not new. The principles on which it depends have been explained in part by Hume, and more at large by Dr. Adam Smith. It has been advanced and applied to the present subject, though not with its proper weight, or in the most forcible point of view, by Mr. Wallace, and it may probably have been stated by many writers that I have never met with. I should certainly therefore not think of advancing it again, though I mean to place it in a point of view in some degree different from any that I have hitherto seen, if it had ever been fairly and satisfactorily answered.

The cause of this neglect on the part of the advocates for the perfectibility of mankind is not easily accounted for. I cannot doubt the talents of such men as Godwin and Condorcet. I am unwilling to doubt their candour. To my understanding, and probably to that of most others, the difficulty appears insurmountable. Yet these men of acknowledged ability and penetration, scarcely deign to notice it, and hold on their course in such speculations, with unabated ardour and undiminished confidence. I have certainly no right to say that they purposely shut their eyes to such arguments. I ought rather to doubt the validity of them, when neglected by such men, however forcibly their truth may strike my own mind. Yet in this respect it must be acknowledged that we are all of us too prone to err. If I saw a glass of wine repeatedly presented to a man, and he took no notice of it, I should be apt to think that he was blind or uncivil. A juster philosophy might teach me rather to think that my eyes deceived me and that the offer was not really what I conceived it to be.

In entering upon the argument I must premise that I put out of the question, at present, all mere conjectures, that is, all suppositions, the probable realization of which cannot be inferred upon any just philosophical grounds. A writer may tell me that he thinks man will ultimately become an ostrich. I cannot properly contradict him. But before he can expect to bring any reasonable person over to his opinion, he ought to shew, that the necks of mankind have been gradually elongating, that the lips have grown harder and more prominent, that the legs and feet are daily altering their shape, and that the hair is beginning to change into stubs of feathers. And till the probability of so wonderful a conversion can be shewn, it is surely lost time and lost eloquence to expatiate on the happiness of man in such a state; to describe his powers, both of running and flying, to paint him in a condition where all narrow luxuries would be contemned, where he would be employed only in collecting the necessaries of life, and where, consequently, each man's share of labour would be light, and his portion of leisure ample.

I think I may fairly make two postulata.

First, That food is necessary to the existence of man.

Secondly, That the passion between the sexes is necessary and will remain nearly in its present state.

These two laws, ever since we have had any knowledge of mankind, appear to have been fixed laws of our nature, and, as we have not hitherto seen any alteration in them, we have no right to conclude that they will ever cease to be what they now are, without an immediate act of power in that Being who first arranged the system of the universe, and for the advantage of his creatures, still executes, according to fixed laws, all its various operations.

I do not know that any writer has supposed that on this earth man will ultimately be able to live without food. But Mr. Godwin has conjectured that the passion between the sexes may in time be extinguished. As, however, he calls this part of his work a deviation into the land of conjecture, I will not dwell longer upon it at present than to say that the best arguments for the perfectibility of man are drawn from a contemplation of the great progress that has already made from the savage state and the difficulty of saying where he is to stop. But towards the extinction of the passion between the sexes, no progress whatever has hitherto been made. It appears to exist in as much force at present as it did two thousand or four thousand years ago. There are individual exceptions now as there always have been. But, as these exceptions do not appear to increase in number, it would surely be a very unphilosophical mode of arguing, to infer merely from the existence of an exception, that the exception would, in time, become the rule, and the rule the exception.

Assuming then, my postulata as granted, I say, that the power of population is indefinitely greater than the power in the earth to produce subsistence for man.

Population, when unchecked, increases in a geometrical ratio. Subsistence increases only in an arithmetical ratio. A slight acquaintance with numbers will shew the immensity of the first power in comparison of the second.

By that law of our nature which makes food necessary to the life of man, the effects of these two unequal powers must be kept equal.

This implies a strong and constantly operating check on population from the difficulty of subsistence. This difficulty must fall some where and must necessarily be severely felt by a large portion of mankind.

Through the animal and vegetable kingdoms, nature has scattered the seeds of life abroad with the most profuse and liberal hand. She has been comparatively sparing in the room and the nourishment necessary to rear them. The germs of existence contained in this spot of earth, with ample food, and ample room to expand in, would fill millions of worlds in the course of a few thousand years. Necessity, that imperious all pervading law of nature, restrains them within the prescribed bounds. The race of plants, and the race of animals shrink under this great restrictive law. And the race of man cannot, by any efforts of reason, escape from it. Among plants and animals its effects are waste of seed, sickness, and premature death. Among mankind, misery and vice. The former, misery, is an absolutely necessary consequence of it. Vice is a highly probable consequence, and we therefore see it abundantly prevail, but it ought not, perhaps, to be called an absolutely necessary consequence. The ordeal of virtue is to resist all temptation to evil.

This natural inequality of the two powers of population and of production in the earth and that great law of our nature which must constantly keep their effects equal from the great difficulty that to me appears insurmountable in the way to the perfectibility of society. All other arguments are of slight and subordinate consideration in comparison of this. I see no way by which man can escape from the weight of this law which pervades all animated nature. No fancied equality, no agrarian regulations in their utmost extent, could remove the pressure of it even for a single century. And it appears, therefore, to be decisive against the possible existence of a society, all the members of which should live in ease, happiness, and comparative leisure; and feel no anxiety about providing the means of subsistence for themselves and families.

Consequently, if the premises are just, the argument is conclusive against the perfectibility of the mass of mankind.

I have thus sketched the general outline of the argument, but I will examine it more particularly, and I think it will be found that experience, the true source and foundation of all knowledge, invariably confirms its truth.

Part
Three

Where
Did We
Go Wrong?

The fault, dear Brutus, is not in our stars, but in ourselves . . .

Shakespeare, *Julius Caesar*

Part Two describes man's failures to live in harmony with nature; this part offers some explanations of why he fails. The explanations are diverse, often contradictory. There is no attempt to pull them all together into a comprehensive answer, merely some conjectures about why man has wrought such havoc on his environment. The selections deal less with specific problems, such as why men litter—although that is touched on—than with general topics such as man's relationship to nature. Although there are a few technical pieces, most selections favor the humanistic explanation over the scientific.

Chapter 10, "People Are No Damn Good," offers a misanthropic view of human nature; man has caused such harm on earth because he is rotten to the core. "We have cancer—cancer of the soul," says Philip Wylie of modern man in his famous jeremiad, *Generation of Vipers*. Wylie, who made his reputation attacking man's most sacred institutions—notably motherhood—believes that man has failed abjectly in his attempt to establish civilization on earth.

Mark Twain and Montaigne focus on the trait which has been primarily responsible for man's assault on the balance of nature—his tendency to separate himself from and elevate himself above his fellow creatures. Montaigne scoffs at the colossal egotism of "the most frail of all creatures . . . [that] dare equal himself to God, that he describeth divine conditions unto himself, that he selecteth and separateth himself from out the rank of other creatures." Man's superiority to the beasts is highly questionable in Montaigne's eyes: "When I am playing with my cat, who knows whether she have more sport in dallying with me than I have in gaming with her." Twain is equally contemptuous of man's presumption of superiority over his fellow creatures. Comparing man to the beasts, he argues the "Descent of Man from the Higher Animals."

Chapter 11, "Virtue is the Root of All Evil," explores the proposition that men do harm not because they are no good, but because they are too good—or at least they try to be. C. P. Snow once said, "When you think of the long and gloomy history of man, you will find more hideous crimes have been committed in the name of obedience than have ever been committed in the name of rebellion." Accordingly, Part Three starts with an exhortation from Genesis which far too many men have followed:

> Be fruitful, and multiply, and fill the earth, and subdue it; and have dominion over the fish of the sea, and over the fowl of the air, and over every living thing that moveth upon the earth.

Here are the roots of many of our present troubles; we have been fruitful and multiplied until we fill the earth to overflowing. In gathering the materials necessary to feed, clothe, and amuse ourselves, we threaten to strip the earth bare. And when the Bible admonishes "subdue, and have dominion over . . . every living thing that moveth upon the earth," man clearly feels justified to treat the animals as if they were his own private chattels.

The selection, "Horses' Hoofs," by the ancient Chinese mystic Chuangtse, is an Oriental parable about the folly and brutality of man's dominion over the beast. Then, in "On Scaring Some Waterfowl in Loch Turit," Robert Burns deplores man who

> *Would be Lord of all below:*
> *Plumes himself in freedom's pride,*
> *Tyrant stern to all beside.*

In "The Damned Human Race," Mark Twain attributes man's ills to his propensity for religion and his chief constitutional defect, the Moral Sense.

Chapter 12, "The Promethean Bind," deals with science and technology. Aeschylus's *Prometheus Bound* is a drama based on the myth of the Titan Prometheus who stole fire from heaven to give it to man. Within the context of the play the gift is seen as the absolute good for man, the possibility for development which saves the human race. However, this gift of fire was the cause of Prometheus's suffering. We now face the horrible and ironic realization that because of our misuse of it, fire, the symbol of science and technology, may be destroying its masters.

Science and technology have been enthroned as the twin deities of the twentieth century. This worship is as true for the Orient, most of whose people are now committed to scientific materialism, as it is for the West, where the breathtaking achievements of the twentieth century—aviation, atomic fission, moon walks—have awed men into a reverential attitude toward science and technology.

One thing that the ecology movement has done, both in this country and abroad, is to raise doubts about science and technology. We now question whether these twin gods have not caused as many problems as they have solved. Congressional rejection of the SST in 1971 may fall short of deicide—science and technology still reign supreme—but this decision does mark an important turning point in Americans' attitude toward science and technology. Chapter 10 includes *Time* magazine's analysis of "the first time in American history that a major technological innovation has been shot down."

In "A Scientist's Sermon" from *The Magic Animal,* Philip Wylie discusses the shortcomings of science as religion. The pieces by Thoreau and Audubon seem to indicate that, like the gods of old, science demands the sacrifice of live animals. Without being an anti-vivisectionist, one can still appreciate Thoreau's self-disgust in "murdering" a turtle for a scientific experiment. If Thoreau is guilty of murder, Audubon participates in mass slaughter when collecting specimens for his work. Unlike Thoreau, however, Audubon has no misgivings about the carnage.

In the selection from *Future Shock,* Alvin Toffler explains the technology of littering. Richard Eberhart concerns himself with man's littering of space with his new devices. In "On Shooting Particles Beyond the World" Eberhart deplores the early nonmanned launchings, the small steps that led to the small step that astronaut Neil Armstrong called a great step for mankind. Eberhart considers it a step in the wrong direction. He is dismayed at the prospect of man's leaving his mark in space.

> *Good Boy Man! Your innards are put out,*
> *From now on all space will be your vomitorium.*[1]

Since Part Three probes the reasons for man's ecological failures, it unavoidably takes a negative tone—misanthropy, cynicism, and despair echo gloomily from selection after selection. Accordingly

[1] From *Collected Poems, 1930–1960* by Richard Eberhart. ©1960 by Richard Eberhart. Reprinted by permission of Oxford University Press and Chatto and Windus, Ltd.

it is important to make it clear here that the editors are not suggesting a mad course like abandoning science and religion. That would be throwing out the baby with the bathwater. Science and religion, whatever their defects, have been a great blessing for man. Science and its handmaiden, technology, have given us the weapons to fight hunger and disease, have protected us from the elements, and, perhaps most important, have afforded us the leisure that allowed the flowering of the arts.

Whatever the shortcomings or hypocrisies of one sect or another, there can be little doubt that religion has inspired much of what man has most right to be proud of on earth. Not only has it given us works like *Paradise Lost,* Michelangelo's paintings, and Bach's masses, it has allowed man to come to terms with the infinite, and helped him discover the meaning of his existence on earth.

Granting that, why then do we assemble these pieces attacking science and religion? Because something is drastically wrong with our civilization. In trying to find the root of the trouble we turned to the experts on disaster, the prophets of gloom. Perhaps much of what they say is frantic and overstated, but they raise questions that need to be raised. Clearly we need a thorough examination of our life style and value system, and their attacks on all we hold sacred can be a salutary spur to starting it.

CHAPTER
TEN
People Are No Damn Good

THE GOOD MAN
H. L. Mencken

H. L. Mencken (1880–1956) was an American journalist, critic, essayist, scholar, and pundit. As editor of *Smart Set* and *The American Mercury* during and after World War I, Mencken lampooned the mores and institutions of American culture, particularly those of the middle classes, whom he referred to as the "booboisie."

Man, at his best, remains a sort of one-lunged animal, never completely rounded and perfect, as a cockroach, say, is perfect. If he shows one valuable quality, it is almost unheard of for him to show any other. Give him a head, and he lacks a heart. Give him a heart of a gallon capacity, and his head holds scarcely a pint. The artist, nine times out of ten, is a dead-beat and given to the debauching of virgins, so-called. The patriot is a bigot, and, more often than not, a bounder and a poltroon. The man of physical bravery is often on a level, intellectually, with a Baptist clergyman. The intellectual giant has bad kidneys and cannot thread a needle. In all my years of search in this world, from the Golden Gate in the West to the Vistula in the East, and from the Orkney Islands in the North to the Spanish Main in the South, I have never met a thoroughly moral man who was honorable.

THE DAMNED HUMAN RACE[1]
Mark Twain

Mark Twain (1835–1910), the American novelist and humorist, is best known for his masterpiece, *The Adventures of Huckleberry Finn*. *The Damned Human Race*, one of Twain's last works, betrays the pessimism and cynicism Twain increasingly felt toward the end of his life. "The Lowest Animal" is part of that work.

V: The Lowest Animal

In August, 1572, similar things were occurring in Paris and elsewhere in France. In this case it was Christian against Christian. The Roman Catholics, by previous concert, sprang a surprise upon the unprepared and unsuspecting Protestants, and butchered them by thousands—both sexes and all ages. This was the memorable St. Bartholomew's Day. At Rome the Pope and the Church gave public thanks to God when the happy news came.

During several centuries hundreds of heretics were burned at the stake every year because their religious opinions were not satisfactory to the Roman Church.

In all ages the savages of all lands have made the slaughtering of their neighboring brothers and the enslaving of their women and children the common business of their lives.

[1]"The Lowest Animal" from *Mark Twain Letters From The Earth* edited by Bernard DeVoto. Copyright © 1962 by The Mark Twain Co. Reprinted by permission of Harper and Row, Publishers, Inc.

Hypocrisy, envy, malice, cruelty, vengefulness, seduction, rape, robbery, swindling, arson, bigamy, adultery, and the oppression and humiliation of the poor and the helpless in all ways have been and still are more or less common among both the civilized and uncivilized peoples of the earth.

For many centuries "the common brotherhood of man" has been urged—on Sundays—and "patriotism" on Sundays and weekdays both. Yet patriotism *contemplates the opposite of a common brotherhood.*

Woman's equality with man has never been conceded by any people, ancient or modern, civilized or savage.

I have been studying the traits and dispositions of the "lower animals" (so-called), and contrasting them with the traits and dispositions of man. I find the result humiliating to me. For it obliges me to renounce my allegiance to the Darwinian theory of the Ascent of Man from the Lower Animals; since it now seems plain to me that that theory ought to be vacated in favor of a new and truer one, this new and truer one to be named the Descent of Man from the Higher Animals.

In proceeding toward this unpleasant conclusion I have not guessed or speculated or conjectured, but have used what is commonly called the scientific method. That is to say, I have subjected every postulate that presented itself to the crucial test of actual experiment, and have adopted it or rejected it according to the result. Thus I verified and established each step of my course in its turn before advancing to the next. These experiments were made in the London Zoological Gardens, and covered many months of painstaking and fatiguing work.

Before particularizing any of the experiments, I wish to state one or two things which seem to more properly belong in this place than further along. This in the interest of clearness. The massed experiments established to my satisfaction certain generalizations, to wit:

1. That the human race is of one distinct species. It exhibits slight variations—in color, stature, mental caliber, and so on—due to climate, environment, and so forth; but it is a species by itself, and not to be confounded with any other.

2. That the quadrupeds are a distinct family, also. This family exhibits variations—in color, size, food preferences and so on; but it is a family by itself.

3. That the other families—the birds, the fishes, the insects, the reptiles, etc.—are more or less distinct, also. They are in the procession. They are links in the chain which stretches down from the higher animals to man at the bottom.

Some of my experiments were quite curious. In the course of my reading I had come across a case where, many years ago, some hunters on our Great Plains organized a buffalo hunt for the entertainment of an English earl—that, and to provide some fresh meat for his larder. They had charming sport. They killed seventy-two of those great animals; and ate part of one of them and left the seventy-one to rot. In order to determine the difference between an anaconda and an earl—if any—I caused seven young calves to be turned into the anaconda's cage. The grateful reptile immediately crushed one of them and swallowed it, then lay back satisfied. It showed no further interest in the calves, and no disposition to harm them. I tried this experiment with other anacondas; always with the same result. The fact stood proven that the difference between an earl and an anaconda is that the earl is cruel and the anaconda isn't; and that the earl wantonly destroys what he has no use for, but the anaconda doesn't. This seemed to suggest that the anaconda was not descended from the earl. It also seemed to suggest that the earl was descended from the anaconda, and had lost a good deal in the transition.

I was aware that many men who have accumulated more millions of money than they can ever use have shown a rabid hunger for more, and have not scrupled to cheat the ignorant and the helpless out of their poor servings in order to partially appease that appetite. I furnished a hundred different kinds of wild and tame animals the opportunity to accumulate vast stores of food, but none of them would do it. The squirrels and bees and certain birds made accumulations, but stopped when they had gathered a winter's supply, and could not be persuaded to add to it either honestly or by chicane. In order to bolster up a tottering reputation the ant pretended to store up supplies, but I was not deceived. I know the ant. These experiments convinced me that there is this difference between man and the higher animals: he is avaricious and miserly, they are not.

In the course of my experiments I convinced myself that among the animals man is the only one that harbors insults and injuries, broods over them, waits till a chance offers, then takes revenge. The passion of revenge is unknown to the higher animals.

Roosters keep harems, but it is by consent of their concubines; therefore no wrong is done. Men keep harems, but it is by brute force, privileged by atrocious laws which the other sex were allowed no hand in making. In this matter man occupies a far lower place than the rooster.

Cats are loose in their morals, but not consciously so. Man, in his descent from the cat, has brought the cat's looseness with him but has left the unconsciousness behind—the saving grace which excuses the cat. The cat is innocent, man is not.

Indecency, vulgarity, obscenity—these are strictly confined to man; he invented them. Among the higher animals there is no trace of them. They hide nothing; they are not ashamed. Man, with his soiled mind, covers himself. He will not even enter a drawing room with his breast and back naked, so alive are he and his mates to indecent suggestion. Man is "The Animal that Laughs." But so does the monkey, as Mr. Darwin pointed out; and so does the Australian bird that is called the laughing jackass. No—Man is the Animal that Blushes. He is the only one that does it—or has occasion to.

At the head of this article we see how "three monks were burnt to death" a few days ago, and a prior "put to death with atrocious cruelty." Do we inquire into the details? No; or we should find out that the prior was subjected to unprintable mutilations. Man—when he is a North American Indian—gouges out his prisoner's eyes; when he is King John, with a nephew to render untroublesome, he uses a red-hot iron; when he is a religious zealot dealing with heretics in the Middle Ages, he skins his captive alive and scatters salt on his back; in the first Richard's time he shuts up a multitude of Jew families in a tower and sets fire to it; in Columbus's time he captures a family of Spanish Jews and—but *that* is not printable; in our day in England a man is fined ten shillings for beating his mother nearly to death with a chair, and another man is fined forty shillings for having four pheasant eggs in his possession without being able to satisfactorily explain how he got them. Of all the animals, man is the only one that is cruel. He is the only one that inflicts pain for the pleasure of doing it. It is a trait that is not known to the higher animals. The cat plays with the frightened mouse; but she has this excuse, that she does not know that the mouse is suffering. The cat is moderate—unhumanly moderate: she only scares the mouse, she does not hurt it; she doesn't dig out its eyes, or tear off its skin, or

drive splinters under its nails—man-fashion; when she is done playing with it she makes a sudden meal of it and puts it out of its trouble.
Man is the Cruel Animal. He is alone in that distinction.

The higher animals engage in individual fights, but never
in organized masses. Man is the only animal that deals in that atrocity
of atrocities, War. He is the only one that gathers his brethren about
him and goes forth in cold blood and with calm pulse to extermi-
nate his kind. He is the only animal that for sordid wages will march
out, as the Hessians did in our Revolution, and as the boyish
Prince Napoleon did in the Zulu war, and help to slaughter strangers
of his own species who have done him no harm and with whom he
has no quarrel.

Man is the only animal that robs his helpless fellow of his
country—takes possession of it and drives him out of it or destroys
him. Man has done this in all the ages. There is not an acre of ground
on the globe that is in possession of its rightful owner, or that has not
been taken away from owner after owner, cycle after cycle, by force
and bloodshed.

AN APOLOGY OF RAYMOND SEBOND
Michel de Montaigne
translated by John Florio

Michel Eyquem, seigneur de Montaigne (1533–1592), was a
French philosopher and writer, famous for his essays. Although
deeply reverent toward God and Nature, Montaigne was bitter and
cynical toward mankind. His motto, "Que sais-je?" (What do I know?),
sums up his skeptical attitude toward human knowledge. "An Apol-
ogy of Raymond Sebond" is ostensibly a defense of a Spanish
theologian whose work Montaigne had translated, but in actuality it is
an extended discussion of man's fallibility.

Let us now but consider man alone without other help, armed
but with his own weapons, and unprovided of the grace and knowledge of God which is all his honor, all his strength, and all the ground
of his being. Let us see what hold-fast or free-hold he hath in this

gorgeous and goodly equipage. Let him with the utmost power of his discourse make me understand upon what foundation he hath built those great advantages and odds he supposeth to have over other creatures. Who hath persuaded him that this admirable moving of heaven's vaults, that the eternal light of these lamps so fiercely rolling over his head, that the horror-moving and continual motion of this infinite, vast ocean, were established and continue so many ages for his commodity and service? Is it possible to imagine anything so ridiculous as this miserable and wretched creature, which is not so much as master of himself, exposed and subject to offenses of all things, and yet dareth call himself master and emperor of this universe, in whose power it is not to know the least part of it, much less to command the same? And the privilege, which he so fondly challengeth, to be the only absolute creature in this huge world's frame, perfectly able to know the absolute beauty and several parts thereof, and that he is only of power to yield the great architect thereof due thanks for it, and to keep account both of the receipts and layings-out of the world. Who hath sealed him this patent? Let him show us his letters of privilege for so noble and so great a charge.

Have they been granted only in favor of the wise? Then concern they but a few. Are the foolish and wicked worthy of so extraordinary a favor? Who, being the worst part of the world, should they be preferred before the rest? Shall we believe him? "For whose cause then shall a man say that the world was made? In sooth, for those creatures' sake which have the use of reason: those are gods and men, than whom assuredly nothing is better" [Cicero, "Of the Nature of the Gods"]. We shall never sufficiently baffle the impudency of this conjoining.

Presumption is our natural and original infirmity. Of all creatures man is the most miserable and frail, and therewithal the proudest and disdainfullest, who perceiveth and seeth himself placed here, amidst their filth and mire of the world, fast tied and nailed to the worst, most senseless, and drooping part of the world, in the vilest corner of the house and farthest from heaven's cope, with those creatures that are the worst of the three conditions; and yet dareth imaginarily place himself above the circle of the moon and reduce heaven under his feet. It is through the vanity of the same imagination that he dare equal himself to God, that he ascribeth divine conditions unto himself, that he selecteth and separateth himself from out the rank of other creatures, to which his fellow-brethren and compeers he cuts out and shareth their parts and allotteth them what portions of means or forces he thinks good. How knoweth he by the virtue of his understanding the inward and secret motions of beasts? By what comparison from them to us doth he conclude the brutishness he ascribeth unto them?

When I am playing with my cat, who knows whether she have more sport in dallying with me than I have in gaming with her? We entertain one another with mutual apish tricks; if I have my hour to begin or to refuse, so hath she hers. Plato, in setting forth the golden age under Saturn, amongst the chief advantages that man had then reporteth the communication he had with beasts, of whom inquiring and taking instruction he knew the true qualities and differences of every one of them; by and from whom he got an absolute understanding and perfect wisdom, whereby he led a happier life than we can do. Can we have a better proof to judge of man's impudency touching beasts? This notable author was of opinion that in the greatest part of the corporal form which nature hath bestowed on them she hath only respected the use of the prognostications which in his days were thereby gathered.

CATASTROPHE, CHRIST, AND CHEMISTRY[2]
Philip Wylie

Philip Wylie (1902–) is an American novelist, philosopher, and prophet of doom. Despite the cliché, Wylie made his way to fame and fortune by attacking Mom and apple pie. *Generation of Vipers* is the best known of his books; *The Magic Animal* his most recent.

A Preliminary and Prejudicial Survey of a Modern, Christian Nation at War, with Notes on the Church, on Science, and on Economics, the New Mysticism.

It is time for man to make a new appraisal of himself. His failure is abject. His plans for the future are infantile. The varied forms of his civilization in this century are smashing each other. In

[2]From *Generation of Vipers* by Philip Wylie. Copyright 1942, © 1955, 1970 by Philip Wylie. Reprinted by permission of Holt, Rinehart and Winston, Inc.

universality and degree, the war he has finally managed to perpetrate surpasses every past similar social disaster. The United States of America is still intact, but its material safety is by no means guaranteed and its psychological future is in black doubt. Plans for what is called the defense of the democracies involve a city-by-city holocaust resembling an Old Testament act of Jehovah.

The war[3] began at a time when society was rapidly disintegrating. American and British democracy had held itself from the center of a chaos which was described as the great depression by a series of stop-gap borrowings and other slip-witted expedients which no sane man believed could be indefinitely maintained. Some nations froze their societies into absolutist schemes of life. Such freezing, in an individual, or a state, or a species, is the inevitable precursor of extinction. The way of hand-out and tax-patching was the step before the last one. Only a fluid and realistic society is evolving. None of the contemporary societies was realistic.

War is, of course, another expedient. It represents an unreasoned and inarticulate attempt of a species to solve its frustrations by exploding. A variety of outcomes can be expected. Some wars reseed populations and, after a gestative period, instill new vitality into stale regions. Some wars destroy the victor, the conquered nation, or both, and thereby simply erase angry causes from the planet. Some leave the combatants exhausted enough to *think,* if they have stopped short of total ruin, and to advance their future by the exercise of reason and goodwill, motivated by the shock of what has happened and the obviousness of what the sick populace requires. But most wars are inconclusive; the psychic trauma which they produce leads to a false era of apparent altruism and peace; old grudges, hypocrisies, greeds, imbalances, jealousies, superstitions and fears slowly erase the briefly necessary sense of safety. War comes again.

We Americans are planning the peace, already. Aside from the utter fatuity of the fact itself, our plans, as announced to date, show so little understanding of the causes of the war we are engaged in, that anybody who contemplates them must realize the peace in view would be as hopeless as the last one.

[3]This refers to World War II, of course. World War III, now in its middle-incipient stages, will obviously bear an even closer resemblance to an "Old Testament act of Jehovah."

We may not win. Or, we may win under circumstances which will make us too dulled and enfeebled to carry out any plan. Or we may win after suffering such ghastly punishment as to turn our altruistic purposes into revenge. Or, again, victory may come so soon, and so easily for the United States of America, that we will sit like a benign Dutch uncle at the peace table and hand out Sunday School rules and diplomas to the infuriated peoples of Europe. We did that the last time.

We have set up as peace aims such ideas as the world-wide institution and maintenance of the "four freedoms"; and the implementation of an "Atlantic Charter." I suppose, when Washington or Winston Churchill gets around to it, there will be a "Pacific Charter," also.[4] These aims are unselfish. The emotions of the men who subscribe to them are decent. But they are fantastically naive aims.

They assume what almost every Briton and American assumes: that civilized man has reached the edge of the dawn—that goodness and virtue and nobility are *almost* ready for universal realization—that we are a Christian and a scientific people who need only a few more years and a slight increment of intelligence in Parliament and Congress to produce a millennium. Our concepts of our own constitutions and our own ideals of freedom include perfectionism, or something near to it. We believe that we, as individuals and as the inhabitants of states, shires, townships and nations, are wedded to human dignity and acquainted with truth.

One could point out that Germany was, until recently, a so-called Christian nation. Catholicism and Protestantism were firmly rooted there. Germany, indeed, has produced more than its share of martyrs and protesting reformers. In its churches, the same gospels were preached that the people of London and New York hearkened to, on Sunday. It sang the same hymns and practiced the same rites. Its Bible was interchangeable with our own. Germany, too, was a great "scientific" nation. Until the beginning of the last war, a quarter of a century ago, Germany was the *leading* exponent of science, both applied and classical.

[4] As I write (September, 1954), this "Pacific Charter" has come into a state of murky being and Churchill recently made a quick trip to Washington concerning its architecture. I did not foresee, however, that the Prime Minister would be by this time more or less opposed to *any* arrangement which would offend Russia—owing to an Utter Vulnerability of the British Isles which, nowadays, amounts to military nonexistence.

In ten years, Germany exorcised the church for all practical purposes, substituted a widely practiced and self-acknowledged paganism, put a stop to every branch of classical science save that which was deemed fruitful to the war effort, and set up a state policy denying the holy tenets to which the democracies paid lip service.

From that, and other similar national regressions, a detached citizen of the world might draw the conclusion that our own premises and practices were shaky. Such an observer might infer that neither Britain nor America held over the bones of barbarism much but a rotting cloak of clericism and a deceptive scientific advancement. The lesson is so plain, as a matter of fact—the analogy so exact—that it ought not to be necessary to examine any other aspect of man's current society than the German in order to find the causes of our universal despair. However, owing to the basic flaw in the modern approach to consciousness, no list of parallels between Germany and, say, the United States, however long and explicit, would convince one single American that Americans need to worry themselves about such immediate future possibilities as Iowa pogroms, the national glorification of instinctualism, the enwhorement of American womanhood, Boston church raids, and a federal Gestapo.[5]

Americans think Germans are foreigners who live in funny-looking cities and have little locomotives that couldn't pull a line of boxcars up the foothills of the Rockies. University professors, scientists, medical men, pompous doodles, many of whom hold Heidelberg degrees, think that about the Germans—even though they trouble themselves to invent in addition a latent, inherent *difference*[6] between Germans and ourselves which they describe in elaborated terminology. Thus, to use the German analogue for the purpose of showing

[5]These matters (with the possible exception of Iowa pogroms) have come to be the occasional worries of some millions of Americans.

[6]During World War II it was generally assumed that the "differentness" of the Germans would remain self-evident for some centuries. Genocide alone, taken as a national principle, gave Germany a distinction shared in kind and scale only with the Soviets. Today, however, owing to a fearful need of allies to stand against the red tide, those Hitlerian eccentricities have been glossed over. Men like Dulles have fitted Germany into the "defense picture" (against the remembering reluctance of France) and words like "Dachau" are losing their emotional impact. This change in viewpoint is one more evidence of the emotional nature of our age which, if it stemmed from the principle of *laissez faire* before the War, now surely has the earmarks of that even more urgent motive: *sauve qui peut*.

how near the United States is to barbarism would be hopeless. Acting on the assumption that we are different and better, we, the American people, educated or unlettered, hold to the asinine premise of "thank God I am not as other men," above all other postulates.

But we are as other men, exactly. Of one blood, one species, one brain, one figure, one fundamental set of collective instincts, one solitary body of information, one everything. Superiority and inferiority are individual, not racial or national. Only deliberate, human breeding over periods of thousands of years could alter that fact. However, since our ability to learn by projection and parallel has been stifled from the top to the bottom of our society, it will be necessary to demonstrate the shakiness of our civilized fundaments and the thinness of our Christian veneer by taking an attitude slightly unlike the usual approach of ourselves to ourselves.

This shift of viewpoint will provide much illumination, both profound and superficial, although there is nothing new about it. It is a shift to an attitude that has been tested by millennia. It has never been found wanting. It is not my personal and private attitude. To say so, after reading this book, will be to revert to the nonsensical postulate that you are not as other men. Not, in *this* instance, as *I* am. Unluckily for the comfort of the hour, but luckily for the history of man, the spread of the theory of human differentness invariably precedes the pratfall of the proud.

I am going to write somewhat about the world but mostly about you—your home and kiddies, mom and the loved ones, old Doc Smith and the preacher, the Brooklyn Dodgers and the Star-Spangled Banner—in short, the American scene. But I am going to ask you to look at it through my eyes, and through the eyes of certain far wiser men than I, whose sight I have borrowed, as you can. For a great number of pages, I am going to examine, with you, the debit side of our ledger. Some people will think this is unpatriotic and some will be certain that it is dangerous. But none can deny that we are in a horrid mess and all will agree that to remedy disaster and to prevent its recurrence, it is essential to study the true causes, no matter what they may be.

I happen to believe, after much study, hard thought, and a variety of miserable experiences, that the attention of modern man has been so far diverted from nature and reality as to make the even momentary refocus of his eye a difficult proceeding. I can only try—with such faculties and facilities as I possess. I am proud of mankind for his good points. I am deeply concerned over his blindness to his evil attributes. I beg you to attack them with me in a mood of honest urgency and courage, the mood of a man, say, who submits to a perilous operation because his only chance of existence depends upon it.

We have cancer—cancer of the soul.

Religion has failed. Indeed, its widespread adoption and the holocausts which followed strongly suggest that religion, as we have known and thought about it, will never reappear importantly in the councils of man. Germany, as I said, was religious. So was Russia; so was Italy. But the behavior of Germany is in no way different today from the behavior of Japan, a country known to be heathen, barbaric, and full of grisly mummery.

Some time ago, the organized churches of the world took a body blow from science. Science revealed their orthodoxy as sham—a business largely pagan in origin, and partly cheap psychology in practice. The subsequent retreat of the church, or its demoralization, had a more sinister effect upon people than is generally imagined.

Science has not actually stricken any real human ideal or philosophical hypothesis from the realm of possibility. It has made no startling discovery in the field of good and evil, right and wrong, decency and obscenity, courage and cowardice, altruism and nihilism, or the relation of man's consciousness to the preultimate ingot which blasted itself apart into a cosmos. Few scientists, in fact, have studied such matters, and those who have done so, with a handful of exceptions, have produced nothing more than a vast literature of measurements of objective human behavior. The handful who proceeded deeper into the investigation of man's personality have written a small but amazing collection of books which show that psychological honesty, put in practice even before the invention of the internal combustion motor, produced truth then, as, indeed, it always must.

But the truths uttered in antiquity were not sorted out from antique error by the church, or the scientists, or anybody—and nearly all old thought was thrown away by bright new man in his brave new world on the unscientific principle that some old thought was manifest rubbish, therefore all of it could be ignored. It is a peculiar fumble, typical of the last century and a half. No doubt Archimedes uttered as much nonsense in his life as any man; but his investigation of displacement led to conclusions which are still accepted. Sound old values in the material world have been maintained. Equally sound old values in the world of human personality have not. Jesus Christ, who probably also uttered much unrecorded nonsense in his time, clearly conveyed a great deal of truth. We retained Archimedes' law but not Christ's. I will show you why, in due course.

Such Christianity as we professed—forms, rituals, buildings, mottoes on our coins, and the like—obviously has not been enough to save our world from horror. Instead, out of a Christian era was born the uttermost horror of man's hard story—the hellishness of these days and the hellishness—largely unrecognized—of 1930, 1920, 1910, and 1900. For, in our years of peace the seeds of war did not lie dormant; they grew grotesquely everywhere in the land and only the blind failed to see the crop. Unfortunately, practically all men were blind.

You have considered this a Christian nation, all your life. Our constitution implies as much. But a minute's thought might have shown you years ago—decades ago—that the United States of America was not in any *real* sense a Christian nation at all. Numerically? Less than half the people had even a nominal church membership. There goes the sacred majority. Dogmatically? Those who belonged to churches belonged to so many different faiths at swords' points with each other on matters of creed and technique that even the definition of Christianity crumples to absurdity. You laughed over the medieval theologians who argued about the number of angels who could dance on a pinpoint—and then deliberated petulantly on whether or not proper baptism consisted of a sprinkling with Holy Water, a complete immersion in a small swimming pool with the preacher in rubber boots, or a mere symbolic laying on of a minister's hand wet in something that came unblessed out of a faucet. Even if you personally avoided these mighty encounters, your fellowmen engaged in them, wherefore it was up to you either to stop their nonsense or take the consequences of it. Religion in our Christian land was mostly puerile fiddle-faddle before science kicked it apart.

The kick—or the repeated kicks—which made it inescapable to all but abject dupes that "the things that you're liable to read in the Bible . . . ain't necessarily so" had no refining effect. The dross of sentiment, fable, error and fundamentalism (which was everything but fundamental) was not discarded for the pure gold of exquisite logic and insight which remained in the Scriptures. The whole business was thrown overboard. And the church did not try to retain *any* integrity, because its bishops, priests, canons, and ushers had never known which parts possessed integrity. Nobody had shown them. They tried, rather, to meet the iconoclasm of modern religious criticism by a process of adaptations which have brought them to a position that is tragic, repulsive, and very funny.

On the contemporary pulpit, shrouded for Sundays, there is apt to be a bingo wheel for weekday lotteries. The service house of the up-to-date church is a combination basketball court and dance hall. The symbolic blood of the Lamb is still sipped on Easter, but on other days the punch at the ladies' aid is sometimes spiked. Where the Buchmanites have left their spoor is often a "modern approach toward sex living" which leads to all sorts of miscellaneous gropes in the gloom, neuroses, and confessional orgasms. Not yet a place of open assignation, assignation is the next logical step for the church—as it was once a primitively logical part of temple routine. A bolder clergy might revive it. But the desuetude of the church is such that in recent years few bold men have been attracted by its "challenge." The real challenge was too profound for the contemporary undergraduate even to know about. The superficial challenge was too silly for him to accept. Mentors became, as they always do on a decaying social limb, the maladjusted, the weak, the misfits, the confused, the dangerously well-intentioned, the squirting extroverts, the cloyed, the greedy, and the exponents of laziness—pipsqueaks, in short.

Millions of human beings have been emotionally exalted, "uplifted," or even, sometimes, worthily instructed in small affairs, by the church. But the over-all uplift was deleterious in the end because its source, its mechanism and its validity were not understood and the very incomprehensibility of the elation set up an equal decline, adding one more factor to the schizoid world of modern people—one more bump in our now established set of infinitely superimposed cycles of manic-depression.

The church has failed. It failed to create an individual philosophy acceptable to an "educated" modern man. It failed to enlist an American majority. Its component parts failed to agree with each other on any basis. So our Christian civilization is neither Christian nor civilized. Look at it.[7]

The failure of science is even more grotesque.

A detached brain, contemplating science and scientists these days, could scarcely stay maddened lampoons and inspirational japes. Science did away with the church by throwing it into widely accepted default. That certain truths which had long ago given rise to the church might have prevented the occurrence in no way alters the fact. Mankind abandoned the true with the false and made his place of worship into a joke because science had revealed that not all its ceremonies and offices were "rational." The average man was shorn of his Sunday lecture, his conscience, his logarithms of right and wrong. "Intellectual" men stamped upon the grave of religion so that the ghost would never rise: the business was done with, they decreed.

Science made almost no study of the thing it had destroyed, or of the vacuum left in the spirit of man by the confiscation. Science, by God, was science, and religion was positively not scientific! Down with it!

What science did achieve is no secret. Science took the atom apart. It put together a relativistic definition of the tangible universe. It ruled out as nonexistent all elements it could not detect by machinery, even though man is preoccupied with such matters throughout his days. That renaissance, enlightening in its way, was accompanied by a thorough pulling of the blinds in half the human house. What you could see through the front windows was scientific. What you

[7]It did not occur to me, as I wrote the foregoing passage in 1941, that orthodox religion, by 1955, would have become a new refuge for masses of Americans who, out of sheer panic, had refused to look at themselves or to study science. I was well aware of the coming "atomic age" and its horrifying probabilities, but I was not able to perceive then that unconscious fear would shatter the common sense of multitudes.

I did not realize, that is, how the chief menace of communism would be seen as its "godlessness" and how, in magical countermeasure, "godliness" would become more or less consonant with "Americanism"—how even an actual pledge to God would be added by the Congress to our pledge to the Flag. It is a lapse for which I apologize (and one for which I have tried to make amends in the years between). But who could have imagined, early in World War II that, as the American need for clear and detached thought became imperative, Americans would be frightened *away* from thinking, from science and from scientists—abandoning their one decent hope to gain the presumed sanctuary of godliness? In this connection, one recalls Stalin's acid query about the number of divisions possessed by the Pope. God surely will not do what man could and should and will not.

were not allowed to examine through the darkened rear windows was not merely nonscientific—it simply did not exist. No medieval theologian ever touched off a sophistry of greater magnitude!

The results of scientific endeavor piled up, however, in such variety and size as to be convincing evidence of the efficacy of the method. On the outermost fields of speculation, science did not reach any conclusions much more satisfying to the average man than some of the postulates in, say, the Vedas, which are at least three thousand years old. But the new measurements satisfied the scientific passion for description. And, if the Aryans of 1000 B.C. somehow got onto corpuscular and radiant speculation—if they meditated the firmamental origin in somewhat the same terms as Abbé Le Maître—it is nothing against science that it should derive the same notion and express it even better, ninety generations later.

Shunning the difficult terrain of the intangible and the impalpable, science undertook the tangible and the describable. It was not only easier, but it was fashionable. The renaissance of science took place at the beginning of a European age of trade. A man of wealth was then, as usually, more of a personage than a man of wisdom—and many brave commercial pioneers had the foresight to perceive that science could be turned into a tidy thing. Born among a materialistic people, science consequently throve on matter and even its purest forms were usually subsidized to create more wealth or, at least, subsidized by wealth in patronage.

Science set out to increase worldly goods. Classical men in the business may grow black in the face denying this, but—so far—science has contributed virtually nothing else to mankind and I hold that a ninety-nine per cent total of circumstantial evidence is fairly convincing. Man's physical senses were extended enormously by science. The degree and the speed of that achievement are, indeed, the most common sources of our contemporary vanity; they form the whole preposterous case for the claim that we are civilized. No other attributes of man were, in any way, either extended or vitalized by science. Man's personality, his relations with other men, his private ethics, his social integrity, his standards of value, his love of truth, his dignity or his contentment, were not even potentially improved by the scientists—if the almost unknown work of a few men be excepted.

The effect is, of course, alarming. (At least, I am alarmed by it. And I hold that any man, these days, who does not live every hour in a condition of alarm—however detached or icy—is either a traitor or an idiot.) The electron tube, the locomotive, the internal combustion engine, the suspension bridge, vaccine and the glass giant of Palomar were turned over to the cruel bumpkin of the Middle Ages and his pal, the naked bushman leaping around his tribal fire. True, those characters were stuffed into good waistcoats and somewhat circumscribed by municipal law—but inside their heads they were living fossils—obsolete in the presence of their accouterments—intact specimens, in so far as science had anything to do with their psyches. A few suits of clothes, some money in the bank, and a new kind of fear constitute the main differences between the average American today and the hairy men with clubs who accompanied Attila to the city of Rome. The behavior of Attila's boys has been duplicated by millions upon millions of Nazi soldiers and laymen, in detail. They are Western men, remember—scientific and Christian, like ourselves. Each acted from an environment as modern as that of Chillicothe, or my own city of Miami Beach.[8] Each had studied science and each had gone to church—each of millions—and yet each was able to embrace rape, murder, torture, larceny, mayhem and every other barbarous infamy the minute opportunity spelled itself in letters acceptable to him.

Americans are no different, underneath.

In another passage soon to appear, I propose to point this out more graphically. Here, I merely wish to indicate that the science-built world of engines and laboratories in which man lives has grown up apart from man himself. Science has not instructed man—it has only implemented him.

A very proper sense of confusion has thus fallen upon mankind. His elected representatives do not understand the gadgets and machines which have come into being, or their consequences, or their social implications, or even the reason for the existence of many of them. Soil erodes away. States become dust bowls. People are unemployed and famished. Prices rise. Bread grows scarce. The radio blats away all day and night without the dimmest notion of responsibility for the effect of what it says. Men and women harbor in their houses machinery the workings of which they do not have the intelligence quotient to learn to comprehend by any possible means of instruction. Men and women drive automobiles which are so much better and more dependable, as natural objects, than the minds of the drivers

---

[8] We have since moved to the country.

that the net result, aside from universal escapism, is a homicide total higher than that of all our war casualties put together.

But science continues irresponsibly to tender new tools—airplanes, for example—and it is not bright of science. There is nothing wrong with the tools. The trouble is with the people. I would declare no truce against discovery. But I do suggest new lines for scientific investigation. Men unequipped internally but overloaded by objects are sure to stumble and fall to fighting. Again—one should not hand loaded pistols to the youngsters in a day nursery; but that is the learned procedure of this century. The proliferation of goods mounts and mounts again. Avarice, imitation, the lust for money, power and glamour—all primitive and unrestrained impulses —control the consumer public. The demented dogma of classicism reimbues the scientists with the urge to continue the proceeding irrespective of all result. And so they burn late oil, to freedom's glory—or Hitler's.

Our boots are not merely seven league: they stride the globe. Our eyes see through light years. Our ears hear voices from every city on the planet. Our biceps tear down cliffs. In every material sense, we have reached the end of the legends, the finale of the fairy tales. All the physical imagining of man, when he was limited to the power of his own body, has been realized. But not any good whatever has come of it—only the greatest evil man has yet endured.

During the decade before the onslaught of the current war, society was very near to collapse, and one thing was certain: in that prewar society of ours, not one per cent of the population really understood the material advances of their time, and of that one per cent, scarcely a man in ten thousand was giving any large part of his effort to an *intelligent* study of the hysterical dilemma. I say intelligent, advisedly. There were myriad panacea-makers but almost none mentioned as the cause—individual man.

Science had convinced itself that *only* the field of matter, or energy, was worth exploring with its new instrument: truth. Not one physical scientist in a thousand made a suggestion for attacking the manifest shambles of the individual. Salvation was expected even by the savants from a loosely associated group of pseudo-scientific quacks who called themselves economists or sociologists. The plans of those persons, probably, will go into the formulation of the next peace—making that peace as unrealistic as its numberless precursors. For this is the era when man subscribes his whole body and soul, in so far as he can, to materialism, and farms out the remnant to somebody called an economist.

The economist poses as a scientist and is so accepted. He tries to view man as a consumer of goods, and nothing else. Economic reasons, he says, start wars, set up national boundaries, build churches, create cities, destroy nations, and bring plagues of locusts. The correct economic system for the manufacture and distribution of goods, according to these wizards, is all that is needed to make life one long throb of happy motoring. Here, disguised as science, is the mystical motif—the witch-doctor prerogative—religion in its worst sense. Through such be-all-ism, economists have become the clergy of the twentieth century. In them we have placed our faith.

There has never been a democratic school of economics. Instead, in every democracy, are many schools, all interested in narrowing democracy, rather than in promulgating it. None agrees with any others, even concerning a definition of terms. On every public problem our great economists (and there are no mediocre economists—as Marcus Goodrich once pointed out—which in itself neatly implies the absurdity of economics) solemnly take all possible sides: the positive, the negative, the converse, and the contraposite, which is logical as a device, but gets the public nowhere.

However, even where there is one system, the theory of the amenability of all man's problems to fixed trade rules breaks down. We have before us two notable examples: communism and fascism— the left and the right. Both are economic systems, basically. Both are absolutist—one compelled upon the state by the people, and the other compelled upon the people by a small, impassioned group which declares itself to be the state.

Apologists for communism explain that it broke down in Russia because Russia was not an industrial nation. That seedy and specious argument needs no more rebuttal. The Soviet itself has furnished it. Communism broke down because men are not created equal, do not work equally, cannot be paid equally, do not have equal social and financial deserts, will not produce their best effort in a society that is not competitive, and cannot be made to work long or hard or with brilliance if they are not permitted to own, possess, buy, sell, and do business with each other.

All the illuminating work of Pavlov on dogs merely seemed to show that dogs were machines; but none of it undertook to destroy the instinctual patterns of dogs. Later work of the same sort, attempting exactly that, showed that when even the best-conditioned reflexes of pigs were set in conflict with their instincts, pigs had nervous breakdowns and went insane. The Russians *had* to quit trying to squeeze human life into the patterns of Pavlov and of Marx because men have instinct, too. Men are not machines. A few months of Marxism showed with ghastly clarity that his economic theory, which depended upon the presumption that men could be made to operate as ants do, was phony, and Russia abandoned communism.

Fascism is, of course, old stuff. Communism was, too, but Marx knew little of anthropology. In any case, he was so furious at the outrages of nineteenth-century industrialism that he was unable to think lucidly. Fascism is communism compelled by state violence and put to any use for which the state sees fit, from the doling out of candy to the citizenry to the enactment of war upon the citizens of other states.

Absolute dominion of a powerful people by a minority always produces national aggression. The psychology of that phenomenon is simple in essence even when it is complex in expression. A king and his nobles, or a Hitler and his unsqueamish satraps, having snatched the power, must brandish it to emboss the fact on the local populace. Next, they must protect their luster by impressing outsiders, lest a peripheral human titter undo them. Conquest is a most impressive procedure. It is useful to them, also, to start wars as a diversion; the people would study the high cost of tyranny, if they did not. War is by far the most diverting exercise man has thought of—and for such reasons, aggression goes hand in hand with autocracy.

Fascism—or rightism—is in essence the legalization of larceny, as has been said. That is why we find the czars of our American monopolies have rightist tendencies. A monopoly, being a strict contradiction of nature and acceptable only as an emergency measure, requires the legalization of larceny for its maintenance. All living things are in competition to live at all times—even man—and even man today—but truces are essential for mutual tolerance. Fascism, like monopoly, denies the right of truce. Plundering at home is quick work for every totalitarian administration. Plundering abroad is a constant temptation. So fascism—or state capitalism—will always be neighbor-raping.

The economic system of theft has one immense advantage: it works. But it also has one great disadvantage: it works only while there is something to steal. Thus, if Germany or Japan conquered the whole world, the winner would take all[9]—including the problem of man and science, unsolved, and further boggled by whatever medieval nonsense would be added by the Germans or the Japs. They would be nowhere—which is to say, they would be, at best, just where we were when the war began, and at worst, some thousand or more years behind that, which in truth, is not very far.

I do not mean that a thousand years is a short time in biology or geology—although it is. I mean that man, except for his possibly fatal accretion of machinery, has really advanced almost not at all in the *last* one thousand years. Even the dreadful specter of Hitler's Tausend-Jahr Reich is, in that relation, tiddlywinks. If we in America were busy spreading through our population some powerful forward step of consciousness, we might look selflessly at the Hitler proposal of a millennium of slavery as a most dismal threat. But we are not busy with anything more valuable to mankind than private security and prosperity.

We could be.

The proposition I wish to make could and would start just such a movement and give rise to exactly that result: a general increase in the consciousness of man. It is a simple proposal. It has been made over and over for many thousands of years by thoughtful people. It has not, however, been put forward, so far as I know, by any popular contemporary author in terms acceptable to the average doctor of philosophy, high school graduate, or reader of the New York *Times*. I am going to try here, by various means, to set forth an old and basic idea in such a way that it can be understood by that travesty of wisdom and catastrophe of misguidance, the modern educated man.

All I shall suggest is that man—individual man—enlarge his attitude toward himself.

---

[9] This is the point overlooked by many erudite but foolish people who nowadays assume that we—and the democracies—ought to have let Hitler conquer Russia. To those of us who cannot manage to select amongst tryants a preferred foe, let alone a preferred American führer (or commissar), the point seems cogent.

In order to do so most rapidly and effectively he should use the tool at hand: science. He should employ the scientific method for the purpose of studying himself and teaching himself what he learns about himself. He should apply logic and integrity to his subjective personality—just as he has done to the objective world. He would find that laws parallel to physical principles rule his inner life. He would find that truth cannot be escaped within, any more than it can be escaped without. He would learn that when he kids himself, or believes a lie, or deceives another man, he commits a crime as real and as destructive as the crime of deliberately running down a person with an automobile.

Our civilization has not yet even dreamed of applying science to *itself*. Science is exact. It measures and weighs. It admits every error instantly, when error is detected. It understands that knowledge is fluid and changing. It recognizes the relativity of data. It perceives that objects are not at all what they appear to be and that their nature is bizarre and changing. It knows that nothing stands still. Only the principle of fluid integrity, of eternal openmindedness, is fixed, in science. Everything else can be dismissed at any time by every scientist. The objective world, viewed by him, holds no dogma save that one: I will pursue the truth, and the truth only, because all else is by definition false, and I am a mind of too much dignity to limit myself by awarenesses based on falsehood.

The great American oaf—be he college president, bank teller, race track tout, or missionary—assumes that he has *already* been converted into this state of mind by science. The number and excellence of the products of science on every hand lead him to identify *himself* with the scientific principle. His civilization is scientific. So he is.

No more pitiful fallacy could be imagined. An automobile represents an immensely greater body of honesty than the salesman who sells it or the jerk who drives himself to doom in it. Most men are literally too crooked with themselves to be allowed to drive cars. Since they *are* allowed—cars contribute their share of calamity to man. The integrity of thinking and acting that enters into the radio set on the common man's bedside table is a thundering rebuke to the reliability of the cluck beside it and the macaroon singing over it.

Man must now approach himself, if he still has a chance, with the detached and sincere passion he has applied to the world of things. He must give as much energy to his soul as he does to his job. And the best men with the best brains must research as feverishly into themselves and each other as they have into atoms.

The blame for Armageddon lies on man. And the millennium will come only when the average man exhibits a scientific integrity about *all* he is and does—instead of half of it. Many a psychological Archimedes has put signposts on the hard road man must follow if he is to avoid self-destruction and come into his own. A few very great modern scientists have added to the lore. Indications of what man may expect of himself are everywhere at hand. But most men must first be persuaded that the task lies ahead and not behind—that we are infants, still, with loaded guns for toys. Toward that persuasion I shall now set myself. I have said that we civilized men are still medieval—cruel bumpkins and dancing savages. I would like to elucidate that point, first, because no other can be made until it is somewhat accepted.

FROG[10]
Zinaida Nikolayevna Hippius
translated by Vladimir Markov and Merrill Sparks

Zinaida Nikolayevna Hippius (1869–1945) has been called "the greatest religious poet of Russia"; the major theme of her poetry is "the story of the soul's journey to a complete finding of God."[11] Because of her piety and her anti-Bolshevism she is virtually unread in Russia today.

Some kind of frog (They're all the same to me.)
Is whistling long and loud and thoughtfully.
Beneath a black damp sky his chatter . . .

What if it's about things that most matter?

[10]From *Modern Russian Poetry* edited by Vladimir Markov and Merrill Sparks, copyright © 1966, 1967 by MacGibbon & Kee, Ltd., reprinted by permission of The Bobbs-Merrill Company, Inc., and Granada Publishing, Ltd.

[11]Vladimir Markov and Merrill Sparks, *Modern Russian Poetry*, p. lvi.

And what if —grasping what he'd say—
All would change and change would move through me?
I'd see the world in a different way,
And new things in the world would be shown to me?

But annoyed, I shut the window with a bang.
All this —a southern night's illusion
During a languid, sleepless sleep . . . Then pang!

Some kind of frog! So what! Big deal intrusion!

THE SHOOTING[12]
Robert Pack

Robert Pack (1929–) was born in New York and is currently on the faculty of Middlebury College, Vermont. His books of poetry include *The Irony of Joy, Stranger's Privilege,* and *Guarded by Women.*

I shot an otter because I had a gun;
The gun was loaned to me, you understand.
Perhaps I shot it merely for the fun.
Must everything have meaning and be planned?

Afterwards I suffered penitence,
And dreamed my dachshund died, convulsed in fright.
They look alike, but that's coincidence.
Within one week my dream was proven right.

At first I thought its death significant
As punishment for what I'd lightly done;
But good sense said I'd nothing to repent,
That it is natural to hunt for fun.

[12]"The Shooting" by Robert Pack. Copyright © 1960 by Robert Pack. Reprinted from *Guarded by Women,* by Robert Pack, by permission of Random House, Inc.

Was I unnatural to feel remorse?
I mourned the otter and my dog as one.
But superstition would not guide my course;
To prove that I was free I bought the gun.

I dreamed I watched my frightened brother die.
Such fancy worried me, I must admit.
But at his funeral I would not cry,
Certain that I was not to blame for it.

I gave my friend the gun because of guilt,
And feared then that my sanity was done.
On fear, he said, the myth of hell was built.
He shot an otter because he had a gun.

CHAPTER ELEVEN
Virtue Is the Root of All Evil

*And God blessed them, and God said unto them, Be fruitful,
and multiply, and fill the earth, and subdue it; and have dominion over
the fish of the sea, and over the fowl of the air,
and over every living thing that moveth upon the earth.*

*And God said, Behold, I have given you every herb bearing
seed, which is upon the face of all the earth, and every tree, in which is
the fruit of a tree yielding seed; to you it shall be for food.*

*And to every beast of the earth, and to every fowl of the air, and
to every thing that creepeth upon the earth, wherein there is life, I have
given every green herb for food: and it was so.*

Genesis 1:28–30

HORSES' HOOFS[1]
Chuangtse
translated by Lin Yutang

Chuangtse (d. ca. 275 B.C.), Chinese philosopher and mystic, stands in relation to Laotse, the founder of Taoism, as Paul does to Jesus, or Plato to Socrates—he recorded and developed the doctrines of the master and, in doing so, added the indelible stamp of his own personality and ideas. Chuangtse's extant writings consist of 33 chapters, all of which mix philosophical disquisition with anecdotes and parables.

Horses have hoofs to carry them over frost and snow, and hair to protect them from wind and cold. They eat grass and drink water, and fling up their tails and gallop. Such is the real nature of horses. Ceremonial halls and big dwellings are of no use to them.

One day Polo (famous horse-trainer) appeared, saying, "I am good at managing horses." So he burned their hair and clipped them, and pared their hoofs and branded them. He put halters around their necks and shackles around their legs and numbered them according to their stables. The result was that two or three in every ten died. Then he kept them hungry and thirsty, trotting them and galloping them, and taught them to run in formations, with the misery of the tasselled bridle in front and the fear of the knotted whip behind, until more than half of them died.

The potter says, "I am good at managing clay. If I want it round, I use compasses; if rectangular, a square." The carpenter says, "I am good at managing wood. If I want it curved, I use an arc; if straight, a line." But on what grounds can we think that the nature of clay and wood desires this application of compasses and square, and arc and line? Nevertheless, every age extols Polo for his skill in training horses, and potters and carpenters for their skill with clay and wood. Those who manage (govern) the affairs of the empire make the same mistake.

I think one who knows how to govern the empire should not do so. For the people have certain natural instincts—to weave and

---

clothe themselves, to till the fields and feed themselves. This is their common character, in which all share. Such instincts may be called "Heaven-born." So in the days of perfect nature, men were quiet in their movements and serene in their looks. At that time, there were no paths over mountains, no boats or bridges over waters. All things were produced, each in its natural district. Birds and beasts multiplied; trees and shrubs thrived. Thus it was that birds and beasts could be led by the hand, and one could climb up and peep into the magpie's nest. For in the days of perfect nature, man lived together with birds and beasts, and there was no distinction of their kind. Who could know of the distinctions between gentlemen and common people? Being all equally without knowledge, their virtue could not go astray. Being all equally without desires, they were in a state of natural integrity. In this state of natural integrity, the people did not lose their (original) nature.

And then when Sages appeared, crawling for charity and limping with duty, doubt and confusion entered men's minds. They said they must make merry by means of music and enforce distinctions by means of ceremony, and the empire became divided against itself. Were the uncarved wood not cut up, who could make sacrificial vessels? Were white jade left uncut, who could make the regalia of courts? Were Tao and virtue not destroyed, what use would there be for charity and duty? Were men's natural instincts not lost, what need would there be for music and ceremonies? Were the five colours not confused, who would need decorations? Were the five notes not confused, who would adopt the six pitch-pipes? Destruction of the natural integrity of things for the production of articles of various kinds—this is the fault of the artisan. Destruction of Tao and virtue in order to introduce charity and duty—this is the error of the Sages. Horses live on dry land, eat grass and drink water. When pleased, they rub their necks together. When angry, they turn round and kick up their heels at each other. Thus far only do their natural instincts carry them. But bridled and bitted, with a moon-shaped metal plate on their foreheads, they learn to cast vicious looks, to turn their heads to bite, to nudge at the yoke, to cheat the bit out of their mouths or steal the bridle off their heads. Thus their minds and gestures become like those of thieves. This is the fault of Polo.

In the days of Ho Hsü, the people did nothing in particular at their homes and went nowhere in particular in their walks. Having food, they rejoiced; tapping their bellies, they wandered about. Thus far the natural capacities of the people carried them. The Sages came then to make them bow and bend with ceremonies and music, in order to regulate the external forms of intercourse, and dangled charity and duty before them, in order to keep their minds in submission. Then the people began to labor and develop a taste for knowledge, and to struggle with one another in their desire for gain, to which there is no end. This is the error of the Sages.

THE DAMNED HUMAN RACE[2]
Mark Twain

Man is the Religious Animal. He is the only Religious Animal. He is the only animal that has the True Religion—several of them. He is the only animal that loves his neighbor as himself, and cuts his throat if his theology isn't straight. He has made a graveyard of the globe in trying his honest best to smooth his brother's path to happiness and heaven. He was at it in the time of the Caesars, he was at it in Mahomet's time, he was at it in the time of the Inquisition, he was at it in France a couple of centuries, he was at it in England in Mary's day, he has been at it ever since he first saw the light, he is at it today in Crete . . . he will be at it somewhere else tomorrow. The higher animals have no religion. And we are told that they are going to be left out, in the Hereafter. I wonder why? It seems questionable taste.

In truth, man is incurably foolish. Simple things which the other animals easily learn, he is incapable of learning. Among my experiments was this. In an hour I taught a cat and a dog to be friends. I put them in a cage. In another hour I taught them to be friends with a rabbit. In the course of two days I was able to add a fox, a goose, a squirrel and some doves. Finally a monkey. They lived together in peace; even affectionately.

Next, in another cage I confined an Irish Catholic from Tipperary, and as soon as he seemed tame I added a Scotch Presbyterian from Aberdeen. Next a Turk from Constantinople; a Greek Christian from Crete; an Armenian; a Methodist from the wilds of Arkansas; a Buddhist from China; a Brahman from Benares. Finally, a Salvation Army Colonel from Wapping. Then I stayed away two whole days. When I came back to note results, the cage of Higher Animals was all right, but in the other there was but a chaos of gory odds and ends of turbans and fezzes and plaids and bones and flesh—not a specimen left alive. These Reasoning Animals had disagreed on a theological detail and carried the matter to a Higher Court.

One is obliged to concede that in true loftiness of character, Man cannot claim to approach even the meanest of the Higher Animals. It is plain that he is constitutionally incapable of approaching that altitude; that he is constitutionally afflicted with a Defect which must make such approach forever impossible, for it is manifest that this defect is permanent in him, indestructible, ineradicable.

I find this Defect to be *the Moral Sense.* He is the only animal that has it. It is the secret of his degradation. It is the quality *which enables him to do wrong.* It has no other office. It is incapable of performing any other function. It could never have been intended to perform any other. Without it, man could do no wrong. He would rise at once to the level of the Higher Animals.

Since the Moral Sense has but the one office, the one capacity—to enable man to do wrong—it is plainly without value to him. It is as valueless to him as is disease. In fact, it manifestly *is* a disease. *Rabies* is bad, but it is not so bad as this disease. Rabies enables a man to do a thing which he could not do when in a healthy state: kill his neighbor with a poisonous bite. No one is the better man for having rabies. The Moral Sense enables a man to do wrong. It enables him to do wrong in a thousand ways. Rabies is an innocent disease, compared to the Moral Sense. No one, then, can be the better man for having the Moral Sense. What, now, do we find the Primal Curse to have been? Plainly what it was in the beginning: the infliction upon man of the Moral Sense; the ability to distinguish good from evil; and with it, necessarily, the ability to *do* evil; for there can be no evil act without the presence of consciousness of it in the doer of it.

And so I find that we have descended and degenerated, from some far ancestor—some microscopic atom wandering at its pleasure between the mighty horizons of a drop of water perchance—insect by insect, animal by animal, reptile by reptile, down the long highway of smirchless innocence, till we have reached the bottom stage of development—namable as the Human Being. Below us—nothing.

ON SCARING SOME WATERFOWL IN LOCH TURIT
Robert Burns

Robert Burns (1759–1796) was a Scotch poet, best known for his dialect poems, such as "The Holy Fair," "Holy Willie's Prayer," and "To a Mouse."

A Wild Scene Among the Hills of Oughtertyre

Why, ye tenants of the lake,
For me your wat'ry haunt forsake?
Tell me, fellow-creatures, why
At my presence thus you fly?
Why disturb your social joys,
Parent, filial, kindred ties? —
Common friend to you and me,
Nature's gifts to all are free:
Peaceful keep your dimpling wave,
Busy feed, or wanton lave;
Or, beneath the sheltering rock,
Bide the surging billow's shock.

Conscious, blushing for our race,
Soon, too soon, your fears I trace.
Man, your proud usurping foe,
Would be lord of all below:
Plumes himself in freedom's pride,
Tyrant stern to all beside.

The eagle, from the cliffy brow,
Marking you his prey below,
In his breast no pity dwells,
Strong necessity compels:
But Man, to whom alone is giv'n
A ray direct from pitying Heav'n,
Glories in his heart humane —
And creatures for his pleasure slain!

In these savage, liquid plains,
Only known to wand'ring swains,
Where the mossy riv'let strays,
Far from human haunts and ways;
All on Nature you depend,
And life's poor season peaceful spend.

Or, if man's superior might
Dare invade your native right,
On the lofty ether borne,
Man with all his pow'rs you scorn;
Swiftly seek, on clanging wings,
Other lakes and other springs;
And the foe you cannot brave,
Scorn at least to be his slave.

CHAPTER
TWELVE
The Promethean Bind

THE MAGIC ANIMAL[1]
Philip Wylie

3 / A Scientist's Sermon

There have always been a few scientists who, from time to time, leaned out of their towers to attempt the act of participation in man's affairs. Rachel Carson was one. She broke the territorial rules in that endeavor and was roundly scolded from the tall towers.

Another example intrigued me as I edited this work. In the technical, but not exactly disciplined, pages of *Playboy* magazine for January 1967, Sir Julian Huxley offered his thoughts on "The Crisis

[1] From *The Magic Animal* by Philip Wylie, copyright © 1968 by Philip Wylie. Reprinted by permission of Doubleday & Company, Inc.

in Man's Destiny." And a more articulate scientist could not be found for the job.

In the piece Huxley points out early on that the greatest shock to mankind science has so far occasioned was its proof that men are part of nature, and within it, bound to it and by it—not, as men had always thitherto assumed, supranatural.

What Huxley means by the reminder is that man must adapt to nature since man cannot hope to alter the order of reality by managerial, technical, rational, religious, or other means. However, multitudes who assume they are knowledgeable, including multitudes of scientists, have not reached that high a state of shocked awareness. And most men survived by simply ignoring the import of such news altogether.

For example, in a somewhat earlier issue of *Saturday Review*, there appeared an article entitled "What Modern Science Offers the Church," by Emmanuel G. Mesthene, executive director of the Harvard University Program on Technology and Society. In it, the author held that man could, should and would conquer and control nature by technology. The fellow wrote as if that assumption were not only universal and valid but not open any longer even to question.

Just what that might offer the church, even if true, I was not able to discern. But I could see that the author's point of view was opposite to that which Huxley presumed basic among scientists, at least. And I could guess that the director's attitude relates to the program directly, one financed by a long-term grant from the International Business Machines Corporation, a firm obsessed with the idea that technology is the means to all human good.

Sir Julian Huxley had a better idea. His essay lists many of the familiar but grievous blunders of present-day technology and many aspects of civilized behavior that represent threats to our species. He includes the swiftly stepped-up ruination of our living environment, the rapid exhaustion of resources, the pollution of air and water, the population explosion, and the geophysical certainty that unless we soon change our industrial techniques entirely we shall make the planet uninhabitable. He also mentioned the uncontrolled aggressive and nationalistic postures of an animal equipped with H-bombs.

Another of his observations especially beguiled me since it is as sinister as it is strangely obscure to the layman. Our expectation of boundless atomic power from present-style reactors is not warranted. The process involves dealing with highly radioactive reactor components by their hazardous, long-term sequestering. That produces an ever-bigger storage problem, one likely to concern men for centuries and one that will grow while power reactors multiply until it creates a cost factor unacceptable to our debited heirs and assigns. Since the fossil fuels are already earmarked for short-term squandering and since fission is clearly not an unlimited yet practical power source, we must hope that fusion will lend itself to power generation in the relatively near future.

The engineer-physicists in that field are fairly confident it will. Should they fail, however, our hopes even for an ever-greater supply of electrical power will be shattered. In that case we shall be thrown back, at last, on such energy as we can take directly from the sun and from water sun-lifted to turn turbines, along, doubtless, with devices to collect tidal power. These will be costly and their power-yield relatively low. At the moment, then, even man's hopes of an expanding industrial society rest on the possible but unsure exploitation of thermonuclear energy.

Huxley's index of crisis-realities is, however, merely a multiple alarm in the ivory towers, not a program or plan for action. He sees and foresees these certain physical perils, along with some others innate but undefined, within man, yet his suggestions for remedy are near nil.

Humanity must change these ways, and swiftly, or the collision courses cited by Sir Julian will lead to just that, crash, and repeated crashes. One agrees.

But we cannot begin to do anything, the author admits, till we find out what to do. Find out from ethology, he suggests, or Zen, or psychedelic revelation. Broad-minded, that man! Or is he? Psychology offers no hopeful answer, he indicates—which seems rather odd in view of the various fields he puts forward.

Once we get the proper value system for action, though, we mere lay human beings must make the correct changes and in a generation or two, evidently, if Sir Julian's schedule for imminent desperations is sound. Those changes would involve a revolution in a brief period of a magnitude approximately equal to that represented by all the changes men have managed from the Old Stone Age to the present.

By what means are we to find the light and pursue it in a manner that would alter all our goals and shut down or rebuild our factories? Suppose Zen fails us, and LSD?

In Huxley's words, we must do it, "somehow or other."

If that is not a clear illustration of the territorial jail of science, no jail exists. Huxley is in such control of local reason that he is almost nitwitted about unreason even in the territory of scientific minds.

Pure science?

Pure piety!

"You must," sayeth the man in the ivory tower, "for if ye do not, ye shall suffer hell on earth in punishment for your sins!"

So says the preacher in his pulpit. So calls the muezzin from his minaret. The Pope on the balcony. Obey God, Allah, Huxley.

Who the hell's in charge here, and responsible? Who's ethical? The moral superiority of all beings but men has been plain since primates started to do what they still call thinking. To say an end is mandatory and means thereto must be found somehow is to ignore the central point of all such effort, and here, what Huxley isn't.

From OF THE CANNIBALS
Michel de Montaigne
translated by John Florio

As life through simplicity becometh more pleasant, so (as I erewhile began to say) becometh it more innocent and better. The simple and the ignorant, saith St. Paul, raise themselves up to heaven and take possession of it, whereas we, with all the knowledge we have, plunge ourselves down to the pit of hell. I rely neither upon Valentinianus, a professed enemy to knowledge and learning, nor upon Licinius, both Roman emperors, who named them the venom and plague of all politic estates; nor on Mohammet, who, as I have heard, doth utterly interdict all manner of learning to his subjects. But the example of that great Lycurgus and his authority ought to bear chief sway, and the reverence of that divine Lacedaemonian policy, so great, so admirable, and so long time flourishing in all virtue and felicity without any institution or exercise at all of letters. Those who return from that new world which of late hath been discovered by the Spaniards, can witness unto us how those nations, being without magistrates or law, live much more regularly and formally than we, who have amongst us more officers and laws than men of other professions or actions:

> Their hands and bosoms with writs and citations,
> With papers, libels, proxies, full they bear,
> And bundles great of strict examinations,
> Of glosses, counsels, readings here and there.
> Whereby in towns poor men of occupations
> Possess not their small goods secure from fear;
> Before, behind, on each sides, advocates,
> Proctors, and notaries hold up debates.
>
> Ariosto XIV. 84

It was that which a Roman senator said, that their predecessors had their breath stinking of garlic and their stomach perfumed with a good conscience; and contrary, the men of his times outwardly smelt of nothing but sweet odors, but inwardly they stunk of all vices.

A SLOWDOWN IN THE TECHNOLOGY OF HASTE[2]

From the early days of the Republic, when Thomas Jefferson backed Inventor Eli Whitney's design for mass-produced muskets with interchangeable parts, public support for technological progress has been an American tradition. Out of this tradition has grown an obsession with speed, a consequence of the nation's great distances and the rush to cover them quickly, producing what Historian Daniel J. Boorstin calls "a technology of haste" that dates back to the pioneering steamboats of nearly two centuries ago. Add to those themes the national desire to win, to be first. A natural consequence was the

[2]Reprinted by permission from TIME, The Weekly Newsmagazine; Copyright Time Inc., 1971.

historic landing of men on the moon, an event that meant to Eric Hoffer the triumph of the squares, to Norman Mailer the consummation of WASP values. But now, not even two years after Apollo 11, the nation seems to find that kind of victory somewhat hollow.

Such, at least, may be the reason the U. S. Congress has voted to kill the billion-dollar supersonic transport. Rarely before have the lawmakers denied funds for a program billed as essential to American primacy in the world. President Nixon observed last week, after the Senate had joined the House in ending further federal subsidy for the SST, that the congressional action "could be taken as a reversal of America's tradition of staying in the vanguard of scientific and technological advance." Says Paul Seabury, a Berkeley political scientist: "It is the first time in American history that a major technological innovation has been shot down."

Third-Rate. The SST went down despite just such warnings from its backers. "If you're talking about no SST," said Washington's Warren Magnuson just before the Senate voted, "you're talking about no *American* SST. You will be leading America down the road toward becoming a third-rate nation in aviation. We'll be running into a technological Appalachia around here if we're not careful." The vote was another blow to the nation's beleaguered aerospace industry. Afterward Magnuson put a brave face on what had happened—"this isn't a defeat, it's only a setback"—and said that it was the question of national priorities that did him in. "A lot of people talked about mass transit, the need for housing," he grumbled. "Hell, I'm for that, too."

The men who defeated the SST, however, felt that mass transit and the need for housing—and many other urgent domestic issues—far outranked the SST. Several of the House freshmen who unexpectedly tipped the balance against the aircraft said as much. Democrat George Danielson of California: "The need to solve other greater social and economic problems was the most compelling factor. The biggest issues are pollution, better housing, more educational opportunities and mass transit." Democrat Nick Begich of Alaska: "The people do not want this airplane. There are other human resources and public works projects that have a higher priority."

The Los Angeles *Times,* which supported the SST, admitted that the aircraft "became a symbol to a lot of people—a symbol of resistance to the so-called 'military-industrial complex,' a symbol of resistance to technological spoliation of the environment, even a symbol of distaste for President Nixon." Senator Adlai Stevenson III declared: "Congress has not been faced with an issue of such symbolic importance in many years." It was a rare occasion, notes *Time* Senior Correspondent John Steele, for asking some fundamental questions: "Do we really need this? Is it so important to be first in every phase of technology? Are there other things we want and need from life instead? It is obvious to winners and losers alike that something new is afoot—a questioning of old values, old landmarks of progress, old priorities."

Genuine Advance? To John Burke, dean of social sciences at U.C.L.A., the defeat of the SST marks "a change in our civilization's idea of progress." If that is so, it has its dangers, for, as Boorstin points out: "We can't give up the exploring spirit. We can't legislate against progress. Our problem is to find ways of continuing to explore the unknown and still keep our lives decent."

The death of the SST need not be seen as a vote against exploring the unknown. It is not a triumph for the hysterical foes of all technology. For one thing, the SST was vulnerable to the criticism that it does not represent a genuine technical advance. Much of the know-how necessary to build a Mach 3 aircraft—in titanium metallurgy and engine intake design, for example—was already in hand from development of the X-15, the SR-71 and the B-70. Says Harvard Sociologist Daniel Bell: "The technology argument made no sense to anybody who followed it seriously. The SST was not the kind of advance that the jet was over the prop plane."

Seen in that light, the fate of the SST represents a serious break with the compulsion to pursue any technological height only "because it is there." But that is not the same as turning against all progress; it means redefining progress. The new mood could lead to a new sophistication, a new selectivity about what kinds of technology are worth pursuing and at what pace. "Technological wizardry is not an end in itself," Arnold Toynbee observed recently. "It is desirable only if it makes for human welfare, and this is the test that any tool ought to be made to pass." No one can say just yet how firmly the U. S. will henceforth accept that standard, but popular sentiment seems to be moving toward it.

THINGS: THE THROW-AWAY SOCIETY[3]
Alvin Toffler

Alvin Toffler is an American sociologist who specializes in the future. He is currently visiting scholar at the Russell Sage Foundation. He has taught at the New School for Social Research and at Cornell University, and has served as an adviser to IBM and the Institute for the Future.

"Barbie," a twelve-inch plastic teen-ager, is the best-known and best-selling doll in history. Since its introduction in 1959, the Barbie doll population of the world has grown to 12,000,000—more than the human population of Los Angeles or London or Paris. Little girls adore Barbie because she is highly realistic and eminently dressupable. Mattel, Inc., makers of Barbie, also sells a complete wardrobe for her, including clothes for ordinary daytime wear, clothes for formal party wear, clothes for swimming and skiing.

Recently Mattel announced a new improved Barbie doll. The new version has a slimmer figure, "real" eyelashes, and a twist-and-turn waist that makes her more humanoid than ever. Moreover, Mattel announced that, for the first time, any young lady wishing to purchase a new Barbie would receive a trade-in allowance for her old one.

What Mattel did not announce was that by trading in her old doll for a technologically improved model, the little girl of today, citizen of tomorrow's super-industrial world, would learn a fundamental lesson about the new society: that man's relationships with *things* are increasingly temporary.

The ocean of man-made physical objects that surrounds us is set within a larger ocean of natural objects. But increasingly, it is the technologically produced environment that matters for the individual. The texture of plastic or concrete, the iridescent glisten of an automobile under a streetlight, the staggering vision of a cityscape seen from the window of a jet—these are the intimate realities of his existence. Man-made things enter into and color his consciousness. Their number is expanding with explosive force, both absolutely and

[3] From *Future Shock*, by Alvin Toffler. Copyright © 1970 by Alvin Toffler. Reprinted by permission of Random House, Inc.

relative to the natural environment. This will be even more true in super-industrial society than it is today.

Anti-materialists tend to deride the importance of "things." Yet things are highly significant, not merely because of their functional utility, but also because of their psychological impact. We develop relationships with things. Things affect our sense of continuity or discontinuity. They play a role in the structure of situations and the foreshortening of our relationships with things accelerates the pace of life.

Moreover, our attitudes toward things reflect basic value judgments. Nothing could be more dramatic than the difference between the new breed of little girls who cheerfully turn in their Barbies for the new improved model and those who, like their mothers and grandmothers before them, clutch lingeringly and lovingly to the same doll until it disintegrates from sheer age. In this difference lies the contrast between past and future, between societies based on permanence, and the new, fast-forming society based on transience.

The Paper Wedding Gown

That man-thing relationships are growing more and more temporary may be illustrated by examining the culture surrounding the little girl who trades in her doll. This child soon learns that Barbie dolls are by no means the only physical objects that pass into and out of her young life at a rapid clip. Diapers, bibs, paper napkins, Kleenex, towels, non-returnable soda bottles—all are used up quickly in her home and ruthlessly eliminated. Corn muffins come in baking tins that are thrown away after one use. Spinach is encased in plastic sacks that can be dropped into a pan of boiling water for heating, and then thrown away. TV dinners are cooked and often served on throw-away trays. Her home is a large processing machine through which objects flow, appearing and leaving, at a faster and faster rate of speed. From birth on, she is inextricably embedded in a throw-away culture.

The idea of using a product once or for a brief period and then replacing it, runs counter to the grain of societies or individuals steeped in a heritage of poverty. Not long ago Uriel Rone, a market researcher for the French advertising agency Publicis, told me: "The French housewife is not used to disposable products. She likes to keep things, even old things, rather than throw them away. We represented one company that wanted to introduce a kind of plastic throw-away curtain. We did a marketing study for them and found the resistance too strong." This resistance, however, is dying all over the developed world.

Thus a writer, Edward Maze, has pointed out that many Americans visiting Sweden in the early 1950's were astounded by its cleanliness. "We were almost awed by the fact that there were no beer and soft drink bottles by the roadsides, as, much to our shame, there were in America. But by the 1960's, lo and behold, bottles were suddenly blooming along Swedish highways ... What happened? Sweden had become a buy, use and throw-away society, following the American pattern." In Japan today throw-away tissues are so universal that cloth handkerchiefs are regarded as old fashioned, not to say unsanitary. In England for sixpence one may buy a "Dentamatic throw-away toothbrush" which comes already coated with toothpaste for its one-time use. And even in France, disposable cigarette lighters are commonplace. From cardboard milk containers to the rockets that power space vehicles, products created for short-term or one-time use are becoming more numerous and crucial to our way of life.

The recent introduction of paper and quasi-paper clothing carried the trend toward disposability a step further. Fashionable boutiques and working-class clothing stores have sprouted whole departments devoted to gaily colored and imaginatively designed paper apparel. Fashion magazines display breathtakingly sumptuous gowns, coats, pajamas, even wedding dresses made of paper. The bride pictured in one of these wears a long white train of lacelike paper that, the caption writer notes, will make "great kitchen curtains" after the ceremony.

Paper clothes are particularly suitable for children. Writes one fashion expert: "Little girls will soon be able to spill ice cream, draw pictures and make cutouts on their clothes while their mothers smile benignly at their creativity." And for adults who want to express their own creativity, there is even a "paint-yourself-dress" complete with brushes. Price: $2.00.

Price, of course, is a critical factor behind the paper explosion. Thus a department store features simple A-line dresses made of what it calls "devil-may-care cellulose fiber and nylon." At $1.29 each, it is almost cheaper for the consumer to buy and discard a new one than to send an ordinary dress to the cleaners. Soon it will be. But more than economics is involved, for the extension of the throw-away culture has important psychological consequences.

We develop a throw-away mentality to match our throw-away products. This mentality produces, among other things, a set of radically altered values with respect to poverty. But the spread of disposability through the society also implies decreased durations in man-thing relationships. Instead of being linked with a single object over a relatively long span of time, we are linked for brief periods with the succession of objects that supplant it.

JOURNALS
Henry David Thoreau

Aug. 18, 1854

I have just been through the process of killing the cistudo[4] for the sake of science; but I cannot excuse myself for this murder, and see that such actions are inconsistent with the poetic perception, however they may serve science, and will affect the quality of my observations. I pray that I may walk more innocently and serenely through nature. No reasoning whatever reconciles me to this act. It affects my day injuriously. I have lost some self-respect. I have a murderer's experience in a degree.

March 23, 1856

I spend a considerable portion of my time observing the habits of the wild animals, my brute neighbors. By their various movements and migrations they fetch the year about to me. Very significant are the flight of geese and the migration of suckers, etc., etc. But when I consider that the nobler animals have been exterminated here—the cougar, panther, lynx, wolverene, wolf, bear, moose, deer, the beaver, the turkey, etc., etc.—I cannot but feel as if I lived in a tamed, and, as it were, emasculated country. Would not the motions of those larger and wilder animals have been more significant still? Is

[4]Box turtle

it not a maimed and imperfect nature that I am conversant with? As if I were to study a tribe of Indians that had lost all its warriors. Do not the forest and the meadow now lack expression, now that I never see nor think of the moose with a lesser forest on his head in the one, nor of the beaver in the other? When I think what were the various sounds and notes, the migrations and works, and changes of fur and plumage which ushered in the spring and marked the other seasons of the year, I am reminded that this my life in nature, this particular round of natural phenomena which I call a year, is lamentably incomplete. I listen to [a] concert in which so many parts are wanting. The whole civilized country is to some extent turned into a city, and I am that citizen whom I pity. Many of those animal migrations and other phenomena by which the Indians marked the season are no longer to be observed. I seek acquaintance with Nature—to know her moods and manners. Primitive Nature is the most interesting to me. I take infinite pains to know all the phenomena of the spring, for instance, thinking that I have here the entire poem, and then, to my chagrin, I hear that it is but an imperfect copy that I possess and have read, that my ancestors have torn out many of the first leaves and grandest passages, and mutilated it in many places. I should not like to think that some demigod had come before me and picked out some of the best of the stars. I wish to know an entire heaven and an entire earth. All the great trees and beasts, fishes and fowl are gone. The streams, perchance, are somewhat shrunk.

March 15, 1860

A hen-hawk sails away from the wood southward. I get a very fair sight of it sailing overhead. What a perfectly regular and neat outline it presents! an easily recognized figure anywhere. Yet I never see it represented in any books. The exact correspondence of the marks on one side to those on the other, as the black or dark tip of one wing to the other, and the dark line midway the wing. I have no idea that one can get as correct an idea of the form and color of the under sides of a hen-hawk's wings by spreading those of a dead specimen in his study as by looking up at a free and living hawk soaring above him in the fields. The penalty for obtaining a petty knowledge thus dishonestly is that it is less interesting to men generally, as it is less significant. Some, seeing and admiring the neat figure of the hawk sailing two or three hundred feet above their heads, wish to get nearer and hold it in their hands, perchance, not realizing that they can see it best at this distance, better now, perhaps, than ever they will again. What is an eagle in captivity!—screaming in a courtyard! I am not the wiser respecting eagles for having seen one there. I do not wish to know the length of its entrails.

DELINEATIONS OF AMERICAN SCENES AND CHARACTER
John James Audubon

St. John's River, in Florida

The Florida Keys

As the "Marion" approached the inlet called "Indian Key," which is situated on the eastern coast of the peninsula of Florida, my heart swelled with uncontrollable delight. Our vessel once over the coral reef that every where stretches along the shore like a great wall reared by an army of giants, we found ourselves in safe anchorage, within a few furlongs of the land. The next moment saw the oars of a boat propelling us towards the shore, and in brief time, we stood on the desired beach. With what delightful feelings did we gaze on the objects around us!—the gorgeous flowers, the singular and beautiful plants, the luxuriant trees. The balmy air which we breathed filled us with animation, so pure and salubrious did it seem to be. The birds which we saw were almost all new to us; their lovely forms appeared to be arrayed in more brilliant apparel than I had ever before seen, and as they gambolled in happy playfulness among the bushes, or glided over the light green waters, we longed to form a more intimate acquaintance with them.

Students of nature spend little time in introduction, especially when they present themselves to persons who feel an interest in their pursuits. This was the case with Mr. Thruston, the Deputy Collector of the island, who shook us all heartily by the hand, and in a trice had a boat manned at our service. Accompanied by him, his pilot and fishermen, off we went, and after a short pull landed on a large key. Few minutes had elapsed, when shot after shot might be heard, and down came whirling through the air the objects of our desire. One of us thrust himself into the tangled groves that covered all but the beautiful coral beach that in a continued line bordered the island, while others gazed on the glowing and diversified hues of the curious inhabitants of the deep. I saw one of my party rush into the limpid element, to seize on a crab, that with claws extended upwards, awaited his approach, as if determined not to give way. A loud voice called him back to the land, for sharks are as abundant along these shores as pebbles, and the hungry prowlers could not have got a more savoury dinner.

The pilot, besides being a first-rate shooter, possessed a most intimate acquaintance with the country. He had been a "conch-diver," and no matter what number of fathoms measured the distance between the surface of the water and its craggy bottom, to seek for curious shells in their retreat seemed to him more pastime than toil. Not a Cormorant or Pelican, a Flamingo, an Ibis, or Heron, had ever in his days formed its nest without his having marked the spot; and as to the Keys to which the Doves are wont to resort, he was better acquainted with them than many fops are with the contents of their pockets. In a word, he positively knew every channel that led to these islands, and every cranny along their shores. For years his employment had been to hunt those singular animals called Sea Cows or-Manatees, and he had conquered hundreds of them, "merely," as he said, because the flesh and hide bring "a fair price," at Havannah. He never went anywhere to land without "Long Tom," which proved indeed to be a wonderful gun, and which made smart havoc when charged with "groceries," a term by which he designated the large shot which he used. In like manner, he never paddled his light canoe without having by his side the trusty javelin, with which he unerringly transfixed such fishes as he thought fit either for market or for his own use. In attacking turtles, netting, or overturning them, I doubt if his equal ever lived on the Florida coast. No sooner was he made acquainted with my errand, than he freely offered his best services, and from that moment until I left Key West he was seldom out of my hearing.

While the young gentlemen who accompanied us were engaged in procuring plants, shells, and small birds, he tapped me on the shoulder, and with a smile said to me, "Come along, I'll shew you something better worth your while." To the boat we betook ourselves, with the Captain and only a pair of tars, for more he said would not answer. The yawl for a while was urged at a great rate, but as we approached a point, the oars were taken in, and the pilot alone "sculling," desired us to make ready, for in a few minutes we should have "rare sport." As we advanced, the more slowly did we move, and the most profound silence was maintained, until suddenly coming almost in contact with a thick shrubbery of mangroves, we beheld, right before us, a multitude of pelicans. A discharge of artillery seldom produced more effect;—the dead, the dying, and the wounded, fell from the trees upon the water, while those unscathed flew screaming through the air in terror and dismay. "There," said he, "did not I tell you so? is it not rare sport?" The birds, one after another, were lodged under the gunwales, when the pilot desired the captain to order the lads to pull away. Within about half a mile we reached the extremity of the key. "Pull away," cried the pilot, "never mind them on the wing, for those black rascals don't mind a little firing—now, boys, lay her close under the nests." And there we were, with four hundred cormorants' nests over our heads. The birds were sitting, and when we fired, the number that dropped as if dead, and plunged into the water was such, that I thought by some unaccountable means or other we had killed the whole colony. You would have smiled at the loud laugh and curious gestures of the pilot. "Gentlemen," said he, "almost a blank shot!" And so it was, for, on following the birds as one after another peeped up from the water, we found only a few unable to take to wing. "Now," said the pilot, "had you waited until *I had spoken* to the black villains, you might have killed a score or more of them." On inspection, we found that our shots had lodged in the tough dry twigs of which these birds form their nests, and that we had lost the more favourable opportunity of hitting them, by not waiting until they rose. "Never mind," said the pilot, "if you wish it, you may load the *Lady of the Green Mantle* [5] with them in less than a week. Stand still, my lads; and now, gentlemen, in ten minutes you and I will bring down a score of them." And so we did. As we rounded the island, a beautiful bird of the species called Peale's Egret, came up and was shot. We now landed, took in the rest of our party, and returned to Indian Key, where we arrived three hours before sunset.

[5] The name given by the wreckers and smugglers to the Marion.

The sailors and other individuals to whom my name and pursuits had become known, carried our birds to the pilot's house. His good wife had a room ready for me to draw in, and my assistant might have been seen busily engaged in skinning, while George Lehman was making a sketch of the lovely isle.

Time is ever precious to the student of nature. I placed several birds in their natural attitudes, and began to delineate them. A dance had been prepared also, and no sooner was the sun lost to our eye, than males and females, including our captain and others from the vessel, were seen advancing gaily towards the house in full apparel. The birds were skinned, the sketch was on paper, and I told my young men to amuse themselves. As to myself, I could not join in the merriment, for, full of the remembrance of you, reader, and of the patrons of my work both in America and in Europe, I went on "grinding"—not on an organ, like the Lady of Bras d'Or, but on paper, to the finishing, not merely of my outlines, but of my notes respecting the objects seen this day.

The room adjoining that in which I worked, was soon filled. Two miserable fiddlers screwed their screeching silken strings—not an inch of catgut graced their instruments; and the bouncing of brave lads and fair lasses shook the premises to the foundation. One with a slip came down heavily on the floor, and the burst of laughter that followed echoed over the isle. Diluted claret was handed round to cool the ladies, while a beverage of more potent energies warmed their partners. After supper our captain returned to the Marion, and I, with my young men, slept in light swinging hammocks under the eaves of the piazza.

It was the end of April, when the nights were short and the days therefore long. Anxious to turn every moment to account, we were on board Mr. Thruston's boat at three next morning. Pursuing our way through the deep and tortuous channels that every where traverse the immense muddy soap-like flats that stretch from the outward Keys to the Main, we proceeded on our voyage of discovery. Here and there we met with great beds of floating seaweeds which shewed us that Turtles were abundant there, these masses being the refuse of their food. On talking to Mr. Thruston of the nature of these muddy flats, he mentioned that he had once been lost amongst their narrow channels for several days and nights, when in pursuit of some smugglers' boat, the owners of which were better acquainted with the place than the men who were along with him. Although in full sight of several of the Keys, as well as of the main land, he was unable to reach either, until a heavy gale raised the water, when he sailed directly over the flats, and returned home almost exhausted with fatigue and hunger. His present pilot often alluded to the circumstance afterwards, ending with a great laugh, and asserting that had he "been there, the rascals would not have escaped."

Coming under a Key on which multitudes of Frigate Pelicans had begun to form their nests, we shot a good number of them, and observed their habits. The boastings of our pilot were here confirmed by the exploits which he performed with his long gun, and on several occasions he brought down a bird from a height of fully a hundred yards. The poor birds, unaware of the range of our artillery, sailed calmly along, so that it was not difficult for "Long Tom," or rather for his owner, to furnish us with as many as we required. The day was spent in this manner, and towards night we returned, laden with booty, to the hospitable home of the pilot.

The next morning was delightful. The gentle sea-breeze glided over the flowery isle, the horizon was clear, and all was silent save the long breakers that rushed over the distant reefs. As we were proceeding towards some Keys, seldom visited by men, the sun rose from the bosom of the waters with a burst of glory that impressed on my soul the idea of that Power which called into existence so magnificent an object. The moon, thin and pale, as if ashamed to show her feeble light, concealed herself in the dim west. The surface of the waters shone in its tremulous smoothness, and the deep blue of the clear heavens was pure as the world that lies beyond them. The Heron heavily flew towards the land, like the glutton retiring at day-break, with well-lined paunch, from the house of some wealthy patron of good cheer. The Night Heron and the Owl, fearful of day, with hurried flight sought safety in the recesses of the deepest swamps; while the Gulls and Terns, ever cheerful, gambolled over the water, exulting in the prospect of abundance. I also exulted in hope, my whole frame seemed to expand; and our sturdy crew shewed, by their merry faces, that nature had charms for them too. How much of beauty and joy is lost to them who never view the rising sun, and of whose wakeful existence the best half is nocturnal!

Twenty miles our men had to row before we reached "Sandy Island," and as on its level shores we all leaped, we plainly saw the

the southernmost cape of the Floridas. The flocks of birds that covered the shelly beaches, and those hovering over head, so astonished us that we could for a while scarcely believe our eyes. The first volley procured a supply of food sufficient for two days' consumption. Such tales, you have already been told, are well enough at a distance from the place to which they refer; but you will doubtless be still more surprised when I tell you that our first fire among the crowd of the Great Godwits laid prostrate sixty-five of these birds. Rose-coloured Curlews stalked gracefully beneath the mangroves; Purple Herons rose at almost every step we took, and each cactus supported the nest of a White Ibis. The air was darkened by whistling wings, while, on the waters, floated Gallinules and other interesting birds. We formed a kind of shed with sticks and grass, the sailor cook commenced his labours, and ere long we supplied the deficiencies of our fatigued frames. The business of the day over, we secured ourselves from insects by means of musquito-nets, and were lulled to rest by the cackles of the beautiful Purple Gallinules!

ON SHOOTING PARTICLES BEYOND THE WORLD[6]
Richard Eberhart

Richard Eberhart (1904–), born in Austin, Minnesota, currently lives in Hanover, New Hampshire, where he is professor of English at Dartmouth College. He was founder and first president of The Poets' Theater in Cambridge, Massachusetts, and served a term as Consultant in Poetry at the Library of Congress from 1959 to 1961.

"White Sands, N. M. Dec. 18 (UP). 'We first throw a little something into the skies,' Zwicky said. 'Then a little more, then a shipload of instruments—then ourselves.'"

On this day man's disgust is known
Incipient before but now full blown
With minor wars of major consequence,
Duly building empirical delusions.

[6]From *Collected Poems, 1930–1960* by Richard Eberhart. © 1960 by Richard Eberhart. Reprinted by permission of Oxford University Press and Chatto & Windus, Ltd.

Now this little creature in a rage
Like new-born infant screaming compleat angler
Objects to the whole globe itself
And with a vicious lunge he throws

Metal particles beyond the orbit of mankind.
Beethoven shaking his fist at death,
A giant dignity in human terms,
Is nothing to this imbecile metal fury.

The world is too much for him. The green
Of earth is not enough, love's deities,
Peaceful intercourse, happiness of nations,
The wild animal dazzled on the desert.

If the maniac would only realize
The comforts of his padded cell
He would have penetrated the
Impenetrability of the spiritual.

It is not intelligent to go too far.
How he frets that he can't go too!
But his particles would maim a star,
His free-floating bombards rock the moon.

Good Boy! We pat the baby to eructate,
We pat him then for eructation.
Good Boy Man! Your innards are put out,
From now all space will be your vomitorium.

The atom bomb accepted this world,
Its hatred of man blew death in his face.
But not content, he'll send slugs beyond,
His particles of intellect will spit on the sun.

Not God he'll catch, in the mystery of space.
He flaunts his own out-cast state
As he throws his imperfections outward bound,
And his shout that gives a hissing sound.

Part
Four

Solutions:
Variations on a
Theme of the
Simple Life

Never anything can be amiss
When simpleness and duty tender it.

Shakespeare,
A Midsummer Night's Dream

By now we are all familiar with proposals to solve our ecological problems. We have been bombarded with advice: avoid pesticides, use biodegradable soap, recycle bottles, paper, and scrap. All of this is good advice, of course, but it doesn't really get to the heart of the problem. What is needed is a fundamental change in attitude among the peoples of the world. The problems of pollution and urban blight will not vanish until a majority of the people on this earth strip away the veneer of materialistic civilization with which they have encrusted themselves and get back to nature and the simple life. Accordingly, we begin this part with American naturalist John Burroughs's description of the simple life: "direct and immediate contact with things, life with the false wrappings torn off—the fine house, the fine equipage, the expensive habits, all cut off."

Oriental religious tradition has long stressed the holiness of the simple life: "Reveal thy Simple Self," says the Book of Tao, the Chinese Bible. Much Oriental poetry reflects this idea. T'ao Ch'ien, Chinese poet, begins "A Fire":

> *For a hut on a poor lane*
> *I would willingly give up a mansion.*[1]

T'ao Ch'ien's tale of the lost village reflects the desire to escape the toils of civilization for a simple paradise where

> *The children sang without restraint*
> *The aged relaxed and roamed in peace.*[2]

An important part of the Oriental conception of simple life is working with nature. Masters of Oriental literature generally held the

---

[1] From *The Poems of T'ao Ch'ien*, translated by Lily Pao-Hu Chang and Marjorie Sinclair. Reprinted by permission of the University of Hawaii Press, © 1953.

[2] From *The Poems of T'ao Ch'ien*, translated by Lily Pao-Hu Chang and Marjorie Sinclair. Reprinted by permission of the University of Hawaii Press. © 1953.

belief that great art springs from man's ability to commune with nature. Bashō, the great seventeenth-century Japanese poet, explains the necessity to lose one's sense of self and become immersed in nature.

> Go to the pine if you want to learn about the pine, or to the bamboo if you want to learn about the bamboo. And in doing so, you must leave your subjective preoccupation with yourself. Otherwise you impose yourself on the subject and do not learn. Your poetry issues of its own accord when you and the object have become one—when you have plunged deep enough into the object to see something like a hidden glimmering there. However well phrased your poetry may be, if your feeling is not natural—if the object and yourself are separate—then your poetry is not true poetry but merely your subjective counterfeit.[3]

The Narrow Road to the Deep North and Other Travel Sketches is a prose and verse record of Bashō's decision to leave his comfortable but stultifying life and become a lonely, possessionless wanderer whose itinerary was governed only by nature. He walked for weeks to experience the blooming of the famous cherry blossoms of Yoshino or the beauty of Kisagata lagoon. He delighted in the treasures disguised as weeds beside the road. Nature, as his sensitive writing attests, became for Bashō the source of artistic excellence as well as the source of life.

An important part of the simple life is repose and contemplation. In "Life as Visionary Spirit" contemporary American poet Richard Eberhart urges man to free himself from action:

> *Nothing like the freedom of vision,*
> *To look from a hill to the sea,*
> *Meditating one's bile and bible: free*
> *From action, to be . . .*
>
> *Let the soul softly idle,*
> *Beyond past, beyond future. . . .*[4]

[3]Matsuo Bashō: *The Narrow Road To The Deep North and Other Travel Sketches* translated by Nobuyuki Yuasa (Penguin Classics 1966) pp. 97-117: *The Narrow Road to the Deep North.* Copyright © Nobuyuki Yuasa, 1966.

[4]From *Collected Poems, 1930*–1960 by Richard Eberhart. © 1960 by Richard Eberhart. Reprinted by permission of Oxford University Press and Chatto & Windus, Ltd.

Bertolt Brecht asserts that repose, particularly in the midst of nature, leads to communion. In "Of Swimming in Lakes and Rivers," he says:

> *You must float inert in a pool or in a river*
> *Like the waterweeds in which pike are lying*

To float and drift aimlessly leads man to God, "When at evening He swims in His rivers here below."

A corollary of the idea of the simple life is the idea of "reverence for life," to use Albert Schweitzer's phrase. Schweitzer, who left the comforts of upper-class German civilization for the primitive life of the African jungle, makes reverence for life the basis of his spiritual relationship with the universe.

CHAPTER
THIRTEEN
Idling

LIFE AS VISIONARY SPIRIT[1]
Richard Eberhart

Nothing like the freedom of vision,
*   To look from a hill to the sea,*
Meditating one's bile and bible: free
*   From action, to be.*

The best moment is when
*   Stillness holds the air motionless,*
So that time can bless
*   History, blood is a caress.*

[1]From *Collected Poems, 1930–1960* by Richard Eberhart. © 1960 by Richard Eberhart. Reprinted by permission of Oxford University Press and Chatto & Windus.

Neither in landwork nor in seawork
Believe. Belief must be pure.
Let the soul softly idle,
Beyond past, beyond future.

Let it be said, "A great effulgence
Grows upon the sandspit rose.
A rare salt harrows the air.
Your eyes show divine shows."

OF SWIMMING IN LAKES AND RIVERS[2]
Bertolt Brecht
translated by H. R. Hays

Bertolt Brecht (1898–1956) was a German dramatist and poet. A Marxist exile from Hitler, Brecht lived in the United States until after World War II, when he moved to East Germany. His brilliant talents and penchant for experimentation have made him one of the major influences on contemporary drama. Among his best-known works are *Mother Courage*, *Beggar's Opera*, and *The Good Woman of Setzuan*.

In the pale summertime, when far above you
In only the largest trees the winds are sighing,
You must float inert in a pool or in a river
Like the waterweeds in which pike are lying.
Your flesh grows light in water. Thrust your arm
Softly from water into air and now
The little wind cradles it forgetfully,
Seeming to take it for a brown bough.

[2]From *Of Swimming in Lakes and Rivers* by Bertolt Brecht. Reprinted by permission of Suhrkamp Verlag. Copyright © 1960 Suhrkamp Verlag, Frankfurt am Main.

At midday the sky proffers a great stillness.
You close your eyes when the swallows pass you.
The mud is warm. When the cool bubbles rise up
You know that a fish has just swum across you.
Your body, your thigh and motionless arm
Lie in quiet unity, only when the cool
Fish are swimming lazily across you
Can you feel the sun shine down upon the pool.

In the evening when, from long lying,
You grow so lazy that all your limbs prickle
Without a backward glance you must fling yourself,
Splashing, into a blue river where the rapids ripple.
It is best to hold out until evening comes
For then, like a shark over stream and shrubbery,
The pale sky looms, angry and gluttonous,
And all things are just as they should be.

You must, of course, lie on your back quietly
As is usual and let yourself go on drifting.
You must not swim, no, but only act as if
You were a mass of flotsam slowly shifting.
You must look up at the sky and act as if
A woman carried you, and it is so.
Quiet, without disturbance, as the good God himself does
When at evening he swims in his rivers here below.

SHADY, SHADY THE WOOD IN FRONT OF THE HALL[3]
T'ao Ch'ien
translated by Arthur Waley

Shady, shady the wood in front of the Hall:
At midsummer full of calm shadows.
The south wind follows summer's train:

[3] From *Translations from the Chinese*, by Arthur Waley. Copyright 1919, 1941 by Alfred A. Knopf, Inc., and renewed 1947 by Arthur Waley. Reprinted by permission of the publisher.

With its eddying puffs it blows open my coat.
I am free from ties and can live a life of retirement.
When I rise from sleep, I play with books and harp.
The lettuce in the garden still grows moist:
Of last year's grain there is always plenty left.
Self-support should maintain strict limits:
More than enough is not what I want.
I grind millet and make good wine:
When the wine is heated, I pour it out for myself.
My little children are playing at my side,
Learning to talk, they babble unformed sounds.
These things have made me happy again
And I forget my lost cap of office.
Distant, distant I gaze at the white clouds:
With a deep yearning I think of the Sages of Antiquity.

A FIRE[4]
T'ao Ch'ien
translated by Lily Pao-Hu Chang and Marjorie Sinclair

In the Middle of the Sixth Month
In the Year Wu Shêng

For a hut on a poor lane
I would willingly give up a mansion!
In summer a wind came quickly,
And my house was suddenly burned.
Of the whole house, not one room was left—
Only the boat anchored under the shade in front of my gate.
High is the sky of the new autumn evenings,
When the delicate moon will be full again.
Fruits and vegetables are growing.
The startled birds have not yet returned.

[4]From *The Poems of T'ao Ch'ien*, translated by Lily Pao-Hu Chang and Marjorie Sinclair. Reprinted by permission of the University of Hawaii Press, © 1953.

In the middle of the night, I stand alone with far-off thoughts;
In one glance I embrace the nine heavens.
When young, I made my own decision,
And forty years have passed since I left home.
Form and shape are gone with change,
But the house of the spirit is tranquil.
Truth and fortitude certainly have substance;
Even jade and rock are not comparable.
I think of the good times
When there was grain left in the open fields overnight,
And people had full stomachs and nothing to worry about.
They got up early and returned late.
I am not living in that time,
So it is better to water the western garden.

MOVING[5]
T'ao Ch'ien
translated by Lily Pao-Hu Chang and Marjorie Sinclair

[2]

Many are the beautiful days in spring and autumn
For climbing hills and composing new poems!
When we pass each other, we call out cheerfully.
If we have wine, we pour it out and drink.
When the farm work is done, we return to our homes,
And when there is leisure, we miss each other.
When we miss each other, we call on each other,
And talk and laugh endlessly;
Nothing can surpass such happiness.
How can I leave this?
To have food and clothing enough,
I need only to cultivate the land.

[5]From *The Poems of T'ao Ch'ien*, translated by Lily Pao-Hu Chang and Marjorie Sinclair.
Reprinted by permission of the University of Hawaii Press, © 1953.

A HEIFER CLAMBERS UP[6]
Gary Snyder

a heifer clambers up
        nighthawk goes out
                horses
trail back to the barn.
        spider gleams in his
                new web
dew on the shingles, on the car,
        on the mailbox—
the mole, the onion, and the beetle
        cease their wars.
                worlds tip
into the sunshine, men and women
        get up, babies crying
children grab their lunches
                and leave for school.
the radio announces
        in the milking barn
                in the car bound for work
"tonight all the countries
        will get drunk and have a party"
russia, america, china,
                singing with their poets,
pregnant and gracious,
        sending flowers and dancing bears
                to all the capitals
fat
        with the baby happy land

TO THE CHINESE COMRADES[7]
Gary Snyder

Chairman Mao, you should quit smoking.
    Dont bother those philosophers
Build dams, plant trees,
    dont kill flies by hand,
Marx was another westerner.
    it's all in the head.
You dont need the bomb.
    stick to farming.
Write some poems. Swim the river.
    those blue overalls are great.
Dont shoot me, let's go drinking.
    just
Wait.

[7]Gary Snyder, *The Back Country. Copyright* © 1965 by Gary Snyder. Reprinted by permission of New Directions Publishing Corporation.

CHAPTER FOURTEEN
Shangri-Las

ALL WATCHED OVER BY MACHINES OF LOVING GRACE[1]
Richard Brautigan

I like to think (and
the sooner the better!)
of a cybernetic meadow
where mammals and computers
live together in mutually
programming harmony
like pure water
touching clear sky.

[1]From *The Pill Versus the Springhill Mine Disaster* by Richard Brautigan. Copyright © 1968 by Richard Brautigan. A Seymour Lawrence Book/Delacorte Press. Reprinted by permission of the publisher.

I like to think
      (right now, please!)
of a cybernetic forest
filled with pines and electronics
where deer stroll peacefully
past computers
as if they were flowers
with spinning blossoms.

I like to think
      (it has to be!)
of a cybernetic ecology
where we are free of our labors
and joined back to nature,
returned to our mammal
brothers and sisters,
and all watched over
by machines of loving grace.

LET'S VOYAGE INTO THE NEW AMERICAN HOUSE[2]
Richard Brautigan

There are doors
that want to be free
from their hinges to
fly with perfect clouds.

There are windows
that want to be
released from their
frames to run with
the deer through
back country meadows.

There are walls
that want to prowl
with the mountains
through the early
morning dusk.

There are floors
that want to digest
their furniture into
flowers and trees.

There are roofs
that want to travel
gracefully with
the stars through
circles of darkness.

PEACH BLOSSOM FOUNTAIN[3]
T'ao Ch'ien
translated by Lily Pao-Hu Chang and Marjorie Sinclair

In the reign of T'ai-yüan of the Chin Dynasty, there lived in Wuling a fisherman. One day he sailed up a stream and, forgetful of the distance he had gone, suddenly came upon a grove of blossoming peach trees. The grove, which contained only peach trees, extended a hundred feet along the banks. The flowers were fresh and beautiful, dropping their petals everywhere. The fisherman was curious about the grove and continued through it to the other side. There he found the source of the stream. Just beyond it lay a mountain, and in the mountain he saw a small opening which glimmered, as if light shone through.

He stepped from his boat and went into the opening; the entrance was very narrow, barely room enough for one person. After walking some distance along the passageway, he came suddenly upon the brilliance of daylight. He saw before him a broad and level land,

[3]From *The Poems of T'ao Ch'ien*, translated by Lily Pao-Hu Chang and Marjorie Sinclair. Reprinted by permisssion of the University of Hawaii Press, © 1953.

with the houses neatly laid out, rich fields and beautiful ponds, mulberry trees, bamboos, and many other things. There were paths between the fields, and the clamor of crowing chickens and barking dogs mingled. He saw men and women, wearing clothes like those of the outsiders, coming and going, and working together. Old and young, all seemed to be happy and contented. When they noticed the fisherman, they were startled and asked where he had come from. After he had answered, they wanted to return immediately to their homes to prepare wine and kill chickens for a feast.

The villagers, hearing of the arrival of this person, came to see him. They told him that their ancestors, in order to avoid the trouble of Ch'in, had come to this hidden place with their wives and children. They had never returned and were cut off completely from the outside. They asked him what dynasty was reigning now. They had never heard of the Han Dynasty or of Wei and Chin. The fisherman told them what he knew, and they sighed and were moved. They wanted to invite him to their homes, and they all laid out wine and food.

He stayed on for several days and then said goodbye. The people cautioned him, "It is not worthwhile to tell the outsiders." After he came out, he stepped into his boat and sailed back down the stream, recording the landmarks on the way. When he reached the city, he went to the governor and told him what he had seen. The governor then sent men with him to find the place; they hunted for the landmarks but lost their way and could not continue.

Liu Tzu-chi of Nanyang, a learned scholar, heard of this and happily set out to go there. But he had no success, and soon afterwards he died of an illness. Since then no one has asked for the way.

During the reign of the despotic Emperor Ying,
Virtuous men shunned this world.
Huang and Chi took refuge in Mount Shang.
People died, it is said,
And the road became lost.
The path on which they set out had grown weedy.
They followed their destiny and farmed the fields.

When the sun set, they rested;
Bamboo and mulberry cast a shade.
With seasonal farming, they rotated the crops,
And in the spring, silk was gathered.
Autumn harvests were not given for taxes.
The weedy land discouraged travelling;
Roosters crowed and dogs barked together.
The people retained the ancient way of living,
And they made no new gowns.
The children sang without restraint;
The aged relaxed and roamed in peace.
When the grass was green, they knew the season was good,
And when the trees were sere, they knew the wind was sharp.
Although they kept no record of time,
The rotation of the four seasons naturally made a year.
There was peace and harmony.
Why should one work for knowledge and wisdom?
In this beautiful land five hundred people hid themselves.
One day the heavenly place was opened.
The life was simple and seemed to have a different origin;
Before long it was again closed.
May I ask you travellers
What you think of this land beyond the dust and the noise?
I want to drift with the gentle wind
And go searching for this place.

CHAPTER FIFTEEN
Back to Nature

A WISH[1]
Robert Creely

      Robert Creely (1926–) was born in Massachusetts, attended college at Harvard and Black Mountain, and presently teaches at the University of New Mexico.

So much rain
to make the mud again,
trees green
and flowers also.

[1]"A Wish" is reprinted with the permission of Charles Scribner's Sons from *For Love* by Robert Creely. Copyright © 1962 Robert Creely.

The water which
ran up the sun
and down again,
it is the same.

A man of supple
yielding manner
might, too, discover
ways of water.

SOME THOUGHTS ON WILD FOOD[2]
Euell Gibbons

Euell Gibbons is a contemporary American naturalist and champion of foraging for wild foods. Gibbons argues that searching woods and meadows for food is not only entertaining but also helps put man back in close contact with nature.

Why bother with wild food plants in a country which produces a surplus of many domestic food products? With as much reason, one might ask, why go fishing for mountain trout when codfish fillets are for sale in any supermarket? Or why bother with hunting and game cookery when unlimited quantities of fine meat can be purchased at every butcher counter?

Why do millions of Americans desert their comfortable and convenient apartments and split-level houses for a time each year to go camping under comparatively primitive conditions in our forests and national parks? For that matter, why does anyone go for a walk on a woodland trail when one could be speeding along a superhighway in a high-powered automobile?

We live in a vastly complex society which has been able to provide us with a multitude of material things, and this is good, but people are beginning to suspect that we have paid a high spiritual

[2] From *Stalking The Wild Asparagus,* by Euell Gibbons. Copyright © 1962 by Euell Gibbons (New York: David McKay Company, Inc.) Used by permission of the publisher.

price for our plenty. Each person would like to feel that he is an entity, a separate individual capable of independent existence, and this is hard to believe when everything that we eat, wear, live in, drive, use or handle has required the cooperative effort of literally millions of people to produce, process, transport, and, eventually, distribute to our hands. Man simply must feel that he is more than a mere mechanical part in this intricately interdependent industrial system. We enjoy the comfort and plenty which this highly organized production and distribution has brought us, but don't we sometimes feel that we are living a secondhand sort of existence, and that we are in danger of losing all contact with the origins of life and the nature which nourishes it?

Fortunately, there is a saving streak of the primitive in all of us. Every man secretly believes that if he were an Adam, set down in a virgin world, he would not only be able to survive but could also provide well for his Eve and any number of little Cains and Abels. Who has not dreamed of escaping the increasing complexities and frustrations of modern life by running off to some South Sea isle and living on coconuts, fish and breadfruit?

I have tried the lotus-eating life of a Pacific beachcomber and found it lacking. I'm sure it will surprise many when I assert that it is easier to "go native" in many sections of the United States than in the South Seas. There are thousands of spots in this country where, with the requisite knowledge, a man could live solely on the bounty of nature far more easily than on any Pacific island I know. With the judicious, if incongruous, use of a home freezer, he could stay fat the year around by "reaping where he did not sow."

Probably very few of us will ever be faced with the necessity of living off the country for any extended period of time. The outdoor skills, necessary to the survival of our ancestors, are now utilized in the service of recreation. In recent years there has been a great renewal of interest in hunting, fishing and camping. I do not consider this a deplorable atavism, but a creative protest against the artificiality of our daily lives. A knowledge of wild food gathering can contribute greatly to our enjoyment of this back-to-nature movement. It can add new meaning to every camping trip, to every hike or even to a Sunday drive in the country. It involves no dangerous or expensive equipment and is an activity that can be shared by the whole family. Even those too gentle or too squeamish to kill and dress game or fish can enjoy gathering and preparing wild plant food for the camp table. Those who remember when they packed a picnic lunch and went out for a day's berrying or nutting will never deny the possibilities of wild food gathering as a family recreation.

Children, especially, are intrigued with the idea of garnering their food from the fields and byways. The child's unspoiled sense of wonder is excited when he discovers the possibility of living, at least in part, as our more primitive forebears did. His enjoyment and appreciation of nature are vastly increased when he knows her secrets and how she can minister to his needs. I have seen several feeding problems cured merely by interesting the child in the gathering and preparation of wild food plants. Food takes on a new meaning to the child who has participated in this fundamental method of acquiring it. Children who have the opportunity of sharing this fascinating hobby with an interested family for only a single season will learn a great deal more about the basic processes of nature than many years of classroom instruction can teach them.

Another point in favor of foraging as a family hobby is the handiness with which it can be practiced. One doesn't need to go to the mountains or virgin forests to find wild food plants. In fact, mountains and dense forests are among the poorer places to look. Abandoned farmsteads, old fields, fence rows, burned-off areas, roadsides, along streams, woodlots, around farm ponds, swampy areas and even vacant lots are the finest foraging sites.

I have lived at my present address for only a few months and I am not as familiar with the area as I would like to be. But, just for fun and to escape from the typewriter for a while, I interrupted this writing to take my notebook and go for an hour's walk. Without going more than a half mile from the house, I saw, identified and recorded more than sixty species of plants good for human food and several of these had more than one edible part.

A look at this list tells me that I could gather edible fruits, nuts, leaves, buds, blossoms, sprouts, stems, sap, grain, roots, tubers, bulbs and seeds. I could prepare salads, vegetables in all shapes, forms and colors, root vegetables, starchy vegetables, high-protein vegetables, cereals, breadstuffs, beverages, condiments, sugar, desserts, pickles, jams, jellies and preserves from the plants growing in the small area I covered on my walk. Many of these raw materials were present in great quantities. One could forage all the vegetable food a family could use in a season from these few acres and never have the same menu twice.

Of course, not all the plants I saw were in the edible stage when I observed them in early June. However, about half of them were offering nutritious and palatable food right then, and all the rest were fairly shouting promises of plenty to come to anyone who understood their language.

Some might contend that I live in an especially favored locality, but this is not true. Come with me for an hour's walk in almost any rural or suburban area in the eastern half of our country, and I will point out as many edible wild plants to you, though not necessarily the same ones. I have collected fifteen species that could be used for food on a vacant lot right in Chicago. Eighteen different kinds were pointed out in the circuit of a two-acre pond near Philadelphia. We actually gathered—and later ate—eleven different kinds of wild food, in an afternoon spent strolling along Chesapeake Bay. The hunter or fisherman may often come home empty-handed, but the forager, although he may fail to find the particular plant he is seeking, can always load his knapsack with wholesome and palatable food. The species of plants which the forager finds will change as the seasons advance, but the fields and forests can always furnish something good to eat.

The fact that this food costs nothing but the labor of gathering and preparing it will appeal to many. There is seldom a day in the year when wild food, in one form or another, does not grace our table, and I must admit that it helps to keep our budget within the bounds imposed by the income of a free-lance writer, but that is not the primary reason I seek it. Foraging to me, is a sport, a hobby and my chief source of recreation. One must approach wild food with the right attitude, both in the woods and on the table. Don't try it solely as a means of economizing on food bills, when you hate the necessity for being economical. Unless you approach wild food with genuine interest and love, you will never become a skilled forager. If you dislike the activity of gathering and preparing these natural dainties, you will end up with an unpleasant-tasting mess that will satisfy only half your hunger.

There are a number of wild plants that are cooked and served like asparagus, some starchy roots and tubers that are cooked like potatoes, and many green vegetables that are prepared in the same manner as spinach. Don't make the error of thinking of these foods as *substitutes* for asparagus, potatoes and spinach, or you will fail to appreciate them for their own very real merits. Each species has a flavor, aroma and texture all its own, and is a good food in and of itself and doesn't have to pose as a substitute for something else.

Learn to appreciate new flavors. Relegating good food to the category of "an acquired taste" and refusing to eat it for this reason is reactionary. All tastes are acquired tastes, as is easily seen when one examines the bills of fare of populations in different parts of the world. We are not born with a preference for any food except human milk, and, since this product hardly figures in the diet of adults, we have had to learn to like all that we eat. When one says, in effect, that he will refuse to touch any food for which he did not acquire a taste in early childhood, he is showing symptoms of mental and emotional hardening of the arteries.

I consider the mango and the papaya two of the most delectable fruits with which God graced an already bountiful world. Yet, when I was in the tropics, I saw tourists from temperate regions refuse mangoes because they didn't taste like peaches, and show disgust at papayas because they thought they should taste just like muskmelons and didn't. Such people have my pity, but hardly my respect.

Many of the staple foods we eat today, and even some that we consider luxurious dainties, were once refused on the grounds of prejudice. Wild rice was considered very poor fare as long as it was thought of as a substitute for the polished product of cultivated fields and processing plants. Yet today if you tried to buy any sizable amount of wild rice, you would proably have to make some arrangement with a finance company. One of the earliest reports on maple sugar as made by the Indians, written about 1700, says that the sugar "lacks the pleasing, delicate taste of cane sugar." Now we meekly pay many times the price of cane sugar for this finest of sweets.

Some readers will claim that they prefer to buy their fruit and vegetables from a supermarket for reasons of sanitation and cleanliness. This is the most illogical prejudice of all, as is easily demonstrated. The devitalized and days-old produce usually found on your grocer's shelves has been raised in ordinary dirt, manured with

God-knows-what, and sprayed with poisons a list of which would read like a textbook on toxicology. They were harvested by migrant workers who could be suffering from any number of obnoxious diseases, handled by processors and salespeople and picked over by hordes of customers before you bought them.

By contrast, wild food grows in the clean, uncultivated fields and woods, and has never been touched by human hands until you come along to claim it. No artificial manures, with their possible sources of pollution, have ever been placed around it. Nature's own methods have maintained the fertility that produced it and no poisonous sprays have ever come near it. Wild food is clean because it has never been dirty. You'll have to find a better argument than the one on sanitation before you persuade me that I shouldn't eat wild foods, for, in the matter of cleanliness, wild products are so far ahead of those that are sold for a profit as not to be within speaking distance.

But doesn't it take a great deal of specialized knowledge in order to recognize the wild plants that are good for food, and isn't that knowledge hard to acquire? Did you ever stop to think how much specialized knowledge and fine discrimination are required in order to tell a head of cabbage from a head of lettuce on a grocer's shelf? How would you describe the difference, so someone who had never seen either could be certain what he is getting? Or how would you go about telling someone the difference between Swiss chard, beet tops, spinach and turnip greens? Yet most of us are not aware of ever having made an effort to learn to discriminate between the common vegetables. We recognize them intuitively, just as we do other familiar things. The same thing becomes true of wild food plants after a short acquaintance.

But isn't there danger of eating a poisonous plant by mistake? A person could get poisoned in his own vegetable garden if he didn't know poison hemlock from parsley. The fields and woods are not nearly so full of poisonous plants as the average city dweller seems to think. True, a person who can't tell the difference between poison ivy and a wild grapevine has no business trying to gather wild food, unless he is accompanied by someone who knows considerably more than he does; just as a person who can't tell one vegetable from another has no business shopping alone, but one is no harder to learn than the other. A forager doesn't have to be a graduate botanist. You don't have to be able to call every plant in the woods by its Latin name before you are ready to begin. As soon as you can be sure that you recognize a single edible specimen, you are ready to start gathering food.

Right here, let me allay any fear that an increase in interest in wild food would result in the depletion or extinction of any of our valuable wild plant life. This mistaken idea arises from the outmoded conception of conservation as nonuse. In the past half century we have witnessed a great upsurge of interest in hunting, but far from leading to a depletion of wild life, this has resulted in the adoption of conservation measures which have led to tremendously increased supplies of available game. Similarly, a genuine interest in wild food plants would lead to conservation measures and extension of areas where these plants grow, while protection and propagation would lead to increased supplies.

Adventurous epicures can expect to find flavors and textures in wild foods that can't be obtained elsewhere. Here are new gustatory thrills that can't be purchased at a restaurant or food market. Some will think that wild food just can't be as good as I say it is. I don't expect everyone to be delighted with every dish I describe; tastes differ, and *de gustibus non est disputandum,* but give each plant an honest trial before passing judgment.

There are many wild plants reported in the literature to be edible that I don't like at all. In research for this book I tried several hundred different kinds of plants, and disliked most of them. But a number proved to furnish superior food, worthy of inclusion in the most refined diet. These are the plants included in this book with methods of preparing them that I have either evolved or tested in my own kitchen. Many of the recipes presented here were preceded by uncounted failures before I came up with a dish that I thought worthy to pass on to my readers. The reason I say that these dishes are delicious is because I have found them so.

However, the goodness of many of these plants is not so intrinsic as to be independent of the cook's skill. As you will see in the articles on certain individual plants, some require special treatment and skillful preparation to make them acceptable to a discriminating taste. If you are unwilling to take the extra time and trouble required to make these plants into something really edible, then I would advise that you pass on to the more easily prepared kinds.

Wild food is used at our house in a unique method of entertaining. Our "wild parties," which are dinners where the chief component of every dish is some foraged food, have achieved a local fame. Many different meals can be prepared almost wholly from wild food without serving anything that will be refused by the most finicky guest. Such dinners are remembered and talked about long after the most delicious of conventional dinners have been forgotten.

Guests ave invariably surprised to discover that wild plants can be transformed into such agreeable fare. There is no difficulty about maintaining interesting discussion at a meal where every dish is a conversation piece. The guests always want a list of the strange foods they have enjoyed so they can tell their friends about this unusual experience, so I now make up souvenir menus which they can take home. Here are some examples of dinners that have been served to guests in our house.

One, served in April, started off with a Wild Leek Soup served in individual ramekins. Our salad was made of blanched crowns of chicory, young sprouts of day lilies and the tender, inner portions of calamus stalks, served with a French dressing, to which a bare hint of wild garlic had been added. The main dish was Crayfish Tails Tempura, with a sour-cream sauce containing the tenderest, inner portions of green wild onions. For vegetables we had Buttered Poke Sprouts and Boiled Dandelion Crowns. Hot biscuits, made of Cattail Root Flour, were served with Chokecherry Jelly from our jam cupboard. Dessert was Japanese Knotweed Pie and for a beverage we had Sassafras Tea. The meal was ended by nibbling on bits of Preserved Wild Ginger.

Another meal, served in July, started off with a glass of mixed wild fruit juices and Snapping-Turtle Soup. Then came Chicken-fried Frog's Legs and a Water Cress Salad. The vegetables were Boiled Day-Lily Buds and Cattail Bloom Spikes in melted butter. There were golden muffins of cattail pollen spread with Wild Strawberry Jam. For dessert, we ate Blackberry Cobbler from fresh-picked fruit, drank Dandelion Coffee, then finished with little slices of Candied Calamus Root.

An autumn menu started off with Wild Grape Juice and Wild Mushroom (Shaggy-Mane) Soup. This was followed by Bluegill Fillets, battered and fried, and a salad made of sliced wild Jerusalem artichoke tubers and ripe ground cherries, served with a garlic-bleu-cheese dressing. There were Baked Arrowhead Tubers and wild apples, sliced and cooked with butter and brown sugar until they were nearly caramelized. We had dark muffins of lamb's-quarters seed, freshly ground, and amber May-Apple Marmalade. For dessert there was a mile-high Persimmon-Hickory-Nut Chiffon Pie and Chicory Coffee, followed by a bowl of mixed wild nuts for any who still had a vacant cranny to fill.

I know of no other outdoor sport which can furnish me with as much pleasure as foraging wild food which can be made into exquisite dishes to share with family and friends. If your interest has been aroused, then let me welcome you into the growing army of neoprimitive food gatherers who are finding new fascination and meaning in America's great outdoors.

This book makes no pretense of being an exhaustive treatise on this subject. Among the quarter million described species of plants in the world there are thousands that would be a possible source of human food. I have purposely excluded many of these because of their rarity or limited range, or because they were so unpalatable that one would only eat them as an alternative to starvation. However, there are many perfectly good foods to be found in the wilds that you will not find mentioned here, simply because I have had no experience with them and therefore did not feel that I could add anything significant to the excellent literature that already exists in this field. If your favorite wild food has been ignored in these pages, forgive me. Maybe we can meet some day and exchange information and recipes to the mutual benefit of both of us.

REVERENCE FOR LIFE[3]
Albert Schweitzer

Albert Schweitzer (1875–1965) was a German philosopher, theologian, musicologist, organist, and medical missionary. He left Europe in 1913 to set up a hospital at Lambaréné in French Equatorial

[3]From *A Treasury of Albert Schweitzer,* by Thomas Kiernan, Citadel Press. Reprinted by permission.

Africa. He remained there the rest of his life, save for fund-raising trips to Europe. Schweitzer won the Nobel Prize in 1952.

At sunset of the third day, near the village of Igendja, we moved along an island set in the middle of the wide river. On a sandbank to our left, four hippopotamuses and their young plodded along in our same direction. Just then, in my great tiredness and discouragement, the phrase "Reverence for Life" struck me like a flash. As far as I knew, it was a phrase I had never heard nor ever read. I realized at once that it carried within itself the solution to the problem that had been torturing me. Now I knew that a system of values which concerns itself only with our relationship to other people is incomplete and therefore lacking in power for good. Only by means of reverence for life can we establish a spiritual and humane relationship with both people and all living creatures within our reach. Only in this fashion can we avoid harming others, and, within the limits of our capacity, go to their aid whenever they need us.

It also became clear to me that this elemental but complete system of values possessed an altogether different depth and an entirely different vitality than one that concerned itself only with human beings. Through reverence for life, we come into a spiritual relationship with the universe. The inner depth of feeling we experience through it gives us the will and the capacity to create a spiritual and ethical set of values that enables us to act on a higher plane, because we then feel ourselves truly at home in our world. Through reverence for life, we become, in effect, different persons. I found it difficult to believe that the way to a deeper and stronger ethic, for which I had searched in vain, had been revealed to me as in a dream. Now I was at last ready to write the planned work on the ethics of civilization.

For two days, I had been busy treating the sick wife of the missonary. When she showed signs of getting better, I sailed downstream to the ocean. A few days later, my wife and I returned to Lambaréné. There, I began to sketch in the volume on my philosophy of civilization. The plan was simple. First, I would give a general view of civilization and ethics as set forth in the writings of the world's great thinkers. Secondly, I would occupy myself with the essence and the significance of the ethics of reverence for life.

HUMAN AWARENESS[4]
Albert Schweitzer

The fundamental fact of human awareness is this: "I am life that wants to live in the midst of other life that wants to live." A thinking man feels compelled to approach all life with the same reverence he has for his own. Thus, all life becomes part of his own experience. From such a point of view, "good" means to maintain life, to further life, to bring developing life to its highest value. "Evil" means to destroy life, to hurt life, to keep life from developing. This, then, is the rational, universal, and basic principle of ethics.

Ethics up to now had been incomplete because it had held that its chief concern was merely with the relationship of man to man. In reality, however, ethics must also be concerned with the way man behaves toward all life. In essence, then, man can be considered ethical only if life as such is sacred to him—both in people and in all creatures that inhabit the earth.

The actual living of this ethic, with its responsibilities extending toward all living things, is deeply rooted in universal thought. The ethical relationship of man to man is not something in and of itself, but part of a greater concept. The idea of reverence for life contains everything that expresses love, submission, compasssion, the sharing of joy, and common striving for the good of all. We must free ourselves from thoughtless existence.

At the same time, we are all subject to the mysterious and cruel law by which we maintain human life at the cost of other life. It is by this very destruction and harm of other life that we develop feelings of guilt. As ethical human beings, we must constantly strive to escape from this need to destroy—as much as we possibly can. We must try to demonstrate the essential worth of life by doing all we can to alleviate suffering. Reverence for life, which grows out of a proper understanding of the will to live, contains life-affirmation. It acts to create values that serve the material, the spiritual, and ethical development of man.

[4] From *A Treasury of Albert Schweitzer,* by Thomas Kierman, Citadel Press. Reprinted by permission.

ON GARDENING LIFE[5]
Karel Capek
translated by M. and R. Weatherall

Karel Capek (1890–1938) was a Czech playwright, novelist and essayist. He is known in the West for his play, *R.U.R.* *(Rossum's Universal Robots)*, and satirical novel, *The War of the Newts,* one of the greatest books of this century. *The Gardener's Year* is a humorous account of the trials of the amateur gardener.

On Gardening Life

One says that time brings roses; it is true in a way—usually one must wait for roses until June or July; and as for their growth, three years are sufficient for your rose to make quite a nice top. One ought rather to say that time brings oaks; or that time brings birches. I once planted some birches, saying: "Here there will be a grove of birches; and here in this corner a mighty ancient oak will stand." And I also planted a little seedling oak, but two years have passed, and still there is not a mighty ancient oak, nor are those birches yet a centenary birch grove in which fairies would like to dance. Of course, I shall wait some years yet; we gardeners have immense patience. I have a cedar of Lebanon on my lawn almost as big as I am; according to the experts a cedar can grow to a height of three hundred feet and to a width of fifty feet. Well, I should like to see it when it reaches the prescribed height and width; it really would be only fair if I lived as long in good health and, so to speak, reaped the reward of my labours. In the meantime it has grown a good ten inches; well—we must wait.

Take, for example, a little grass plant; if you sow the seed well and sparrows don't pick it up, it pricks through in a fortnight, and in six weeks it needs cutting, but it is not an English lawn yet. I know an excellent recipe for an English lawn—like the recipe for Worcester Sauce—it comes from an "English country gentleman." An American millionaire said to that gentleman: "Sir, I will pay you anything you like if you will reveal to me by what method such a perfect, even, level, fresh, everlasting, in short, such an English lawn as yours is

[5] From *The Gardener's Year* by Karel Capek, pp. 7–11, 158–60. Reprinted by permission of George Allen & Unwin Ltd.

made."—"That's quite simple," said the English squire. "The soil must be well and deeply dug, it must be fertile and porous, not sour or sticky, not heavy or thin; then it must be well levelled so that it is like a table; after that you sow the seed and roll the ground well; then you water it daily, and when the grass has grown you mow it week after week; you collect the cut grass with sweepers and roll the lawn; you must water, sprinkle, wet, and spray it daily; and if you do this for three hundred years you will have as good a lawn as mine."

To this add that each of us gardeners would like and really ought to examine by actual experience all kinds of roses with regard to their buds, flowers, stems, leaves, crowns, and other features; item all the different kinds of tulips, lilies, irises, delphiniums, carnations, campanulas, astilbes, violets, phloxes, chrysanthemums, dahlias, gladioli, paeonies, asters, primulas, anemones, aquilegias, saxifrages, gentians, sunflowers, day lilies, poppies, golden rods, ranunculi, and veronicas; each of which has at least a dozen of the best and most indispensable classes, varieties, and hybrids; to these one ought to add several hundred genera and species which have only from three to a dozen varieties; further, one should pay special attention to the Alpine, water, and bulbous plants, to heathers and ferns and shade-loving plants, to trees and evergreens; if I were to add all this up I should get, at a very mild estimate, eleven hundred years. The gardener wants eleven hundred years to test, learn to know, and appreciate fully all that is his. I can't make it less, unless I discount 5 per cent. That is for you, and perhaps you need not cultivate the whole lot, although it is well worth while; but you must make haste and not waste a single day, if you want to do what is necessary. You ought to finish what you have begun; you owe it to your garden. I shan't give you a recipe, for you must try yourselves and persevere.

We gardeners live somehow for the future; if roses are in flower, we think that next year they will flower better; and in some few years this little spruce will become a tree—if only those few years were behind me! I should like to see what these birches will be like in fifty years. The right, the best is in front of us. Each successive year will add growth and beauty. Thank God that again we shall be one year farther on!

ON WATERING THE GARDEN[6]
Bertolt Brecht
translated by Edwin Morgan

O watering of the garden, to put the green in good heart!
Spraying of thirsty trees! Give more than enough and
Never forget the shrubbery, not even
The shrub without berries, the exhausted
Niggardly bearers. And don't overlook
The weed between the flowers, it too
Knows thirst. Nor should you pour
Only on the fresh turf or only on the parched turf:
You must refresh the naked earth itself.

THE SIMPLE LIFE
John Burroughs

John Burroughs (1837–1921), American naturalist and essayist, wrote on many topics—the habits of the worm-eating warbler, Walt Whitman, Charles Darwin. This selection is taken from his book of essays, *Leaf and Tendril*.

New York

I am bound to praise the simple life, because I have lived it and found it good. When I depart from it, evil results follow. I love a small house, plain clothes, simple living. Many persons know the luxury of a skin bath—a plunge in the pool or wave unhampered by clothing. That is the simple life—direct and immediate contact with things, life with the false wrappings torn away—the fine house, the fine equipage, the expensive habits, all cut off. How free one feels, how good the elements taste, how close one gets to them, how they fit one's body and one's soul! To see the fire that warms you or, better yet, to cut the wood that feeds the fire that warms you; to see the

[6] From *On Watering the Garden* by Berthold Brecht. Reprinted by permission of Suhrkamp Verlag. Copyright © 1960 Suhrkamp Verlag, Frankfurt am Main.

spring where the water bubbles up that slakes your thirst and to dip your pail into it; to see the beams that are the stay of your four walls and the timbers that uphold the roof that shelters you; to be in direct and personal contact with the sources of your material life; to want no extras, no shields; to find the universal elements enough; to find the air and the water exhilarating; to be refreshed by a morning walk or an evening saunter; to find a quest of wild berries more satisfying than a gift of tropic fruit; to be thrilled by the stars at night; to be elated over a bird's nest or a wildflower in spring—these are some of the rewards of the simple life.

A VISIT TO SARASHINA VILLAGE[7]
Matsuo Bashō

Matsuo Bashō (1644–1694), one of the greatest Japanese poets, is generally credited with perfecting the *haiku*, the short (17 syllable) classical form of Japanese poetry. He was also an accomplished prose writer, who specialized in travel sketches.

The autumn wind inspired my heart with a desire to see the rise of the full moon over Mount Obasute. That rugged mountain in the village of Sarashina is where the villagers in the remote past used to abandon their aging mothers among the rocks. There was another man filled with the same desire, my disciple, Etsujin, who accompanied me, and also a servant sent by my friend Kakei to help me on the journey, for the Kiso road that led to the village was steep and dangerous, passing over a number of high mountains. We all did our best to help one another, but since none of us were experienced travellers, we felt uneasy and made mistakes, doing the wrong things at the wrong times. These mistakes, however, provoked frequent laughter and gave us the courage to push on.

[7] An excerpt from Matsuo Bashō: *The Narrow Road to the Deep North and Other Travel Sketches* translated by Nobuyuki Yuasa (Penquin Classics 1966) pp. 91–93. Copyright © Nobuyuki Yuasa, 1966.

At a certain point on the road, we met an old priest—probably more than sixty years of age—carrying an enormously heavy load on his bent back, tottering along with short, breathless steps and wearing a sullen, serious look on his face. My companions sympathized with him, and, taking the heavy load from the priest's shoulders, put it together with other things they had been carrying on my horse. Consequently, I had to sit on a big pile. Above my head, mountains rose over mountains, and on my left a huge precipice dropped a thousand feet into a boiling river, leaving not a tiny square of flat land in between, so that, perched on the high saddle, I felt stricken with terror every time my horse gave a jerk.

We passed through many a dangerous place, such as Kakehashi, Nezame, Saru-ga-baba, Tachitōge, the road always winding and climbing, so that we often felt as if we were groping our way in the clouds. I abandoned my horse and staggered on my own legs, for I was dizzy with the height and unable to maintain my mental balance from fear. The servant, on the other hand, mounted the horse, and seemed to give not even the slightest thought to the danger. He often nodded in a doze and seemed about to fall headlong over the precipice. Every time I saw him drop his head, I was terrified out of my wits. Upon second thoughts, however, it occurred to me that every one of us was like this servant, wading through the ever-changing reefs of this world in stormy weather, totally blind to the hidden dangers, and that the Buddha surveying us from on high, would surely feel the same misgivings about our fortune as I did about the servant.

When dusk came, we sought a night's lodging in a humble house. After lighting a lamp, I took out my pen and ink, and closed my eyes, trying to remember the sights I had seen and the poems I had composed during the day. When the priest saw me tapping my head and bending over a small piece of paper, he must have thought I was suffering from the weariness of travelling, for he began to give me an account of his youthful pilgrimage, parables from sacred *sutras*, and the stories of the miracles he had witnessed. Alas, I was not able to compose a single poem because of this interruption. Just at this time, however, moonlight touched the corner of my room, coming through the hanging leaves and the chinks in the wall. As I bent my ears to the noise of wooden clappers and the voices of the villagers chasing wild deer away, I felt in my heart that the loneliness of autumn was now consummated in the scene. I said to my companions, 'Let us drink under the bright beams of the moon,' and the master of the house brought out some cups. The cups were too big to be called refined, and were decorated with somewhat uncouth gold-lacquer work, so that over-refined city-dwellers might have hesitated to touch them. Finding them in a remote country as I did, however, I was pleased to see them, and thought that they were even more precious than jewel-inlaid, rare-blue cups.

Seeing in the country
A big moon in the sky,
I felt like decorating it
With gold-lacquer work.

On to a bridge
Suspended over a precipice
Clings an ivy vine,
Body and soul together.

Ancient imperial horses
Must have also crossed
This suspended bridge
On their way to Kyōto.

Halfway on the bridge,
I found it impossible
Even to wink my eye,
When the fog lifted.   **Written by Etsujin**